D1570752

Mass-production
Management

Mass-production Management

The Design and Operation of Production Flow-line Systems

Ray Wild
Management Centre, University of Bradford

JOHN WILEY & SONS
London · New York · Sydney · Toronto

Copyright © 1972 by John Wiley & Sons Ltd.
All Rights Reserved. No part of this publication
may be reproduced, stored in a retrieval system, or
transmitted, in any form or by any means, electronic,
mechanical, photo-copying, recording or otherwise,
without the prior written permission of the
Copyright owner.

Library of Congress catalog card number 72-611

ISBN 0 471 94405 X

Printed in Great Britain by Adlard & Son Ltd.
Bartholomew Press, Dorking, Surrey

Preface

This book was prepared with two major objectives in mind—first the development of terminology and definitions appropriate to the field of mass production, and secondly the examination of some of the more important features of one aspect of mass production, namely flow-line production.

During recent years, the characteristics and problems of mass production have increasingly attracted the attentions of writers. However, most writers have dealt only with particular aspects of the subject. Consequently, while some terminology has evolved during this period, appreciable confusion remains. Certain definitions and concepts are widely accepted and these have, where possible, been adopted in this book; elsewhere new or modified terms have been introduced. In attempting to examine the management problems associated with flow-line production, the principal difficulty encountered related to scope and depth. Although, as I shall point out, there are many areas in which insufficient information is available, it was, nevertheless, impossible to include a discussion of all relevant techniques, papers, etc. My objective, therefore, was to cover adequately the scope of the subject and, where necessary, forfeit depth to achieve a balanced coverage. Accordingly, while the Bibliography contains most of the known available references relevant to our subject, many of these are not described in the text. Such selectivity is inevitable within the constraints of size and cost. It will be appreciated that, in an area such as this, new papers and articles are appearing almost continually.

I gratefully acknowledge the assistance and comments provided by numerous colleagues, particularly Dr. G. Buxey, Mr. P. de la Wyche and Mr. N. Slack of the Management Centre of the University of Bradford, but must emphasize that I alone am responsible for any misinterpretations included in the text. My thanks are also due to Mrs. G. V. Woodhead, who prepared most of the typescript, and Mrs. C. A. Wild for assistance in reading both manuscript and proofs.

RAY WILD
Bradford, October 1971

Contents

Notation

i = work-element number ($i=1, 2, \ldots, m$)

j = station number ($j=1, 2, \ldots, N$)

k = model number

k^* = line set of models

l = number of units made ($l=1, 2, \ldots, Q$)

q_k = production rate for model k

r_k = consumption rate for model k

z = constant

C = effective inventory cost per unit of time (a function of N, C_{1k} and the cost of storage space)

C_{1k} = holding cost per unit of model k per unit of time

C_{2k} = line set-up cost for model k

C_3 = delay cost per unit of time

C_v = coefficient of variation of service times

L = balancing loss (%)

N = number of work stations

N_{min} = minimum number of stations

N' = number of complete production cycles

N_{k^*} = number of models included in line set k

Q = quantity output in given time T, or batch quantity

S_{k^*} = similarity index for models in line set k

$\bar{S}_{k^*}$ = mean similarity index for models in line set k

T = production time period

T_C = cycle time

T_{Ei} = work time for element i

T_{Eik} = work time for element i in model k

T_F = feed interval of units

T_{Sj} = service time for station j

T_{Sh} = service time for unit h ($1 < h \leqslant l$)

T_{Sk} = service time for model k (assumed equal for all stations)

T_{Sl} = service time for unit l

T_T = tolerance time at station

$\bar{T}_{Ei}$ = mean time for element i

$\hat{T}_{Eik}$ = maximum time required for element i for the model in time set k^*

$\bar{T}_S$ = mean service time for station, or mean of station service times

U_{k^*} = utilization index for work elements in models in line set k^*

X = buffer capacity (number of units)

X^* = optimum buffer capacity (number of units)

X_l = time of launching unit l onto line

Z = ordinate of standardized normal distribution

α = time interval between successive stations starting work on any one unit

α_1, α_2 = line parameters

γ = launching interval of units onto line

σ_{Ei}^2 = variance of work times for element i

σ_{Sj}^2 = variance of service times at station j

Δ = desirable station length

$\Delta(-)$ = upstream boundary or station length

$\Delta(+)$ = downstream boundary or station length

Part 1

The Nature, Characteristics and Development of Mass and Flow Production

CHAPTER 1

Concepts of Mass Production

Throughout this book the terms production and manufacture will be considered to be synonymous. There is little dispute as to the meaning of 'manufacture', which is generally defined as the 'making of articles by physical labour or machinery'. Such a definition also traditionally applies to 'production'; however, for some purposes production is also considered to embrace the provision of services.

Fundamentally, production is concerned with the conversion or transformation of 'inputs' into 'outputs'. The inputs in question are materials and labour, while the outputs are normally considered to be goods. Recently, however, it has been recognized that all transformation systems have something in common, irrespective of the nature of their outputs. It has been found that the management of transformation processes is, to some extent, independent of the technology involved. In other words, transformation systems for manufacture, transportation, medical care, etc., have methodological similarities. Problems of location, layout, stock control, scheduling and replacement are important features of each of these systems.

The recognition of this fact has led some people to change the traditional definition of production to encompass systems that provide services as well as goods. There are, however, problems connected with the redefinition of terms which are currently in widespread use, and it is fortunate that an alternative term—'operating systems'—is available to describe systems whose outputs are goods *or* services. For our purposes, a production system will be considered to be one type of operating system, and production management will be taken to be a branch of operations management.

Since this book deals, essentially, with management, brief comment on the nature and significance of production management is worthwhile.

Production management is concerned with the *design, construction and operation of production systems*. Such responsibility necessitates two types of decision making or problem solving—*planning* and *control*.

3

Planning, which is of the utmost importance in the type of production that we are to discuss, is essentially a preproduction activity involving functions such as demand forecasting, the location and layout of facilities, job design, production scheduling, etc.

Control follows planning, and its purpose is to ensure that the system operates in the planned manner. Control problems therefore derive from, and occur during, the operation of the production process, and include such tasks as stock control, maintenance, replacement, quantity control, dispatching, progressing, etc.

This dichotomy of tasks or problem areas is, of course, rather abstract, since in practice neither planning nor control are independent functions, and each will contain something of the other. However, this limitation apart, the division of production management into two such fields does provide a useful framework within which to examine the subject. Such a framework has been adopted in this book.

The nature of production-management problems depends to some extent on the nature of the product. The problems encountered by the production manager of a publishing company are likely to differ, at least in their complexity and relative importance, from those faced by his counterpart employed in pharmaceuticals or petrochemicals. There are, as we have previously indicated, many problems common to the various types of production; however, there are also many differences, and not least is the relative importance and difficulty of planning and control. Such differences need not concern us unduly, since we are concerned basically with one type of production, and we shall be concentrating on the problems of production management in that situation. It is not our intention to provide a general production-management text, and consequently we shall concentrate on the peculiarities of mass-production management, and refer only briefly to the solution of problems common to different types of production.

Not only are there several types of production, but also there are several methods of classifying them for descriptive purposes. Perhaps the simplest classification relies on the use of the concepts of *continuous* and *intermittent* processes.

Continuous production, in its purest form, involves the production of a single type of item by using facilities for 24 h per day and 365 days per year. In contrast, the purest form of intermittent production involves the manufacturing of unique items, with absolutely no repetition.

Such extremes are difficult to envisage; however, petroleum refining is a close approximation to the former, while civil-engineering work is a good, but rather special, example of the latter.

A classification which is, perhaps, more useful for our purposes relies on the division of production systems into three broad and overlapping groups, namely *jobbing*, *batch* and *mass*. These three classes lie on the same continuum of repetitiveness evolved above, i.e. pure jobbing production equates to pure intermittent production, while pure mass production is equivalent to continuous production.

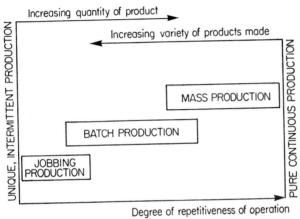

Figure 1.1 Classification of types of production

In practice, since these two extremes rarely exist, jobbing is taken to include those situations which tend towards intermittent operation, and mass production is considered to be production which is almost continuous, or continuous over a limited, but substantial, period of time. Batch production is the term used to describe the territory lying between and overlapping these two opposite classes (see Figure 1.1).

MASS, QUANTITY AND FLOW PRODUCTION

Mass production is a term which came into widespread usage in the early 1900s, and derived largely from America. There has never been a precise, widely adopted definition of the term, yet for most people mass production means the manufacture of products in large quantities by means of purpose-designed manufacturing facilities. Mass production has been adopted as a generic rather than a specific term. Consequently, before we can begin to discuss the subject in detail, we must first look more closely at what is implied or embraced by the term.

Although the term was born around 50 years ago, the type of systems which it now describes are considerably older. Large-quantity production is as old as large-quantity demand. The concept is not new; only the manner in which the concept is translated into practice has any claim to be of recent origin.

Perhaps as early as the 6th century B.C., the Phoenicians were engaged in the production of bricks in vast quantities. However, their production methods differed from those which might be adopted today, in that their 'mass production' was achieved through the use of a massive labour force. This is not mass production in the modern sense of the term, since their mass output was achieved by the multiplication of effort rather than by the adoption of different production principles.

If we were to accept the multiplication of efforts as a means of mass production, we would have to accept that mass production might be achieved by intermittent- and jobbing-production methods. This is clearly in conflict with our previous definition, and we must attempt to explain mass production in terms of the methods, as well as the scale, of production.

The stimulus for mass production derived largely from the invention and increasing availability of mechanized methods of production, a development which, in turn, was dependent on the design and use of power sources. The use of water, and then steam, power accelerated the development of production mechanization. The development of machine tools and other 'mechanical' production equipment came to a climax in the 18th and 19th centuries, and consequently it was around this period that mass production as a 'technology' began to evolve.

The inventions of Kay, Arkwright, Hargreaves and others in the period during and following the Industrial Revolution facilitated the emergence of the textile industry as a mass-production industry. Other inventions and developments had a similar impact on other industries. For example, the development of tools such as lathes, drilling machines, shapers, drop forges, etc., facilitated the production of items in large quantities to high standards of accuracy.

Notice, however, that these examples relate to the mass production of single-piece items or components, destined perhaps for use in the manufacture of more complex products. The production of such items in large quantities is an important feature of mass production. For example, the use of injection-moulding machines to produce plastic items in large quantities is clearly a system of mass production, since it involves the semicontinuous use of special-purpose equipment for the production of large quantities of items.

Examples such as these illustrate one—perhaps the simplest—aspect of mass production. In the interests of clarity and simplicity we shall refer to this aspect of mass production as *quantity production*.

A second aspect of mass production deals with the manufacture of more complex items. The mass production of items such as domestic appliances, motor vehicles, etc., depends on a different type of mass-production technology, the central feature of which is *product flow*, and hence we shall refer to it as *flow production*. Such items cannot usually be manufactured by one tool or piece of equipment because of their complexity or composite nature. They normally require the services of several facilities. For example, the machining of an engine cylinder block requires the use of drilling, tapping, boring and milling facilities. Similarly, a complex assembly such as a motor vehicle will also require a sequence of operations. The mass production of such items, a more recent development than quantity production, is dependent on the use of the flow principle, i.e. the continuous flow of the products through or past a series of production facilities.

Flow production is most easily achieved for products which flow naturally. For example, in petroleum refining, the product and the raw material have a propensity to flow, and the design of the *flow process* is facilitated. Similarly, many foodstuffs, drinks and other products, because of their natural properties, lend themselves to this type of production. In contrast, 'hard' discrete items such as engine cylinder blocks, motor vehicles and domestic appliances do not possess this characteristic. Hence considerable effort must be made to design flow systems for their manufacture.

Nor is the provision of 'flow' the only difficulty to be overcome prior to the mass production of discrete complex items; provision must also be made for the interchangeability of parts. For example, the use of flow production in the assembly of complex products such as motor vehicles would be impractical if it were necessary to modify or adjust the components or parts used to ensure that they would fit together. It is essential that each of the many different types of part used should have been manufactured to sufficient standards of accuracy to ensure interchangeability. Similarly, the flow production of single complex items, such as engine cylinder blocks, must be achieved with a high degree of accuracy, since these items will be required eventually to match and fit together with complementary parts at a subsequent production stage.

The mass production of complex discrete items using the flow principle is one of the most important achievements in manufacturing technology and one of the most important aspects of mass production. Indeed, the importance of this method of manufacture is such that, for many people, the term mass production is synonymous with flow-line production.

On reflection, we can see that the general term 'mass production' embraces two technologies (Figure 1.2), the development of the simpler quantity production having preceded the development of the more complex flow production. Mass production and flow production are not necessarily the same, since mass production only gives rise to flow production when necessitated by the nature of the product.

Flow production consists basically of two subsections, namely, *flow processes* designed for the manufacture of large quantities of bulk, fluid or semifluid products, and *flow lines,* which use the same principle of efficient material and product flow in the manufacture of large quantities of complex, discrete items.

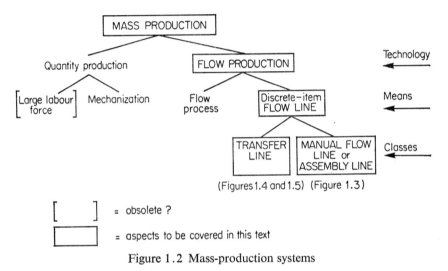

Figure 1.2 Mass-production systems

Figures 1.3 and 1.4 show examples of the two classes of flow-line production that will be examined in later chapters of this book. The flow line in Figure 1.3 is being used for the manual *assembly* of components on printed-circuit boards for colour-television sets; the line shown in Figure 1.4 is engaged in *machining.*

Flow lines such as that shown in Figure 1.3, which are engaged, essentially, in product assembly, are often referred to as *manual flow lines* or *assembly lines,* while those of the type shown in Figure 1.4, using automatic material transfer between the automatic machining 'stations', are normally referred to as *transfer lines.* In addition to the in-line configuration shown in Figure 1.4, such transfer lines have also been designed to operate on a rotary principle (Figure 1.5). These definitions will be enlarged on in Chapter 3.

The use of discrete-item flow lines is a comparatively recent innovation derived from the development of quantity production and the use of interchangeable parts, both of which in their turn depended to a large extent on the mechanization of production processes (Figure 1.6).

Figure 1.3 Manual flow line (reproduced by permission of Thorn Ltd.)

Although flow processes such as chemical and petroleum plants normally involve very considerable capital investment, and although their design is complex and their efficient operation essential, their *production-management* problems are, perhaps, less complex than those associated with discrete-item flow lines.

This is due in part to the fact that, in most cases, there is comparatively

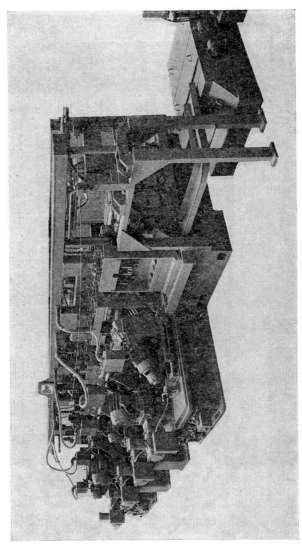

Figure 1.4 Transfer line—'in-line type' [reproduced by permission of Geo. Kingsbury & Co. (Machine Tools) Ltd.]

little flexibility or choice available in the design of process plants, their design often being determined by the nature of the chemical processes which are to take place. Furthermore, such flow processes are often capable of being designed for automatic operation. In contrast, flow lines, especially manual flow lines, present complex design and planning problems of quite a different type to those associated with flow processes.

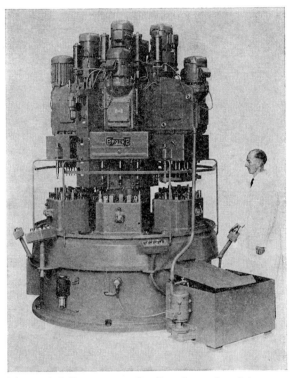

Figure 1.5 Rotary transfer line (reproduced by permission of Brooke Tool Automation Ltd.)

Flow lines are often required to accommodate a variety of products, and are often subject to difficult operating conditions through the occurrence of equipment breakdowns, absenteeism, differing labour performance rates, etc.

Clearly the scale of flow-line operations differs from that of flow processes, but so also do the responsibilities of production management. Production management is only incidentally associated with the design of flow processes, since these processes are largely the responsibility of engineers, chemists, etc. In contrast, the production manager's involvement in flow-line design is considerable, as is the number of alternative strategies available to him, since he is bound only by the nature of the product and the output requirements, and is able to exercise some discretion over the design of the conversion or transformation process.

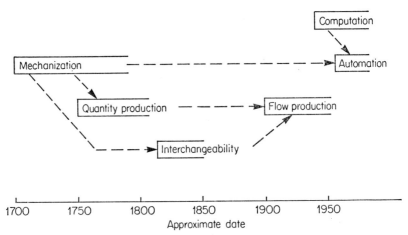

Figure 1.6 Development of technologies for the mass production of discrete items

PRINCIPLES OF FLOW-LINE PRODUCTION

Some of the principles on which flow-line production is based have been mentioned in the previous section. Other writers discussing such principles have evolved very extensive lists, often confusing principles with characteristics. Fundamentally, four general principles are involved:

1. Principle of work flow

Ideally the work, material or products should flow smoothly and regularly through the production process or facilities. Such is the case in flow-process production, but, in flow-line production, motion is normally irregular, the minimization of such irregularity being one objective of flow-line design.

The use of this principle gives rise to certain flow-line characteristics, perhaps the most important of which relates to the amount of *work in progress.* Attempts to achieve a smooth flow will normally reduce the time that an item spends on the flow line, and hence the amount of work in progress is minimized.

Simultaneous operation is a further characteristic deriving from this principle. In flow-line production, all of the operations necessary for the production of the items are being performed simultaneously.

2. Use or provision of interchangeable parts

Assembly lines depend on the availability of interchangeable parts, and flow lines used in 'machining' items are required to produce items to sufficient standards of accuracy to ensure their interchangeability.

3. Principle of minimum distance moved

To ensure continuity of flow, and maximum utilization of available space, it is essential that the flow pattern should be both logical and efficient. This principle normally implies that work areas should be adjacent and linked by materials-handling equipment such as conveyers.

Flow-line production is normally characterized by the *fixed routing of items* because of the inflexibility implied by such a work-flow arrangement. Furthermore, this inflexibility necessitates the manufacture of *standardized items*. In certain types of flow-line production, some product variety is possible; however in general such variety must be minimized in the interests of efficient flow-line design.

4. Division of operation

Although not strictly a principle, the division, rationalization or specialization of operations, or, for manual flow lines, the division of labour, is an important feature of flow-line production. In fact, the principle of the division of operation may be justified in its own right, and thus we can consider it as a feature which complements or facilitates flow-line design. Certainly specialization or division of operation and labour is a characteristic of flow-line design, although, unlike the characteristics already mentioned, it did not derive solely from the development of flow lines.

These principles and characteristics are, of course, in no way essential features of production flow lines. For example, in certain circumstances the minimization of work in progress may be undesirable. Although simple flow lines often conform to the fixed routing characteristic, other more complex lines do not. Nor is the division of labour an essential requirement, or the production of completely standardized items a universal phenomenon. These principles and their associated characteristics, while providing a useful conceptual description of flow lines, do not always apply. In fact, we shall show in later chapters how the recent development of flow-production systems has tended to destroy the validity of many of these principles and characteristics.

PREREQUISITES OF MASS AND FLOW-LINE PRODUCTION

There is only one fundamental prerequisite for mass production, and that is mass demand. Since flow-line production is one means of mass production, its use also depends on mass demand.

The term mass demand must be qualified; in particular, we must consider not only the *level* of demand, but also the *continuity*. In practice, flow-line production will be justified for certain products when demand is both high and reasonably continuous. Nevertheless, in certain circumstances it may be justifiable to establish a flow line to produce items to satisfy one very large order (i.e. to accommodate high-level, but not continuous, demand). In practice such situations are likely to be rare, and some degree of demand continuity will *normally* be a prerequisite for flow-line production. The nature of the product will determine the means of mass production to be used; consequently, a further prerequisite for each of the means of mass production is the availability of a suitable product.

These are the essential prerequisites for flow-line production, but other requirements must be satisfied if flow-line production is to be efficient.

Many of these requirements will be discussed in some detail later; briefly, they relate to line balance, reliability, supply and product design. To manufacture a product on a flow line, the total work required to produce the product—the total work content—must be divided as evenly as possible among the workers or facilities which constitute the line.

This *line balance* is essential if flow is to be continuous, and excessive work in progress is to be avoided. One of the principal features of flow-line systems is the fact that, because the various stages of the system are so interdependent, the failure of any one of them will quickly affect other stations. It is essential, therefore, that the components of such systems should be *reliable* in operation, and that an effective maintenance procedure is adopted.

Similarly, it is essential, for the continued efficient operation of such systems, that the parts or materials required at the various stages of the line are available as and when they are required. The failure of the supply of materials, etc., to the beginning of the line, or to any part of it, will quickly lead to the cessation of production.

Finally, the efficient use of flow-line production depends to a very large extent on the nature of the product. In appropriate circumstances, and with a certain amount of ingenuity, virtually any discrete item can be manufactured on flow lines. Flow lines have been, and still are, used in the manufacture of ships, railway carriages, certain types of houses, aircraft, etc., as well as smaller items such as motor cars, domestic appliances, watches, microelectronic circuits, etc. Many products are ideally suited to this type of manufacture. Even so, the method of manufacture is often an important consideration during the detailed design of such products.

The decision whether or not to adopt flow-line production for a particular product must, of course, be based on economic considerations. The factors to be considered are many, but initial attention will often focus on levels of utilization. Should the decision relate to a flow-line system in which mechanical facilities play an important part, the benefit of using such a system, as compared to, say, a process-type layout, can be explored through an analysis of possible equipment utilization.

The utilization of the equipment currently used in the manufacture of the product can be established by comparing the 'standard hours' value of output with the time available. The number of pieces of equipment required for each operation on the product using a line-type layout could be calculated, and the utilization of this equipment could be calculated for the present and other demand levels. A higher utilization at the present-demand level would suggest the desirability of using this type of layout rather than a process-type layout.

Such an analysis considers only one aspect of the problem, and further factors require examination. We must consider the stability of demand, the reliability of the equipment, etc., as indicated above, and also we must examine the utilization of invested capital. Although the utilization of flow-line equipment might not be substantially higher than the utilization of the existing functionally organized equipment, the use of a flow line might be justified if the equipment involved were less expensive.

Likewise, the labour employed on flow-line equipment may involve lower cost than that required on functionally organized equipment. Furthermore, such labour may be more readily trained and replaced. Material costs may be lower using flow-line production because of lower losses resulting from machine changeovers, and, of course, space utilization may be higher. Thus we see that, although there may be quantitative methods of establishing the benefit of using flow-line production, when considered against limited criteria such as utilization (Deming, 1959), the decision is often of a more complex 'economic trade-off' type.

CLASSES AND VARIETIES OF FLOW LINES

We have previously identified two classes of production flow lines, i.e. *manual or assembly* lines and *transfer* lines. We can now identify various subdivisions of these classes which, for convenience, will be referred to as 'varieties' (see Table 1.1). Each variety may consist of several different *types* of line (see Chapter 5).

Table 1.1 Classes and variety of flow line

Flow-line description		Number of products	Product changes	Flow of items	Setting of equipment and allocation of work
Class	Variety				
Transfer line	Single product	1	None	Regular	No changes required
	Multi-product	>1	Batch changes	Regular within batches	Changes of equipment setting and/or work allocation required on change of batch
Manual flow line	Single product	1	None	Irregular[a]	No changes required
or assembly line	Multi-product	>1	Batch changes	Irregular[a]	Changes of equipment setting and/or work allocation required on batch change
	Mixed product	>1	Continual[c]	Irregular	Changes of equipment setting and/or work allocation normally required[b]

[a] Because of variable work-station times—a characteristic of manual flow lines.
[b] Alternatively, as in 'group technology', tools and equipment might be permanently allocated a specific group of components.
[c] At any time, the line contains a mixture of product types.

Both classes of flow line can be used for the manufacture of either one or more products. The production of one product on either class of line can be accomplished without the need to alter the 'set up' of the line, i.e. without the need to change tools or work allocations, etc. The production of more than one product, however, gives rise to more complex situations. In such cases two alternative strategies are available:

(1) The production of the two or more products in separate batches. This we shall refer to as the *multiproduct* situation, and it necessitates the rearrangement of the flow line between batches.

(2) The production of the two or more products simultaneously on the line. This we shall call the *mixed-product* situation, which gives rise to rather complex design problems, and will be discussed in some detail later.

Whichever strategy is adopted, if more than one product is to be manufactured on the line, these products must have similar work contents. The greater the similarity, the easier it will be to provide either multimodel or mixed-model production. More flexibility is normally available on assembly lines; consequently, in certain circumstances, it may be possible to design such lines for either multimodel or mixed-model operation. For example, many automobile assembly lines work on the mixed-model

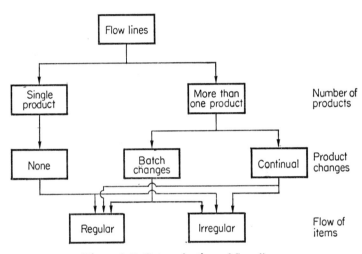

Figure 1.7 Categorization of flow lines

principle, different 'builds' of the same vehicle, and occasionally different types of vehicle, being produced simultaneously on the line. In contrast, transfer lines are far less flexible. They are normally confined to single-model, or occasionally large-batch multimodel operation.

An alternative method of categorizing flow lines is shown in Figure 1.7. Here, as demonstrated previously, we see that flow lines can be used for the production of either one, or more than one, product. Lines on which more than one product is made may be subject to continual product changes (i.e. mixed-model operation) or changes of product batches (i.e. multimodel operation). Continual product change or mixed-model operation may, of necessity, give rise to irregular product flow, whereas for single-product or multiproduct lines it is normally easier to provide a more regular product flow.

Design and use of each of these classes and variety of flow line gives rise to specific production managerial problems, most of which will be discussed in subsequent chapters. Many of these problems are independent of the nature of the line; indeed, some of the problems which will be discussed are a feature of mass production in general rather than flow-line production in particular. However, the following chapters are intended to relate specifically to the design and use of flow-line production systems. The classificatory systems and definitions introduced in this chapter will be used throughout the remainder of the text.

Reference

Deming, D. D. (1959). 'When to shift to straight-line production', *Harvard Bus. Rev.*, 37, No. 6, November/December, 62–68.

CHAPTER 2

Development of Mass and Flow-line Production

It is often suggested that the foundations of modern flow-line production rest at the Highland Park and River Rouge plants of the Ford Company in America. Certainly it is true that Henry Ford I made some notable innovations at these plants in the early 1900s, but it would be incorrect to consider his work, important though it was, to have been the origin of flow-line production, since there are recorded examples of the use of the principle in Europe almost 500 years earlier.

Ford's experiments and innovations are of outstanding importance in the history of technology, since he, more than anyone else, established practical principles for the mass production of consumer goods, which in turn led to far-reaching repercussions in marketing, consumption and society as a whole. Unlike most earlier developments in mass production, Ford's work was not prompted by external pressures such as sudden increases in the demand for his products, or by engineering inventions such as the design of new machine tools, but derived solely from his efforts as a manager to increase the efficiency and productivity of his business. In this respect also his work is of considerable importance, but, before examining it in more detail, we must first look at the changes in manufacture which had taken place during the previous 500 years.

EARLY USE AND DEVELOPMENT OF MASS AND FLOW PRODUCTION

Long before the development of production flow lines, one of the features now associated with this type of production—the division of labour—had been practised in Europe. In 1746, Adam Smith, in his renowned book *Wealth of Nations*, argued the case for the division of labour.

He made no claim to have originated this concept; indeed, he was,

19

perhaps, aware of the fact that the division of labour had been used in Europe some considerable time previously. It had been adopted in Greece as early as the 4th century B.C., noticed in Venice by Marco Polo, and commented upon by Dante as far back as the 1260s. In fact Venice, it seems, had an important part to play in the history of mass production, since, around 1438, the arsenal in Venice is said to have been using the flow or assembly-line principle in equipping galleys. Pero Tafur described the technique in his book *Travels and Adventures*, 1435-9 (Burlingame, 1949):

> 'And as one enters the gate there is a great street on either hand with the sea in the middle, and on one side are windows opening out of the houses of the arsenal, and the same on the other side, and out came a galley towed by a boat, and from the windows they handed out to them, from one the cordage, from another the bread, from another the arms, and from another the balistas and mortars, and so from all sides everything which was required, and when the galley had reached the end of the street all the men required were on board, together with the complement of oars, and she was equipped from end to end. In this manner there came out ten galleys fully armed, between the hours of three and nine. I know not how to describe what I saw there, whether in the manner of its construction or in the management of the workpeople, and I do not think there is anything finer in the world.'

By the time Smith (1746) began to write *Wealth of Nations*, the division of labour in manufacture was probably well known, if not general practice, in certain 'industries'. He described the use of the principle in the manufacture of pins.

> '. . . in the way in which this business is now carried on, not only the whole work is a peculiar trade, but it is divided into a number of branches, of which the greater part are likewise peculiar trades. One man draws out the wire, another straights it, a third cuts it, a fourth points it, a fifth grinds it at the top for receiving the head; to make the head requires two or three distinct operations; to put it on, is a peculiar business, to whiten the pins is another; it is even a trade by itself to put them into the paper; and the important business of making a pin is, in this manner, divided into about eighteen distinct operations, which, in some manufactories, are all performed by distinct hands, though in others the same man will sometimes perform two or three of them.'

Of the workers and the implications of this method of manufacture, Smith commented as follows:

'... a workman not educated to this business, nor acquainted with the use of the machinery employed in it ... could scarce, perhaps, with his utmost industry, make one pin in a day, and certainly could not make twenty. ... But though they were very poor, and therefore but indifferently accommodated with the necessary machinery, they could, when they exerted themselves, make among them ... upwards of forty-eight thousand pins in a day. Each person, therefore, making a tenth part of forty-eight thousand pins, might be considered as making four thousand, eight hundred pins in a day. But if they had all wrought separately, and independently, and without any of them having been educated in this peculiar business, they certainly could not each of them have made twenty, perhaps not one pin in a day ...'

In this discussion Adam Smith recognized and stated some of the principles that were to influence manufacture up until the present day. He recognized the beginning of the disappearance of trades or crafts, the need to minimize movements, the minimization of training requirements and the need to design and use man–machine systems for the production of items in large quantities. Such concepts are now used largely unquestioningly in industry, but two centuries ago they were radical in the extreme.

The advocacy of this type of manufacture during the 17th and 18th centuries was not confined to Europe. It is claimed (Demyanyuk, 1963) that the first conventional manual flow line was used in the Zhirov Company in Moscow in 1731 for the manufacture of buttons and pins in large quantities. Even earlier Leonardo da Vinci is recorded as claiming to have designed a system for the mass, if not flow, production of needles (Usher, 1954):

'Early tomorrow, January 2nd, 1496, I shall make the leather belt and proceed to a trial. ... One hundred times in each hour 400 needles will be finished, making 40,000 in an hour and 480,000 in 12 hours.'

The fact that the majority of these early innovations related to the manufacture of pins and needles is more than mere coincidence.

It was stated in Chapter 1 that the principle requirement of mass production is mass demand or consumption. Unlike the situation which applies at the present time, the pre-Industrial Revolution industrialists were in a position only to respond to, rather than influence, demand. Consequently, we would expect early developments in quantity production to have occurred with items whose consumption was necessarily high. This external stimulus for innovation in manufacture is a common element throughout much of what will be discussed in this chapter.

The efficient flow of work or the automatic or rapid transfer of material between operations, and product-design rationalization or standardization are features of flow-line production. With the exception of the Venice armoury, no examples have yet been provided which demonstrate the use of efficient material or product flow, nor is there any evidence available to suggest that up until this time the requirements of this production had significantly affected product design.

Many of the examples given above, while undoubtedly foreshadowing the advent of flow production, were not themselves characterized by the type of material flow which forms an essential part of present-day assembly or transfer lines. The importance of efficient material and product flow between manufacturing operations increased greatly with the continuing rationalization of manufacturing operations. In fact, attention to flow patterns, inter-operation movement, handling, etc., was to some extent a result of the adoption of labour rationalization.

It has been suggested that one of the earliest examples of a true flow-line system with automatic, or at least mechanical, transfer of material between operations was in operation in a Spanish mint in Segovia. The record of this production systems comes from Sir Kenelm Digby (1644), who is thought to have visited the mint around 1617.

'(It) is so artifically made, that one part of it, distendeth an ingott of silver or gold into that breadth and thickness as is requisite to make coyne of. Which being done, it delivereth the plate it hath wrought, unto an other that printeth the figure of the coyne upon it. And from thence it is turned over to an other that cutteth it according to the print, into due shape and weight. And lastly, the severall peeces fall into a reserve, in another roome: where an officer, whose charge it is, findeth treasure ready coyned; without anything there, to informe him of the severall different motions that the silver or the gold passed before they came to that state. But if he goe on the other side of the wall, into the roome where the other machines stand and are at worke, he will then discerne that everyone of them, which considered by itself might seem a distinct complete engine, is but a serving part of the whole; whose office is, to make money: and that for this work, any one of them separated from the rest, ceaseth to be the part of a minte and the whole is maymed and destroyed.'

This account does not enable us to form any clear picture of the system with which Digby was so obviously impressed. However, his rather didactic discussion which follows this description leaves us in no doubt that he had observed a manufacturing system which contained certain of the principles of the modern transfer line, perfected over 300 years later.

Oliver Evans was undoubtedly a pioneer in the design and use of flow production systems, or more specifically the design and use of *flow processes*, since he was concerned with bulk rather than discrete items. Although his achievements in relation to flour milling are well documented, the precise timing of his developments is somewhat unclear. Evans, an American, was the originator of three types of conveyor, namely belt, screw and bucket, and he is reputed to have designed and built the first 'automatic factory' in which conveyors and other devices were used in the milling of flour.

Whether or not one considers Evans's system as automatic in the present sense of the word, it is beyond doubt that his mill, probably designed around 1785, represents one of the first examples of an integrated flow process. Like most innovations, it was treated with a certain amount of suspicion and scorn in the trade, but nevertheless the flow sequence is said to have cut labour by half and produced a saving, in 1787, of $4875. Eventually the Evans machinery became widely adopted in America, and many of the devices used were translated into other industries, giving rise to the slogan 'untouched by human hand' in many advertisements.

The famous special-purpose machinery designed by Mark Isambard Brunel for the manufacture of ships' blocks is a classic example of the design of a quantity-production system. At that time, the British Admiralty required approximately 100,000 pulley blocks each year to equip their sailing ships. Traditionally, they had been made by hand by 110 craftsmen.

Brunel designed 43 special-purpose machines for the manufacture of these blocks. The machines were made for him by Henry Maudslay, and were driven by a single 32 hp steam engine. Several of these machines are on permanent display at the Science Museum in London. They enabled ten men to undertake the work previously done by 110, and an annual output of 140,000 blocks of various designs to be achieved. The organization of this work was the responsibility of a naval inspector, Samuel Bentham, who had previously been responsible for the production of ships' biscuits in large quantities at the Victualling Office in Deptford. Unlike the block-making machinery, this was very definitely an example of flow-line production, the dough for the biscuits being worked by a machine before being distributed on a flow line to a moulder, marker, splitter, chucker and a depositor, who were reputed to have worked 'with the regularity of a clock' (Armytage, 1961).

B

Here again we see the influence of external pressures in the stimulation of innovation in manufacture. In this case the stimulus was military.

Because of the requirements of the product, it was not necessary for Brunel's equipment to operate as a flow-line system. Unlike many of the products discussed later in this chapter, fine precision was not required in the manufacture of the parts for the wooden blocks, nor was the interchangeability of parts an objective, but rather a consequence, of efficient manufacture.

INTERCHANGEABLE PARTS AND ARMS MANUFACTURE

But for the fact that items or parts can now be economically manufactured to high standards of accuracy, the vast majority of present flow-line manufacture would not be feasible. The ability to make items to close dimensional specifications ensures that such items are interchangeable, and thus the components of a final assembly may be manufactured in the knowledge that they will eventually fit together without the need for subsequent modification or matching. It is this interchangeability which facilitates flow-line production of many products. This principle in interchangeable-part manufacture has been defined (Roe, 1916) as follows:

'... the art of producing complete machines or mechanisms, the corresponding parts of which are so nearly alike that any part may be fitted into any of the given mechanisms ... does not include the manufacture of separate articles, closely alike to each other, but which do not fit together permanently into a mechanism.'

The origins of interchangeable manufacture are somewhat obscure, largely, one suspects, because the need for interchangeable parts was recognized well before such a system of manufacture became feasible, and because some of those who recognized this need were rather optimistic in their claims of having adopted and perfected the system.

Eli Whitney, while not necessarily the first to recognize the importance of interchangeable-part manufacture, nor the first to attempt to use this system, was undoubtedly the most vocal advocate of interchangeable parts. Following his invention of the cotton gin, he turned his attention to the manufacture of arms, which was a booming industry in America in the late 1700s because of that country's race to establish a military protection through fear of the French and British.

On 1 May 1798 Whitney wrote to the American Treasury suggesting that his experience and his ideas for the use of water-powered wood- and metal-cutting machinery would enable him to manufacture large quantities of muskets for the army both quickly and economically. Six weeks after writing to the American Treasury, Whitney received a contract for the manufacture of 10,000 smooth-bore muzzle-loading flintlock muskets for delivery in two lots—4000 in September 1799 and 6000 in September 1800.

Given the existing 'state of the art' of manufacture, it would have been surprising if Whitney had been able to fulfil his contract. He was certainly equipped with ideas and an important principle—the manufacture of interchangeable parts using power-driven machine tools—but at that time it was no more than a principle, and, furthermore, Whitney had no factory. He set up a factory at New Haven, Connecticut, and began to equip it with machine tools, etc., but it soon became clear that Whitney had been somewhat over optimistic about his capabilities. It took him eight, rather than three, years to fulfil this contract.

After the first delivery was due, a Government inspector visited the factory, and found only 500 completed guns. Disturbed by this situation, and probably not understanding Whitney's explanations, the Government invited him to Washington to report in 1800. He took with him parts for ten muskets, and invited his interviewers to pick at random parts, which he then assembled. The Government was obviously impressed by this demonstration of interchangeability, since he was permitted to continue his contract, and was later given a second contract for a further 15,000 muskets.

Whitney undoubtedly did much to establish this method of manufacture in America, but it is equally clear that it took him some considerable time to perfect his manufacturing system. It has been suggested (Battison, 1966), that the parts for Whitney muskets made throughout the period of his first Government contract were not truly interchangeable, but were fitted together while 'soft' after machining, and were then marked for identification purposes to facilitate assembly after hardening.

The Revolution had taken place in France, and the war between England and France had begun in 1793. Consequently, it is not unduly surprising that there are accounts of innovation in arms manufacture in Europe which predate the activities of Whitney. The first attempt to manufacture guns using interchangeable parts is reputed (Roe, 1916) to have taken place around 1717, but it was not until the 1780s that such a manufacturing principle was used with any measure of success. In 1785, Thomas Jefferson, who was then the American Minister in France, wrote to his Government describing the work of one Honoré Blanc, who had made interchangeable parts for musket locks. He reported as follows (Battison, 1966):

'. . . as yet, the inventor (Honoré Blanc) has only completed the lock of the musket, on this plan. He will proceed immediately to have the barrel, stock, and other parts, executed in the same way. Supposing it might be useful to the United States, I went to the workman. He presented me with the parts of fifty locks taken to pieces, and arranged in compartments. I put several together myself, taking pieces at hazzard as they came to hand, and they fitted in a most perfect manner . . . He effects it by tools of his own contrivance, which, at the same time abridge the work, so that he thinks he shall be able to furnish the muskets two livres cheaper than the common price. But it will be two or three years before he will be able to furnish any quantity. I mention it now, as it may have an influence on the plan for furnishing our magazines with this arm.'

In 1789, nine years before Whitney was awarded his first arms contract, Jefferson sent a box of six muskets made on this principle to America, while, on 19 March 1791, a full report based on Blanc's work was submitted to the French Academy of Sciences.

Whether these developments in France were more or less successful than those begun slightly later in America is uncertain. Nor can we be sure of the extent of the independence of these two developments. However, it is beyond dispute that, although Whitney and his contemporaries were unable to translate their principles into practice for many years, they were collectively responsible for establishing an important manufacturing principle, and one that is central to our discussion.

During this period, a whole armaments industry was established in the New England area of America. In 1799, a Government contract for firearms was awarded to Simeon North of Middletown, Connecticut, who, unlike Whitney, was a gunmaker by trade. North eventually began manufacturing guns using the principles advocated by Whitney. In 1808 North was reputedly making pistols using interchangeable parts, and perhaps had taken this principle and that of the division of labour further than Whitney. In his letter that year to the Secretary of the Navy, he stated two of his principles (Roe, 1916):

'I find that by confining a workman to a particular limb of the pistol until he has made two thousand, I save at least one quarter of his labour, to what I should, provided I finished them by small quantities; and the work will be as much better as it is quicker made . . . I have some seventeen thousand screws and other parts of pistols now forged and many parts nearly finished and the business is going on brisk and lively.'

In 1813 North was contracted to supply 20,000 pistols. The agreement contained the following clause, which was probably the first time interchangeable parts had been required by contract, thus leading some people to attribute this development to North.

'The component parts of the pistols are to correspond so exactly that any limb or part of one pistol may be fitted to any other pistol of the twenty thousand.'

Throughout this period Whitney's factory had become a celebrated establishment, visited by people from all parts of the world, including Samuel Colt, who was later to found a small-arms industry which was to influence manufacture in America and Europe.

Colt's first contract for the manufacture of his revolver, invented in 1836, was undertaken in Whitney's factory at Whitneyville near New Haven in 1847. The contract signed between Colt and Whitney Jr. provided that, on completion of manufacture, the equipment designed for the manufacture of the revolvers would become Colt's property and would be installed in his new factory at Hartford. Colt's revolvers or 'six shooters' were used in the war in Mexico, receiving widespread and rapturous acclaim. Demand was enormous, both from the military and from the pioneers struggling against Indian hostility to open up the west of the country.

Colt, who was something of an entrepreneur, having raised money for developing his pistol by lecturing on the subject of laughing gas, was equal to this challenge, although he lacked engineering ability. In 1849 he hired Elisha King Root, who had previously been engaged in the mechanization of the manufacture of axes. The axe had lost its glamour, and Root gave his attention to the organization of Colt's factory at Hartford. He improved many of the Whitney machines, and rationalized operations until, in 1856, the now famous Colt factory occupied 125,000 ft^2 of floor space and utilized about 400 machines producing over 24,000 pistols per year (Haven and Belden, 1940). This factory, which was one of the 'marvels' of the 1850s, was copied widely, and not least in England.

DEVELOPMENTS IN OTHER INDUSTRIES IN AMERICA

During the 60 or 70 years from 1780, the principle of manufacturing interchangeable parts which originated in Europe was developed in America to facilitate the economic production of fairly complex small arms in response to military demand. This principle, which was known for some time as the 'American system of manufacture', together with many of the machine tools developed in the emerging small-arms industry, were adopted in other industries, thus providing a foundation on which to further develop flow-line production.

The transformation of manufacture in many industries began in the early 1800s. For example, until the late 1700s, it was normal for a clock, which was then made almost entirely of wood, to be made and assembled by one craftsman.

Around this time Eli Terry, an American engineer, began to dispel this traditional approach. He began to make clocks in batches, although essentially still using the traditional craft principle. Rationalization of the tasks followed along with the introduction of power-driven machinery, until eventually as many as 10,000 clocks were made each year for a price of $15 compared to the $50 or $60 common beforehand. In 1816 Chauncey Jerome joined Terry's factory at Plymouth and began to further transform the industry. Around 1830 he began to manufacture clocks in brass in large quantities using interchangeable parts, and in 1841 made $35,000 profit out of the manufacture of such clocks selling for $1·50.

With the invention and development of more sophisticated machine tools such as lathes and millers, accuracy, and thus interchangeability, became available to more industries. Prior to the Civil War, an American company began making carriages in Connecticut at a rate of one per hour. Around 1848, pocket watches were being manufactured cheaply and on a large scale, and before 1850 much of the farm machinery made in America was manufactured using interchangeable parts.

In 1830 an important catalyst of mass and flow production was born— the 'penny press'. Previously newpapers were read only by the upper classes, and consequently the tremendous power of the Press to affect attitudes, thought, and behaviour had not been realized. In 1830, a paper designed and priced for a larger proportion of the population was issued in Philadelphia, while in the following ten years many other cities followed suit. Then, as now, mass communication was capable of influencing and creating mass demand, and it became possible for the manufacturer to create or change markets for his products. No longer was manufacture required solely to respond to demand changes, and the movement towards mass production began to escalate, assisted all the time by improvements in transport and distribution. Flow-line production methods began to transform industries such as shoemaking and clothing, and interchange-ability and design standardization became commonplace.

The sewing machine went into quantity flow-line production during this period, total production increasing substantially and a large proportion of the output being exported, largely to Europe.

Throughout this period production began to 'take hold' of demand, not only because of the low prices afforded by the mass production of standardized items, or through mass communication and advertising, but also through innovations such as various types of credit-payment systems, agents, etc. Burlingame (1949) describes the 'marketing' of sewing machines as follows:

'The philosophical and sexual aspects of this machine make a story which it is surprising Hollywood has not exploited. Almost immediately after its production pattern was established it reached what have been called "the little people" in America. No woman, whatever her income or station, was precluded from dreaming of this promise. By national advertising, by skilled agents, by the plan of easy payments, it entered cottages and hall bedrooms where there was scarcely room for it and, having entered, immediately glorified the most sordid environment. It is difficult to imagine anything in the nineteenth century which could have been one half as precious to its owners. It lifted a mass burden from the shoulders of American womankind. We must not be misled by export figures into the belief that it entered European homes on the same level. Its sale abroad to sweaters, to occasional workers and to the rich who employed journeyman seamstresses was another matter. In America it sold to a mass market as a pure luxury and thus began the justification, via the equality doctrine, of the mass production of machines.'

Cyrus McCormick, following the land policies developed by the American Government in which farmers were given land in return for later payment, marketed the reapers he was producing in large quantities in a similar manner. He gave them to the farmers before the harvest for a deposit and an agreement for final payment on the sale of the grain.

Singer, who was largely responsible for the development of the mass production of sewing machines, used a similar arrangement. Both companies made extensive use of the agent system for marketing their products on the scale made possible by developments in manufacturing technology.

DEVELOPMENTS IN BRITAIN

Around 1908, the average worker in the Simeon North small-arms plant at Middletown, Connecticut, made consecutively 2000 parts

(Johnson and Krooss, 1960), whereas in England at about the same time specialization had barely progressed, perhaps only to the extent of one worker undertaking all operations on one part of the product. In England the workers were still virtually craftsmen, unlike those in the arms plants in New England, many of whom had never known craftsmen gunmakers. It is estimated that, by 1860, over 20 American industries were engaged in mass production of products using interchangeable parts, whereas in England there was still only a limited adoption of the 'American system of manufacture'. By the late 1850s, the machines at Colt's armoury at Hartford were largely automatic, and were capable of being operated by women or children. Only a limited amount of handwork was required in finishing items, and labour cost accounted for only 20 per cent of the total manufacturing cost (Johnson and Krooss, 1960).

Certain progress in manufacture had, of course, taken place in Britain. During the 80 years following 1733, when Kay invented his 'flying shuttle', the textile industry in this country was transformed by a series of inventions and machine improvements, all facilitating higher output at less cost. The machine-tool industry thrived in Britain around this time under the influence of engineers such as Maudslay, Whitworth, Nasmyth, Bodmer, Bramah and a host of others. The interrelation among such people was so close that it is possible to trace an unbroken chain from Bramah and Maudslay in England through Whitney and North in New England to later innovators such as Leland and Ford.

Although many of the inventions which gave rise to modern methods of manufacture had their origins in Britain, their widespread and integrated use was to occur first in America. This was doubtless due to some extent to expanding markets, improved transportation, shortages of labour and governmental influence.

Interchangeable-parts manufacture was slow to develop in this country, but efficient product or material flow, another principle on which flow-line production is based, was the subject of some attention in Britain. James Nasmyth, the inventor of the steam hammer, was engaged in the manufacture of machine tools in the Manchester area. Because of the growth of the railways and the expansion of the textile industry at this time, his products were in very great demand and he was obliged to build a new factory at Patricroft—the Bridgewater Foundry, which was finished in 1837. His sales catalogue described a range of standardized machine tools capable of being operated by a 'well-selected labourer' rather than a skilled craftsman. It has been suggested (Musson, 1957) that Nasmyth's tools not only heralded the automatic tools of today, but that his factory pioneered the use of the assembly line. Nasmyth, during the construction of the factory, had suggested that the buildings should be arranged 'in-line' so that 'we will be able to keep in good order'.

Another engineer and inventor operating in Britain at this time was the Swiss-born Johann Georg Bodmer, to whom has been attributed the invention of the travelling crane in 1833. Bodmer, very much a pioneer of flow production, laid out a factory—Chorlton Mills, in Manchester—in which processing and material movement and handling were reputedly integrated (Giedon, 1948):

'It was a sort of model workshop, for which almost everything was newly constructed. Nearly every machine was a patent . . . "the large lathes being provided overhead with small travelling cranes fitted with pulley blocks for the purpose of enabling the workmen more economically and conveniently to set the articles to be operated on in the lathes and to remove them after being finished . . . Small cranes were also erected in sufficient number within easy reach of the planing machines . . . Gradually nearly all of these tools were constructed and were systematically arranged in rows, according to a carefully arranged plan . . . Several lines of rails traversed in shop from end to end for the easy conveyance on trucks of the parts of machinery to be operated upon." '

Bodmer, operating as a consultant, pioneered the moving crane and the endless belt which he was the first to use for continuous fuelling of boilers. He worked on flow systems later adopted in America and advocated by 'pioneers' such as Ford.

Despite the efforts of such pioneers in Britain, it required the influence of war, the consequent demand for arms, and the experience of American manufacturers to move British industry from its craft base. The arsenal largely responsible for the manufacture of arms for the British army in the 1850s stood at Enfield Lock, in Middlesex. In 1851 it was involved, essentially, in forging barrels and in the assembly of non-interchangeable parts made elsewhere. The manufacture of these parts was undertaken by several small companies, each specializing in locks or barrels or bayonets, etc. Some idea of the gulf existing between such methods and those in operation in America at that time can be seen from the fact that, more than 20 years earlier, the American Government armoury at Springfield, which had been designed to incorporate Whitney's and North's principles, had completed its 200,000th firearm incorporating interchangeable parts (Burlingame, 1949). Two events—the 1851 exhibition at Crystal Palace and the Crimean War—undoubtedly helped to change the English system.

The 1851 exhibition was an ironic occasion since, to the layman, it must have provided confirmation of Britain's industrial dominance, while the industrialist and scientist probably came to an entirely different conclusion. America was poorly represented, but even so their exhibits were to have a startling effect on British industry, especially on agriculture (McCormick's exhibits), clothing (the exhibits of Singer) and small arms (the exhibits of Colt and of Robbins and Lawrence). The fame of Colt's weapons had spread ahead of him, while the firm of Robbins and Lawrence was probably less well known in Britain. However it was this latter company, exhibiting under the sign 'Robbins and Lawrence, Windsor, Vermont. Rifles: the various parts made to interchange', which was to have the most startling effect on the British small-arms industry. Robbins and Lawrence demonstrated in London what Whitney had demonstrated in Washington 50 years earlier. They exhibited rifle parts which visitors were invited to assemble.

The year after the exhibition closed, the renovation of the entire British small-arms industry was begun. A committee, including James Nasmyth, was formed in 1853 to advise the Government on this problem and visited the arsenals in America in 1855, reporting to their Government in glowing and enthusiastic terms. Meanwhile (in 1853) Colt, astute as ever, established an arms factory at Pimlico which quickly attracted the interest and enthusiasm of specialists and laymen alike. An article in *Household Words*, the journal run by Dickens, reported as follows (Haven and Belden, 1940):

> 'Neat, delicate handed little girls do the work that brawny smiths still do in other gunshops . . . Even the men have, with scarcely an exception, been hitherto ignorant of gunmaking. No recruiting sergeant ever brought a miscellaneous group into the barrack-yard, to be drilled more rapidly to the same duty . . . Carpenters, cabinet-makers, ex-policemen, butchers, cabmen, hatters, gas-fitters, porters . . . are steadily drilling and boring at lathes all day in upper rooms.'

Reporting on the 'American system of manufacture', Nasmyth said (Armytage, 1961):

> '. . . perfection and economy such as I have never seen before . . . You do not depend on dexterity—all you need is intellect.'

The committee, following its visit to American, resolved to introduce the American system of manufacture in England, and immediately began to remodel the factory at Enfield. The works was largely reequipped with tools obtained from Springfield, and several workers, foremen and managers were also 'borrowed' from the American plant. The Birmingham Small

Arms factory (consisting of 20 firms contracted to supply arms required for the Crimean War) was also established at this time, using largely American machines and, initially, American-made interchangeable parts.

This five-year period of industrial revitalization transformed opinion in Britain, helped the country to win the war in which it was then engaged, established in Britain and throughout the world new principles and standards of mass and flow manufacture and also established America in international trade.

AUTOMOBILE MANUFACTURE

By the mid 1850s, all of the components of flow-line production had been used with success in various industries in several countries. In many cases such components, i.e. work rationalization, efficient material flow and interchangeable parts, had not been combined into one manufacturing system, and, even where such integration had taken place, the level of sophistication common today had not been approached or even conceived. We have seen how mass- and flow-production systems developed in response to mass demand, as well as in anticipation of mass demand. In essence, the situation which existed on quite a widespread scale in 1850 is not far removed from that evident today. However, several important developmental steps were yet to be achieved, and the first, and perhaps most important, of these is associated with Henry Ford, the motor-car magnate.

Although the first commercially successful automobile was made by the French Panhard company in 1891, sometime before automobile production began on the other side of the Atlantic, America was quickly to become the world's leading automobile-producing nation, a fact which, in part, derived from that country's existing expertise in mass manufacture.

The period from 1891 to 1900 was the pioneer phase in automobile production and use, a phase to which America barely contributed. The second phase from 1900 to 1908 represents the beginning of mass production, and the third phase, 1909 to 1925, the expansion of mass production. It was during these latter two phases, particularly the third phase, that the American influence began to dominate. The first motor car intended for the masses, as opposed to the upper classes, was designed by Ranson E. Olds, of Michigan, in 1899. Olds was the first person to attempt to 'manufacture' vehicles. His was a rather complicated car, perhaps too far ahead of its time. Nevertheless, he was successful in setting up a factory at Detroit from which he turned out cars priced at about $1250. His second Oldsmobile car, priced at $650, was assembled from parts bought from other companies, on something approaching an assembly-line principle. Using some division of labour, a moving line and various other innovations, Olds managed to produce 4000 cars in 1904.

Elsewhere mass-production methods had been introduced for the manufacture of automobile parts such as engines, bodies, etc. Henry M. Leland, who had previously worked as a machinist in the Colt factory, began making plans for the manufacture of engines in large numbers using interchangeable parts. Eventually he became so enthusiastic about the emerging automobile industry that he entered it wholeheartedly and began making Cadillacs, perhaps the first truly standardized car. In 1906, to demonstrate his techniques, he sent three vehicles, each with 91 parts, to England, where they were dismantled. His mechanics, equipped with only simple tools, and drawing randomly from the collection of parts, assembled three cars which were then driven on a 500 mile test run.

Henry Ford was a man of considerable insight, determination and genius. He was not responsible for inventing flow-line mass production, since, as

Figure 2.1 Magneto assembly at the Ford Highland Park plant (1913) (reproduced by permission of the Educational Affairs Department, Ford Motor Company, Dearborn, Michigan, U.S.A.)

we have seen, all the ingredients of this method of manufacture were available prior to the time at which Ford began to make the legendary 'Model T'. Ford's contribution, like Whitney's and North's, was developmental rather than inventive. Although by 1904 there were approximately 120 manufacturers assembling cars, none of them was to have quite the same impact as the Ford company formed in Michigan on 16 June 1903.

Although Ford began by making his 'Model A' in the conventional manner, it was not an expensive or elaborate car, and sold for about $1200, less than one-fifth of the price of a four-cylinder Packard of the same year. In 1908, Ford, having declared that he would 'build a motor car for the great multitude', introduced the 'Model T'. Between 1903 and 1913 the managers at the Ford plant extended the techniques developed by Olds and Leland. Work was further rationalized, parts standardized and equipment arranged to facilitate material and product flow. The first assembly line was introduced at the Highland Park plant in 1913. Ford made no claim to have originated this technique, and in fact states (Ford, with Crowther, 1924) that :

'The idea came in a general way from the overhead trolley that the Chicago packers used in dressing beef.'

Figure 2.2 Ford 'Model T' chassis assembly, about 1914 (reproduced by permission of The Educational Affairs Department, Ford Motor Company, Dearborn, Michigan, U.S.A.)

Such disassembly lines incorporating the use of overhead conveyors were known to be in use as early as 1870. The first Ford assembly line (Figure 2.1) was introduced in April 1913 and used in the manufacture of the flywheel magneto for the 'Model T'. Ford describes it as follows:

'We had previously assembled the flywheel magneto in the usual method. With one workman doing a complete job he could turn out from thirty-five to forty pieces in a nine hour day, or about twenty minutes to an assembly. What he did alone was then spread into twenty-nine operations; that cut down the assembly time to thirteen minutes ten seconds. Then we raised the height of the line eight inches—this was in 1914—and cut the time to seven minutes. Further experimenting with the speed that the work should move at cut the time down to five minutes. In short, the result is this: by aid of scientific study one man is now able to do somewhat more than four did only a comparatively few years ago. That line established the efficiency of the method and we now use it everywhere.'

During 1913 other assembly lines were introduced at the Ford works, which enabled 472 workers to produce in an eight-hour day an output previously requiring 1100 workers for a nine-hour day. A moving assembly line enabled the chassis to be produced in 1 h 33 min compared to 12 h 28 min using the previous system. Engine assembly was broken down from one to 84 operations, four times as many engines being produced using the new method. The manufacture of engine parts was similarly 'streamlined.'

Ford describes (Ford, with Crowther, 1924) the development of chassis and body assembly as follows:

'About the best we had done in stationary chassis assembling was an average of twelve hours and twenty-eight minutes per chassis. We tried the experiment of drawing the chassis with a rope and windlass down a line two hundred fifty feet long. Six assemblers travelled with the chassis and picked up the parts from piles placed along the line. This rough experiment reduced the time to five hours fifty minutes per chassis. In the early part of 1914 we elevated the assembly line (Figure 2.2). We had adopted the policy of "man-high" work; we had one line twenty-six and three quarter inches and another twenty-four and one half inches from the floor—to suit squads of different heights. The waist-high arrangement and a further subdivision of work so that each man had fewer movements cut down the labour time per chassis to one hour thirty-three minutes. Only the chassis

Figure 2.3 Ford 'Model T' 'body-drop' operation (reproduced by permission of The Educational Affairs Department, Ford Motor Company, Dearborn, Michigan, U.S.A.)

was then assembled in the line. The body was placed in "John R. Street"—the famous street that runs through our Highland Park factories (Figure 2.3). In the chassis assembling are forty-five separate operations or stations. The first men fasten four mud-guard brackets to the chassis frame—the motor arrives on the tenth operation and so on in detail. Some men do only one or two small operations, others do more. The man who places a part does not fasten it—the part may not be fully in place until after several operations later. The man who puts in a bolt does not put on the nut; the man who puts on the nut does not tighten it. On operation number thirty-four the budding motor gets its gasoline; it has previously received lubrication; on operation number forty-four the radiator is filled with water, and on operation number forty-five the car drives out onto John R. Street.'

The development of manufacturing methods during the life of the 'Model T' was such that the price fell from $780 in 1910 to $290 in 1924. In 1914, after the introduction of the main assembly lines, 264,972 cars were produced, compared with 181,951 in 1913 and 76,150 in 1912. In 1919 over 2,000,000 cars a year were being produced by the company (Ford produced about 400,000 cars in the U.K. in 1970). The one-millionth 'Model T' was produced in 1914, and altogether 15 million 'Model T's were built between 1908 and 1927.

By the mid 1920s, the motor industry had become the largest mass-production industry in America, and a similar trend could be observed in Europe. The number of firms manufacturing cars in the U.S.A. decreased during this period, although the number of factories increased from 178 in 1904 to 2471 in 1923.

Ford's evolutionary work was of paramount importance to the manufacturing industries of the world, and, perhaps more than any subsequent contribution, established the pattern of manufacture which exists today. In the past 40 years further developments have, of course, taken place, but progress during this period has not matched that which took place either between 1795 and 1850 or between 1900 and 1930.

Notable among the developments which have taken place during the last 50 years has been the introduction of the automatic metal-working transfer line. The first fully automatic line was installed by L. R. Smith of Milwaukee for the manufacture of vehicle chassis frames. It was erected between 1919 and 1920, but took several years to bring into full operation. Smith (1924) described his objectives as follows:

'We set out to build automobile frames without men . . . It is highly likely that watching our workers do the same thing over and over again, day in and day out, sent us on our quest for 100 % mechanization of frame manufacture.'

He described the purpose of the line (Figure 2.4), which was capable of producing more than one million frames per year, as follows:

'A completed frame leaves the conveyor end, brushed and cleaned for the paint line, every ten seconds of the production shift. It takes nineteen minutes from the strip of steel as received from the mill to the delivery of an enamelled automobile frame into storage.'

Figure 2.4 A. O. Smith automobile-frame production line (reproduced by permission of the A. O. Smith Corporation)

The fully automatic line (Figure 2.4) performed, on average, about 550 operations in the 1 h 30 min manufacturing cycle, using largely air-powered automatic riveting heads which swung into position over the frame.

Prior to the design of this automatic transfer line, Greenlee and Bros., a company located at Rockford, Illinois, U.S.A., had made what was probably one of the earliest transfer-type machines. It cannot be referred to as a transfer line, since the method of work transfer between work stations was manual rather than automatic; however, it was indisputably an important forerunner of the transfer line. It was originally a two-station machine designed for boring and adzing wooden railway sleepers, and was later extended to four stations.

Around the same time, in England, the Archdale Company was developing transfer-type machines for use by the Morris Company. It is likely that the Archdale Company was the first to manufacture a metal-cutting transfer machine in 1923, in collaboration with Frank Woolard of Morris Engines Ltd. The machine, which was to be used for the machining of cylinder blocks, was 181 ft long, weighed 300 tons and employed 81 electric motors. There were 53 work stations in all, 224 min being required

Figure 2.5 Archdale in-line transfer machine built in 1942 (reproduced by permission of the Archdale Division, Staveley Machine Tools Ltd.)

to complete one cylinder block, with blocks being produced at a rate of one every 4 min. Unlike the chassis-frame line at Milwaukee, this machine was 'hand fed' in that the blocks were moved between stations by hand on 'skidways' and were manually clamped at each station.

This early British machine was not, by our definition, a transfer line. However, two further, somewhat more advanced, machines were built by the same company for Morris at a later date; both of these provided for automatic work transfer between stations. The first of these, a gearbox-machining transfer line (Figure 2.5), was first used in 1924, as also was the line for machining flywheels. Both were ambitious projects, the gearbox line in particular, since it was a double line providing 45 operations for an output of 800 gearboxes in a 47 h week. Neither of these machines was entirely successful and both were eventually broken down into their separate components which were then used individually by the company.

The Archdale Company was also one of the first companies to manufacture rotary transfer machines. Their first machine of this type, delivered to the Ford Motor Company in England in 1933, relied on hand rotation of the circular indexing table. On subsequent designs, automatic rotation or transfer of work was introduced.

Since these pioneering experiments, the automatic transfer of work between stations on transfer lines has become a common and indispensable feature in industry, and thus the trend begun in Venice and Segovia has been brought, via the small-arms manufacturers, Ford and others, to a satisfactory, if not final, conclusion. The principles of work rationalization, efficient material flow, and the manufacture of interchangeable parts have given rise to quantity production using production-flow methods, incorporating either automatic or manual work stations.

It is unlikely that this concept of manufacture, which has taken over 700 years to mature (Table 2.1), has reached its ultimate or final point of development, but, apart from specific engineering and technological developments and design changes, the manual and transfer flow lines presently in existence do not differ substantially from those that might have been observed in certain companies 30 years ago.

Table 2.1 Stages in the development of flow production

Year	Development	Context
1260	Division of labour in Venice commented on by Dante and Marco Polo.	
1438	Flow line at Venice arsenal described.	
1496	Mass production of needles by Leonardo da Vinci.	
1617	Use of automatic straight-line process in Spanish mint.	
1717	Unsuccessful attempt to manufacture guns using interchangeable parts in France.	
1731	Manufacture of buttons and pins on flow line in Moscow.	
1746	Description of flow-line production of pins in England.	
1785	Oliver Evans designs 'automatic' flour mill.	
1785	Production in France of interchangeable parts for muskets.	1793 and 1796 Outbreak of war between France and Britain, and Spain and Britain, respectively.
1798	Eli Whitney's first contract for 10,000 guns (later used interchangeable parts).	
1799	Government contract for gun manufacture to Simeon North (later used interchangeable parts).	
1804	Manufacture of ships' biscuits on flow line in England.	1803 to 1815 Napoleonic Wars
1809	Mass production of ships' blocks in England.	
1830	Manufacture of brass clocks with interchangeable parts—Chauncey Jerome, U.S.A.	1830 'Penny press' launched.
1837	Assembly-line layout principle used at Bridgewater foundry, England.	
1839	Use of flow-line principle at Chorlton Mills, England.	
1846	Use of interchangeable parts in sewing machines.	1845 to 1848 America at war with Mexico
1847	Use of interchangeable parts in farm machinery in U.S.A.	
1848	Use of interchangeable parts in manufacture of watches in U.S.A.	
1851	Crystal Palace Exhibition—interchangeable parts demonstrated.	
1855	Enfield and B.S.A. arms factories modelled on Colt systems.	1854 to 1856 Crimean War
1861	Flow-line production in meat processing in Chicago.	1861 to 1865 American Civil War
1891	Manufacture of freight cars on flow line.	
1899	Design of 'low-cost' Oldsmobile.	
1906	Olds and Cadillac cars made in large quantities.	
1908	First 'Model T' Ford made.	
1913	Use of first assembly line at Ford plant.	
1922	Use of transfer line at A. O. Smith Corporation, U.S.A.	
1923	Use of 'hand' transfer line at Morris Engines, England.	
1924	Use of automatic transfer line at Morris Engines.	

References

Armytage, W. H. G. (1961). *A Social History of Engineering*, Faber and Faber, London.

Battison, E. A. (1966). 'Eli Whitney and the milling machine', *Smithsonian Journal of History*, 1, No. 2, 9–34.

Bright, J. R. (1958). *Automation and Management*, Harvard University Press, Boston, Mass.

Burlingame, R. (1949). *Backgrounds of Power*, Charles Scribner and Sons Ltd., New York.

Burstall, A. F. (1963). *A History of Mechanical Engineering*, Faber and Faber, London.

Demyanyuk, F. S. (1963). *Technological Principles of Flow-line and Automated Production*, Vol. I, Pergamon, Oxford.

Digby, K. (1644). *Of Bodies*, G. Blaizet, Paris.

Ford, H., with Crowther, S. (1924). *My Life and Work*, Rev. Ed., Heinemann, London.

Ford Motor Co. (1956). *The Evolution of Mass Production*, Dearborn, Mich.

Giedon, S. (1948). *Mechanization takes Command*, Oxford University Press, New York.

Haven, C. T., and Belden, F. A. (1940). *A History of the Colt Revolver*, Bonanza Books, New York.

Johnson, E. A., and Krooss, H. E. (1960). *The American Economy*, Prentice Hall, New York.

Musson, A. E. (1957). 'James Nasmyth and the early growth of mechanical engineering', *Econ. Hist. Rev.*, 121–127.

Roe, J. W. (1916). *English and American Tool Builders*, Yale University Press, New Haven.

Smith, A. (1746). *An Inquiry into the Nature and Causes of the Wealth of Nations*, Book 1, Dent's Everyman's Library, London.

Smith, L. R. (1924). 'We built a plant to run without men', *The Magazine of Business*, February, 135–138, 200.

Usher, A. P. (1954). *A History of Mechanical Inventions*, Harvard University Press, Boston, Mass.

Woollard, F. G. (1925). 'Some notes on British methods of continuous production', *Proc. Inst. Automobile Eng.*, 19, February, 419–442.

CHAPTER 3

Definitions and Terminology

In the following chapters the managerial problems peculiar to the design and operation of production flow-line systems will be examined. The chapters in *Part* 2 will deal with the design and operation of single-model lines, and those in *Part* 3 will relate to multimodel and mixed-model lines. Much of what will be discussed in relation to single-model lines will recur during the discussion of the more complex flow lines, indeed *Part* 2 can be considered as a foundation for *Part* 3, in addition to being a self-contained treatment of the problems associated with single-model flow lines. Throughout the following chapters the distinction between transfer lines and manual flow lines will be made as and when necessary; otherwise the discussion will relate to flow lines in general.

To avoid repetition, the remainder of this brief chapter will be devoted to establishing the definitions and terminology which will be used throughout the following chapters.

DEFINITIONS

Throughout the remainder of this book we shall be concerned exclusively with *flow lines*, which, as we have seen in Chapter 1, consist of two related, yet separate, classes of production (Figure 3.1), i.e.

(1) *Transfer lines*, sometimes known as *transfer machines*, since, in effect, this class of production system constitutes one large and complex machine. Transfer lines which may be either of the 'in-line' or 'rotary' type are defined as 'series of automatic manufacturing tools connected by work-transfer devices'. Such lines are normally used for metal (or material) cutting and working, but assembly-type transfer lines are currently being developed. Although early transfer lines relied on the manual movement of the material or product, most contemporary lines utilize automatic movement or transfer methods. This automatic transfer, together with the automatic work cycles of the various

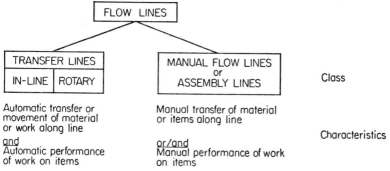

Figure 3.1 Classes of flow line and their characteristics

machines on the line, are the principal characteristics of transfer lines.
(2) *Manual flow lines* or *assembly lines* are characterized by their use of
manual labour, for either or both the transfer of items or material

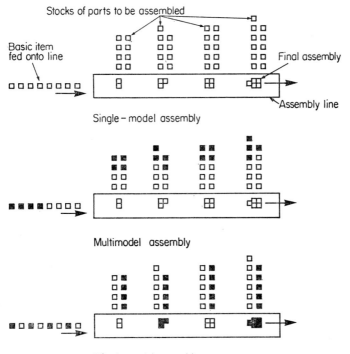

Figure 3.2 Three varieties of flow line (four-station assembly lines)

along the line, and the performance of the necessary work on the material or items. Such lines do not necessarily conform to the in-line pattern; indeed, it is conceivable that successive operations on such lines might not be arranged adjacent to one another.

We have identified three varieties of flow line (Figure 3.2), i.e.

(a) *Single-model lines,* used for the production of a single type or model of item only.
(b) *Multimodel lines,* used for the production, in batches, of two or more usually similar types, models or versions of an item. Each model is made separately in a batch; for large batch sizes, multimodel lines approximate to single-model lines, while, for small batch sizes, multimodel lines approximate to:
(c) *Mixed-model lines,* on which two or more usually similar types or models or versions of an items are manufactured simultaneously.

TERMINOLOGY—SIMPLE LINES

A production flow line consists, essentially, of a series of *work stations,* these stations consisting either of (in a transfer line) one or more machine tools or of (in a manual flow line) one or more workers, probably equipped with some tools.

The *total work content* of the product or item, i.e. the total time required to complete the item, is divided among these stations so that, as the item travels down the line, it becomes incrementally more complete at each station.

One objective in designing flow lines is to attempt to allocate equal amounts of work to each station, i.e. to divide the total work content of the job as evenly as possible between the stations. This is known as *line balancing.* Without such balance, a certain amount of inefficiency or loss must inevitably occur, since some stations will have more work to perform than others. All stations will normally be required to process the same number of items within a given period of time.

The time required to complete the work allocated to each station is known as the *service time.* The time available at each station for the performance of the work is known as the *cycle time*—the cycle time normally being larger than the service time. The cycle time at a station is the time interval between the completion or the starting of work on successive items, and therefore includes both *productive* and *non-productive* work as well as any *idle* time. Non-productive work in both manual flow lines and transfer lines will include the transfer of the product between stations,

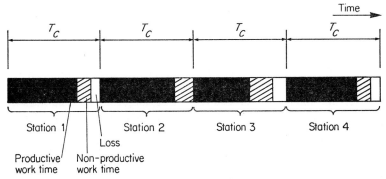

Figure 3.3 Service times and cycle times on a four-station flow line

and in the former will also include a certain amount of handling, movement, etc. (Figure 3.3).

Cycle time = (service time) + (idle time or loss)

$$= \left(\begin{array}{c}\text{productive} \\ \text{work time}\end{array} + \begin{array}{c}\text{non-productive} \\ \text{work time}\end{array}\right) + (\text{idle time or loss})$$

The total work content of the job consists of the total productive work plus the total non-productive work.

Total work content = (productive work) + (non-productive work)

Initially we shall be dealing with situations in which the cycle time is constant and the same for each station, but on more complex lines such a condition may not apply.

The manner in which work can be allocated to stations on the line is influenced by certain constraints. Each job will consist of certain *work elements*, and normally the order in which some of these elements of work can be performed will be influenced by technological or *precedence constraints*. For example, it is necessary to drill a hole before it can be tapped. Such precedence constraints will limit the flow-line designer's ability to achieve balance in allocating work (i.e. work elements) to stations.

The allocation of elements to stations will also be limited by *zoning constraints*. Such constraints will necessitate or preclude the grouping of certain work elements at certain stations. For example, it may be essential that two work elements are not allocated to the same station if they might in some way interfere with one another, e.g. the grouping at one station of a delicate assembly and a heavy forging operation. Such a constraint is known as a *negative zoning constraint*, in contrast to a *positive zoning constraint* which necessitates the grouping of two or more work elements at one station, as might be the case when the maximum utilization of a single expensive piece of equipment is to be achieved. Because of such constraints, perfect line balance is rarely achieved in practice, and a certain amount of *balancing delay* and *balancing loss* is normally inevitable. Balance delay is the difference between the total time available for completion of the job and the total time required. For example, at any one station the balance delay is the difference between the cycle time and the service time. The percentage balancing loss for any station is given by the difference between the cycle time and the service time, expressed as a percentage of the cycle time. Similarly, the balancing loss for a complete line is given by the difference of the total time available (e.g. the sum of the cycle times) and the total time required (i.e. the sum of the service times), expressed as a percentage of the total time available (Figure 3.4).

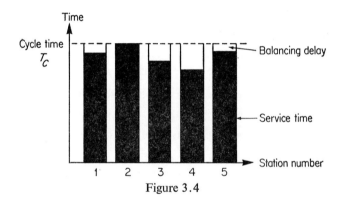

Figure 3.4

TERMINOLOGY—COMPLEX LINES*

To be able to discuss the design and operation of more complex types of line, it will be necessary to introduce some further terminology. We shall see in a later chapter that the principal characteristic which complicates flow-line design is that of operator variability. Unlike transfer lines, where operations are performed automatically, the service time at stations on manual lines is variable.

When the time available to an operator for the completion of work at a station is limited or restricted in some way, a *pacing* situation is said to apply. *Rigid pacing* is defined as the provision of a fixed time, neither

* This section may be omitted on first reading and is required only for Chapter 5 onwards.

more *nor* less, for the completion of work, whereas *pacing with margin* occurs where a time range is provided for the completion of work at stations. In practice, rigid pacing rarely, if ever, occurs, but pacing with margin is common. One method of providing margin is through the use of *buffer stocks* on lines, which, in effect, decouple stations. Stocks are an important feature of many manual flow lines because of the desirability of reducing the pacing effect. In designing such lines, decisions must be made concerning *buffer-stock capacities*, i.e. the maximum number of partially completed items permitted between stations.

Pacing of work is usually considered to result from the manner of operation of the flow line. For example, a conveyor carrying items past workers will give rise to work pacing. A pacing effect may, however, occur even when work is *mechanically unpaced*. This self-imposed *operating pacing* results from a worker's desire to complete his tasks regularly in the time period expected of him.

Many flow lines utilize a moving belt or a conveyor for the transfer of work, as, for example, in the assembly of motor vehicles. The output of such lines is determined by the speed of the belt and the spacing of the items on the belt. Both of these factors can be combined in one term known as the *feed rate*, which is defined as the time interval between items on a moving belt. Where items cannot be removed from the belt, the feed rate for all stations is determined when the items are placed, normally at regular intervals, on the belt prior to the first station. When items can be removed from the belt at each station, the spacing of items after the first station may be irregular, and in such cases a constant feed rate is experienced by only the first station. A further feature of lines which utilize the moving-belt principle is the *tolerance time*, which is defined as the time period during which an item is available for the commencement of work at a station, i.e. it is the period between an item on a moving line coming within reach of an operator at a station and it passing out of the station.

This terminology applies equally to single-model, multimodel or mixed-model flow lines, whereas the following terms relate specifically to multimodel and mixed-model lines. On both of these types of line *sequencing* decisions must be made. In the multimodel line, the decision relates to *batch sequencing*, while on mixed-model lines it relates to *model sequencing*. Batch sequencing deals with the determination of the order in which batches of different models are to be made on the multimodel flow line, while model sequencing deals with the determination of the order in which the different models are to be made on the mixed-model line.

Finally, a term used largely in relation to mixed-model lines is *model launching*. A model is said to be launched onto the line when the basic item or material required for that item is passed to the first station of the line. The *launching interval*, therefore, is the interval between the launching of successive, perhaps different, models onto the line.

Part 2

Single-model Production Flow Lines

CHAPTER 4

The Design of 'Simple' Single-model Lines

We shall be dealing in this chapter with 'simple' flow lines—simple because the problem that we shall deal with is considerably simplified by the assumption that the work-element and service times are constant. This we shall refer to as the *simple* or *deterministic* case. This assumption is valid only for transfer lines, but much of what will be discussed in this chapter will be found to be of relevance in the design of manual flow lines.

The design of a single-model deterministic assembly line is largely a problem of line balancing and the solution of the following problems (although not necessarily in this order):

(1) How are the work elements to be allocated to work stations?
(2) Should any work stations be paralleled, i.e. duplicated, and should multiple manning be employed?
(3) What should the cycle time be?

Problems (1) and (3) can be solved by normal assembly-line balancing procedures, but problem (2) is largely ignored by the presently available balancing techniques, and must therefore be examined as a separate issue.

One of the shortcomings of existing line-balancing techniques and procedures is the rather imprecise nature of their objectives. Comparatively little attention has been paid to the definition of such objectives. In theory, the objective of line balancing is—by allocation of elements to work stations—to obtain a desired production rate at the minimum cost. This objective is itself rather inadequate, first because of the difficulty of identifying and measuring the relevant costs, and secondly because in some cases the production rate to be used is dependent on line balancing.

We shall look at the objectives of line balancing again later, but, for the time being, we shall concentrate on two fundamental approaches to the line-balancing problem, i.e.

(1) Given a required cycle time, allocate work elements to stations so as

53

to (a) minimize the total balancing loss for the line, and (b) distribute the balancing loss incurred as equally as possible between the stations to ensure even loading.

(2) Given the required number of work stations, allocate work to stations so as to minimize the balancing loss and distribute the balancing loss as evenly as possible between stations.

FACTORS AFFECTING LINE BALANCING

Since balancing loss derives from the fact that more time is available for completion of the work than is required, one requirement for perfect balance can be expressed as follows*:

$$NT_C - \sum_{i=1}^{m} T_{Ei} = 0$$

where N = number of stations
T_C = cycle time
T_{Ei} = Work-element time for elements $i = 1, 2, \ldots, m$.

Knowledge of this requirement, however, does little to assist us in achieving line balance. We could, of course, check whether the total work content of the job $\sum_{i=1}^{m} T_{Ei}$ was perfectly divisible by T_C to establish whether perfect balance was feasible. However, this would benefit us little, since, even if the total work content was an exact multiple of T_C, the constraints governing the allocation of work elements to stations as well as the sizes of the work elements would be likely to prevent such a perfect allocation of work. In other words, the achievement of perfect balance such as that depicted in Figure 4.1 (for a five-station line) depends not only on the nature of the relationship of work content to cycle times, but also on other factors. Perfect balance is rarely achieved because of these factors, and situations such as those depicted in Figures 4.2 and 4.3 are more usual. Figure 4.2 shows a situation in which four of the five stations incur some balancing loss, while Figure 4.3 demonstrates a worse situation in which loss is incurred at all five stations. It could be argued, of course, that the latter situation is unnecessary since, by reducing the cycle time, a situation such as that shown in Figure 4.2 could be obtained. However, remember that we may be concerned with the balancing of lines for a given cycle time.

The optimum division of the total work content between workers or stations is influenced by many factors. Several of these factors, deriving basically from human or behavioural considerations, are discussed in

* The notation used throughout the book is listed on p. ix.

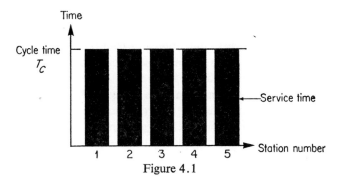

Figure 4.1

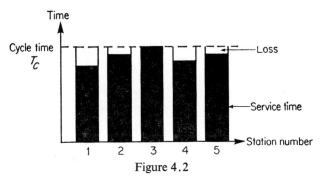

Figure 4.2

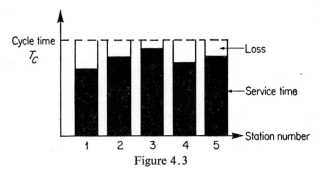

Figure 4.3

some detail in Chapter 9. Two factors, namely *work imbalance* and *non-productive work*, can be discussed here since they may influence the extent of the division of the total work content and thus the change of cycle time and the balancing problem.

The difficulty of achieving a good *balance* depends on the freedom or choice that the designer has in allocating work elements to stations. Two factors limit this freedom—the constraints which exist and the nature of

c

the work elements. Other things being equal, a better balance will be achieved by allocating a large number of small elements to stations than by allocating the same work content in large elements to the same stations. Thus the size of elements in comparison to the cycle time, and also the range of sizes are important factors influencing the success of line balancing. Work-element size is also important with respect to 'learning costs', which will be discussed in Parts 3 and 4. The allocation of elements to stations will also be influenced by precedence and zoning constraints. The more extensive such constraints are, the less is the likelihood of obtaining a good line balance.

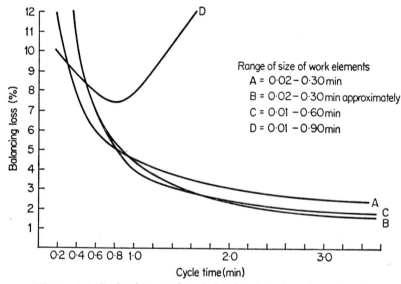

Figure 4.4 Cycle time against balancing loss [based on M. D. Kilbridge and L. Wester (1962). 'The balance delay problem', *Mgt. Sci.*, **8**, No. 1, 69–84]

The relationship between cycle time, work-element and balancing loss is demonstrated by Figure 4.4, which shows the results obtained from four empirical studies (Kilbridge and Wester, 1962). Curve A, for example, is plotted from data relating to 108 television- and radio-chassis assembly lines operating in one company. The curve shows the relationship between the line cycle time and the balancing loss incurred in the line design. Curve B relates to television-chassis assembly lines in another company, while curves C and D derive from the study of lines used in the assembly of a gas stove and an automatic washing machine, respectively.

Curves A, B and C suggest that, other things being equal, the line designers had been able to achieve a better line balance for longer cycle times, i.e. cycle times considerably in excess of the element times, than they had for shorter times or times closer to the element times.

The researchers responsible for this work also investigated the constraints influencing the design of these lines. They found that such constraints were more rigid and restricting for the washing-machine assembly line, and they suggest that curve D takes a 'U' shape because high balancing loss is inevitable at low cycle times, because of the difficulty in allocating the (then) comparatively large work elements. At high cycle times, high loss is a result of the inflexibility caused by zoning constraints deriving from the fact that much of the mechanized equipment used was fixed at a certain part of the line. Notice also that the greater range of work-element times for curve D perhaps contributes to the fact that the balancing loss on these lines was higher than that on the other three groups of lines.

While not providing irrefutable proof of the influence of relative element-cycle-time size and constraint rigidity on the success of line balancing, this research does lend substantial support to what is an intuitively very reasonable argument. The suggested importance of these two factors in line design is of considerable practical significance, since it is often found that line designers, prior to allocating work to stations, do not break down the total work content of the product into minimum rational work elements. It is more usual to break the total work content down into somewhat larger tasks, and this, of course, limits the success of the ensuing balancing, because of the larger relative size of the work 'elements' and also because fewer 'elements' are likely to give rise to more restricting precedence and zoning constraints.

Choice of cycle time might also be influenced by considerations of the importance of *non-productive work*. We have previously noted that the service time at stations will consist of both productive and non-productive work. The latter includes

(1) Product handling (excluding handling of components), e.g. removing or replacing a product from a line or moving a product between stations.
(2) Tool handling.
(3) 'Return-to-position' time. This class of non-productive work occurs only on powered conveyor or moving-belt-type flow lines. The worker may move with the product along the line, returning to a position to pick up the next item, or a return to position may simply involve a body swing.

(4) Station-size allowance, which is the allowance given to compensate for the increased movement necessary to pick up components, etc., as the cycle time, and hence the number of components and the area of the work place, increases.

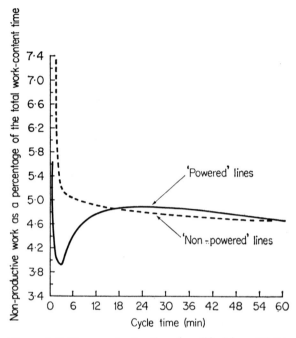

Figure 4.5 Non-productive time (modified from M. D. Kilbridge, 'Non-productive work as a factor in the economic division of labour', *The Journal of Industrial Engineering*, May–June, 1961. Copyright American Institute of Industrial Engineers Inc. Published by permission)

The proportion of the non-productive work content of a job has been found to be related to the cycle time employed. Figure 4.5 shows the relationship obtained in a study conducted in two electronics plants. The solid curve relates to powered or moving-belt-type lines and shows the total non-productive work content [(1), (2), (3) and (4) above] as a percentage of total (productive plus non-productive) work content for various cycle times. The broken curve constructed from the same data relates to non-powered or non-mechanical lines, and differs from the previous curve only in that return-to-position non-productive time is not included. For the non-powered line, the proportion of non-productive time is least around a 2·5 min cycle time, below which it rises quite steeply, and above which it rises to a maximum at a cycle time of approximately 24 min. This 'U'-shaped curve is not evident in the case of the non-powered line; however, in this case also the proportion of non-productive work rises considerably for cycle times of less than 2·5 min. The indication would therefore seem to be that, for this type of work, cycle times below 2–2·5 min should be avoided if non-productive work is considered to be an important cost consideration.

LINE BALANCING AGAINST A GIVEN CYCLE TIME

The requisite cycle time for a flow line will normally be determined by line output requirements, i.e. the cycle time $T_C = T/Q$, where Q is the output required in a period of time T. Now, if T_{Ei} is the time required for the ith element ($i = 1, 2, \ldots, m$) of work, the total work content of the job is

$$\sum_{i=1}^{m} T_{Ei}$$

and if all stations on the line are to have the same maximum cycle time T_C

$$T_{Ei} \leqslant T_C \text{ (for } i = 1, 2, \ldots, m).$$

Achievement of a good line balance for a certain cycle time involves identifying the minimum number of work stations required to accommodate the work content of the job. The theoretical minimum number of stations required by a line operating with a cycle time T_C is given by:

$$\text{theoretical } N_{\min} = \frac{Q \sum_{i=1}^{m} T_{Ei}}{T}.$$

However, there are two points to consider here. First, the theoretical $N_{\min}$ must be an integer; hence normally

$$\frac{Q \sum_{i=1}^{m} T_{Ei}}{T} \leqslant \text{theoretical } N_{\min} < \frac{Q \sum_{i=1}^{m} T_{Ei}}{T} + 1.$$

Secondly, and more importantly, the size of the work elements T_{Ei} and the constraints governing their allocation to stations will also influence the minimum possible number of stations. For example, the number of stations required will be governed by the number of elements whose size is greater than half the cycle time (the number of stations used must be greater than or equal to the number of such elements). The importance of these influences will be considered later.

The service time T_{Sj} (where j = station number = 1, 2, . . ., N) is the time required per unit made at the station. Thus

$$T_C \geqslant T_{S1, S2, \ldots, SN}.$$

The average service time

$$\bar{T}_S = \frac{\sum_{j=1}^{N} T_{Sj}}{N} = \frac{\sum_{i=1}^{m} T_{Ei}}{N}.$$

The balance delay at a station $= T_C - T_{Sj}$.

The balance delay for the line $= NT_C - \sum_{j=1}^{N} T_{Sj}$.

The balancing loss L at a station is given by the following formula:

$$L_j = \left(\frac{T_C - T_{Sj}}{T_C}\right) \times 100 \text{ per cent.}$$

The balancing loss for the line $L = \left(\frac{T_C - \bar{T}_S}{T_C}\right) \times 100 \text{ per cent.}$

Hence the objective of this, the first approach to line balancing, is the minimization of

$$L = \frac{T_C - \bar{T}_S}{T_C} \times 100$$

or

$$L = \frac{NT_C - \sum_{i=1}^{m} T_{Ei}}{NT_C} \times 100$$

for a given cycle time T_C.

Notice that although balancing loss derives from the difference between the time available for work (the cycle time) and the time required (the service time), such loss is not necessarily represented by idle time. Certainly idle time may occur, but equally it is possible that a 'Parkinson's Law' situation might occur in which the work to be done expands to occupy the time available. Either case, however represents an underutilization of resources.

METHODS OF LINE BALANCING

The flow-line balancing problem is complex and important, yet it is only since 1955 that the problem has attracted the attentions of research workers. Since then over a dozen techniques and procedures have been developed, each of which has its own particular advantages and disadvantages. Many of the early attempts at devising balancing techniques are now of academic interest only in that they do not provide a satisfactory means of tackling practical line-balancing problems. Many recent techniques have forfeited some of the rigour which characterized early techniques in order to be capable of accommodating practical problems. In such cases the objective is the provision of a good, but not necessarily optimum, solution, perhaps to provide a basis for subsequent 'manual' manipulation and improvement. A good survey of many line-balancing problems, including most of those discussed here, has been made by Ignall (1965).

The first published treatment of the problem was by Salveson (1955), who, like Bowman (1960), relied on the use of linear programming. In 1956 Jackson presented a conceptually very simple balancing technique, the procedure for which is essentially as follows:

(1) Determine all the possible feasible allocations of elements for the first station.
(2) For each of these possible first stations, determine all the possible second-station allocations.
(3) For each combination of possible first and second stations, design all the possible and feasible third stations.
(4) Continue as above to fourth and subsequent stations until it is found that, in one of the balances, all elements have been allocated to stations, i.e. until the minimum number of stations for the given cycle time is found.

Jackson developed certain procedures which limited the number of possible line balances to be considered. Even so, for large problems, his procedure may well involve considerable computation.

Several other interesting balancing techniques have been developed (see References and Bibilography), and perhaps the best known among these are those which rely on heuristic procedures. Four of these will now be described in some detail. All four are capable of accommodating zoning constraints, although we do not explicitly refer to such constraints, in our descriptions. As with any other heuristic procedures, these techniques do not guarantee an optimum solution in that a balance with the minimum number of stations is not ensured. Nevertheless, in each case one or more 'good solutions' can be obtained fairly easily, and these can then be used as a basis for 'manual' improvement or further modification.

The Kilbridge and Wester method (1961)

This simple *heuristic* method of flow-line balancing is best described by means of an example.

Assembly of a simple component requires the performance of 21 work elements which are governed by certain precedence constraints, as shown in Figure 4.6. This precedence diagram has been constructed according

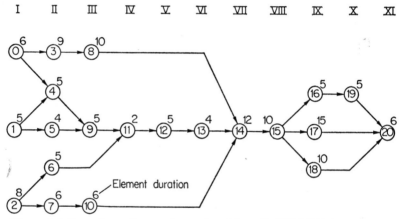

Figure 4.6 Precedence diagram [reproduced from R. Wild (1971). *Techniques of Production Management*, Holt, Rinehart and Winston, London]

to the procedure described by Jackson (1956), namely that circles representing work elements are placed as far to the left as possible, and that all of the arrows joining circles point to the right and are not vertical. The Roman figures above the diagram are column numbers. Elements appearing in column I can be started immediately, those in column II can be begun only after one or more in column I have been completed, and so on.

The data shown on this diagram can now be represented in tabular form as shown in Table 4.1. Column (c) of this table describes the lateral transferability of elements among columns. For example, element 6 can be performed in column III as well as in column II without violating precedence constraints. Element 8 can also be performed in any of the columns IV to VI, likewise element 10. Element 3 can also be performed in any of

Table 4.1 [Reproduced from R. Wild (1971). *Techniques of Production Management,* Holt, Rinehart and Winston, London]

Column number in precedence diagram (a)		Element number (b)	Transferability of element (c)	Element duration (d)	Duration for column (e)	Cumulative duration (f)
I	⎰	0		6		
	⎨	1		5		
	⎱	2		8	19	19
II	⎰	3	III–V (with 8)	9		
	⎪	4		5		
	⎨	5		4		
	⎪	6	III	5		
	⎱	7	III–V (with 10)	6	29	48
III	⎰	8	IV–VI	10		
	⎨	9		5		
	⎱	10	IV–VI	6	21	69
IV		11		2	2	71
V		12		5	5	76
VI		13		4	4	80
VII		14		12	12	92
VIII		15		10	10	102
IX	⎰	16		5		
	⎨	17	X	15		
	⎱	18	X	10	30	132
X		19		5	5	137
XI		20		6	6	143

the columns III and V, provided that element 8 is also transferred, and so can element 7.

Suppose that it is our objective to balance the assembly line for a cycle time of 36. We would proceed as follows:

(1) Is there a duration in column (f) of Table 4.1 equal to the cycle time of 36? *No.*

(2) Select the largest duration in column (f) less than 36 *i.e. 19 for column I.*

(3) Subtract 19 from 36 = *17.*

(4) Does one or more of the elements in the next column (II) equal 17? *No, the nearest is 16 for elements 4, 6 and 7, which will give a work-station time of 35.*

(5) Select the smallest duration from column (f) which is larger than 36 *i.e. 48 for columns I and II.*

(6) Can one or more of the elements in columns I and II be transferred beyond column II so as to reduce the duration to 36? *No, but element 3 (with 8) plus 6 can be transferred to give a work station time of 34.*

(7) Select the next largest duration from column (f) *i.e. 69 for columns I, II and III.*

(8) Can one or more of the elements in columns I, II and III be transferred beyond column III so as to reduce the duration to 36? *No, the nearest is elements 3, 8, 7 and 10 which would give a duration of 38, which is too large.*

(9) Will an improved allocation of elements for station 1 be obtained by considering a large duration from column (f)? *No.*

(10) Adopt the best allocation found previously *i.e. step 4, which gave a work-station time of 35.*

(11) Rewrite Table 4.1 to show this allocation and calculate new cumulative figures for column (f). *Table 4.2.*

Table 4.2 [Reproduced from R. Wild (1971). *Techniques of Production Management,* Holt, Rinehart and Winston, London]

Column number in precedence diagram (a)	Element number (b)	Transferability of element (c)	Element duration (d)	Duration of column (e)	Cumulative duration (f)	
I	0		6			⎫
	1		5			⎪
	2		8			⎪
	4		5			⎬ Station 1
II	6		5			⎪
	7		6		(35)	⎪
III	3	IV–V (with 8)	9			⎭
	9		5			
	5		4			
IV	10	IV–VI	6	24	24	
	8	V–VI	10			
	11		2	12	36	
V	12		5	5	41	
VI	13		4	4	45	
VII	14		12	12	57	
VIII	15		10	10	67	
IX	16		5			
	17	X	15			
	18	X	10	30	97	
X	19		5	5	102	
XI	20		6	6	108	

(12) Is there a duration in column (f) of the new table equal to 36? *Yes, for columns III and IV.*

(13) Allocate the elements in these columns to the second work station and redraw Table 4.2 showing new figures for column (f). *Table 4.3.*

(14) Is there a duration in column (f) of Table 4.3 equal to the cycle time of 36? *No.*

Table 4.3 [Reproduced from R. Wild (1971). *Techniques of Production Management*, Holt, Rinehart and Winston, London]

Column number in precedence diagram (a)	Element number (b)	Transferability of element (c)	Element duration (d)	Duration of column (e)	Cumulative duration (f)	
	0					⎫
	1					⎪
	2					⎬ Station 1
	4					⎪
	6					⎪
	7			35	(35)	⎭
	3		9			⎫
	9		5			⎪
III	5		4			⎬ Station 2
	10		6			⎪
	8		10			⎪
IV	11		2	36	(36)	⎭
V	12		5	5	5	
VI	13		4	4	9	
VII	14		12	12	21	
VIII	15		10	10	31	
	16		5			
IX	17	X	15			
	18	X	10	30	61	
X	19		5	5	66	
XI	20		6	6	72	

(15) Select the largest duration in column (f) which is less than 36 *i.e. 31 from columns V, VI, VII and VIII.*

(16) Subtract 31 from 36 = 5.

(17) Does one or more of the elements in the next column (IX) equal 5? *Yes, element 16.*

(18) Allocate the columns concerned and that element to the work station and redraw Table 4.3. *Table 4.4.*

(19) Is there a duration in column (f) of the new table equal to 36? *Yes, for columns IX, X and XI.*

(20) Allocate the element in these columns to the work station.

All 21 elements have now been assigned to four work stations in the manner shown Figure 4.7, the balancing loss involved being:

$$\frac{NT_C - \sum_{i=1}^{m} T_{Ei}}{NT_C} \times 100$$

$$= \frac{4(36) - 143}{4(36)} \times 100 = 0{\cdot}7 \text{ per cent.}$$

Table 4.4 [Reproduced from R. Wild (1971). *Techniques of Production Management*, Holt, Rinehart and Winston, London]

Column number in precedence diagram (a)	Element number (b)	Transferability of element (c)	Element duration (d)	Duration of column (e)	Cumulative duration (f)	
	0					⎫
	1					⎪
	2					⎬ Station 1
	4					⎪
	6					⎪
	7			35	(35)	⎭
	3					⎫
	9					⎪
	5					⎬ Station 2
	10					⎪
	8					⎪
	11			36	(36)	⎭
V	12	5				⎫
VI	13	4				⎪
VII	14	12				⎬ Station 3
VIII	15	10				⎪
IX	16	5		36	(36)	⎭
IX	17	15				
	18	10		25	25	
X	19	5		5	30	
XI	20	6		6	36	

As can readily be seen from the example, this heuristic method is rapid, easy and often quite efficient. The allocation of elements is basically determined by precedence relationships, lateral transferability of elements being used to aid allocation when necessary. The originators of this method offer the following comments to aid in the application of the method.

(1) Permutability within columns is used to facilitate the selection of elements (tasks) of the length desired for optimum packing of the work stations. Lateral transferability helps to deploy the work elements (tasks) along the stations of the assembly line so they can be used where they best serve the packing solution.

(2) Generally the solutions are not unique. Elements (tasks) assigned to a station which belong, after the assignment is made, in one column of the precedence diagram can generally be permuted within the column. This allows the line supervisor some leeway to alter the sequence of work elements (tasks) without disturbing the optimum balance.

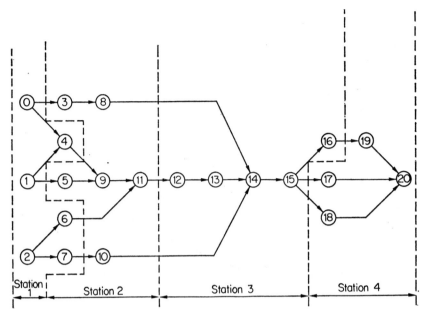

Figure 4.7 Allocation of work elements to stations [reproduced from R. Wild (1971). *Techniques of Production Management*, Holt, Rinehart and Winston, London]

(3) Long time elements (tasks) are best disposed of first, if possible. Thus, if there is a choice between the assignment of an element of duration, say 20 and the assignment of two elements of duration, say, 10 each, assign the larger element first. Small elements are saved for ease of manipulation at the end of the line. The situation is analogous to that of a paymaster dispensing the week's earnings in cash. He will count out the largest bills first. Thus, if the amount to be paid a worker is $77, the paymaster will give three $20 bills first, then one $10, one $5 bill and two $1 bills, in that order.

(4) When moving elements laterally, the move is best made only as far to the right as is necessary to allow a sufficient choice of elements for the work station being considered.

In view of point (3) above, the *ranked-positional-weight* (r.p.w.) method of flow-line balancing described next might be considered a logical extension to the present method, in that, in the r.p.w. method, a heuristic procedure is used which allocates elements to stations according to both their position in the precedence diagram and their duration.

Ranked positional weights

The ranked-positional-weight procedure was developed by Helgeson and Birnie (1961) of the General Electric Company of the U.S.A. in the late 1950s. It is a rapid, but approximate, method which has been shown to provide acceptably good solutions more quickly than many of the alternative methods. It is capable of dealing with both precedence and *zoning* constraints. The procedure is best illustrated by considering a simple example.

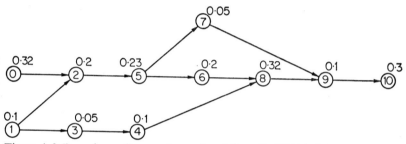

Figure 4.8 Precedence diagram [reproduced from R. Wild (1971). *Techniques of Production Management*, Holt, Rinehart and Winston, London]

Assembly of a very simple component involves 11 minimum rational work elements. There are constraints on the order in which these elements are to be undertaken, but there are no zoning constraints. Figure 4.8 is a precedence diagram in which the circles depict work elements. Element 2 must follow elements 0 and 1 and must precede element 5, etc. The standard element times (in hours) are also shown in Figure 4.8. The same

Table 4.5 Precedence matrix [reproduced from R. Wild (1971). *Techniques of Production Management*, Holt, Rinehart and Winston, London]

Element number	Element time (h)	0	1	2	3	4	5	6	7	8	9	10	Positional weight
0	0·32						+	+	+	+	+	+	1·72
1	0·1		|	|		+	+	+	+	+	+	+	1·65
2	0·2						|	+	+	+	+	+	1·40
3	0·05					|				+	+	+	0·87
4	0·1									|	+	+	0·82
5	0·23							|	|	+	+	+	1·20
6	0·2									|	+	+	0·92
7	0·05										|	+	0·45
8	0·32										|	+	0·72
9	0·1											|	0·40
10	0·3												0·30

information is listed in Table 4.5. The element number is given in the first column and its standard time is given in the second. The middle of the table shows the element precedences; for example, element 0 is immediately followed by element 2, which in turn is followed by 5, which is followed by 6 and 7, and so on. A single mark indicates the element which follows immediately, and crosses indicate elements which follow because of their relationship with other elements. The final column of the table gives the *positional weight* (p.w.) for each element. This is calculated by summing the element's own standard time and the standard time for all following elements. Thus, for element 0:

$$
\begin{aligned}
\text{p.w.} = \text{element} \quad & 0(= 0\cdot32) \\
+ \text{element} \quad & 2(= 0\cdot20) \\
+ \text{element} \quad & 5(= 0\cdot23) \\
+ \text{element} \quad & 6(= 0\cdot20) \\
+ \text{element} \quad & 7(= 0\cdot05) \\
+ \text{element} \quad & 8(= 0\cdot32) \\
+ \text{element} \quad & 9(= 0\cdot10) \\
+ \text{element} \quad & 10(= 0\cdot30) = 1\cdot72
\end{aligned}
$$

The *positional weight* is, therefore, a measure of the size of an element and its position in the sequence of elements.

The elements, their times and immediate predecessors are given in order of decreasing positional weight in Table 4.6.

Table 4.6 [Reproduced from R. Wild (1971). *Techniques of Production Management*, Holt, Rinehart and Winston, London]

Element number	0	1	2	5	6	3	4	8	7	9	10	Total
Element time	0·32	0·1	0·2	0·23	0·2	0·05	0·1	0·32	0·05	0·1	0·3	1·97
P.W.	1·72	1·65	1·4	1·2	0·92	0·87	0·82	0·72	0·45	0·40	0·30	
Predecessors (immediate)	—	—	0, 1	2	5	1	3	4, 6	5	7, 8	9	

We are required to design an assembly line with the minimum number of stations to provide a cycle time of 0·55 h (i.e. an output of 1·82 per hour). Using Table 4.6, elements are allocated to work stations in order of decreasing positional weight and without violating precedence constraints. Element 0 with the highest p.w. of 1·72 is allocated first to station 1. This allocation is acceptable because element 0 has no immediate predecessors, and furthermore its element time is less than the spare time available in station 1 (see Table 4.7).

Table 4.7 Allocation of elements to stations [reproduced from R. Wild (1971). *Techniques of Production Management*, Holt, Rinehart and Winston, London]

Work station	Element	P.W.	Immediate predecessor	Element time	Cumulative element times (X)	Unassigned cycle time $(T_C - X)$
1	0	1·72	—	0·32	0·32	0·23
	1	1·65	—	0·1	0·42	0·13
	3	0·87	1	0·05	0·47	0·08
2	2	1·4	0, 1	0·2	0·2	0·35
	5	1·2	2	0·23	0·43	0·12
	4	0·82	3	0·1	0·53	0·02
3	6	0·92	5	0·2	0·2	0·35
	8	0·72	4, 6	0·32	0·52	0·03
4	7	0·45	5	0·05	0·05	0·50
	9	0·4	7, 8	0·1	0·15	0·40
	10	0·3	9	0·3	0·45	0·10

$T_C = 0·55$

$$\text{Balancing loss} = \frac{4(0·55) - 1·97}{4(0·55)} \times 100 = 10·4 \text{ per cent}$$

Element 1 is next to be allocated since it has the next highest p.w. It is acceptable in station 1 since no precedence constraints are violated and there is sufficient unassigned cycle time left to accommodate it.

The next highest p.w. belongs to element 2, but this cannot be assigned to station 1, even though its immediate predecessors have been assigned, because the unassigned station time remaining (0·13) is less than the element time (0·2).

Element 5 cannot be allocated because it must follow element 2, nor is there sufficient time available.

Element 6 cannot be allocated to station 2 for the same reasons.

Element 3 can be allocated to station 1 since its immediate predecessor is already allocated and there is sufficient time available.

Of the remaining elements, only 7 is short enough for accommodation in station 1, but it cannot be allocated here because it must follow element 5.

The same procedure is now repeated for the remaining stations.

Four work stations are required for this assembly line, and the initial allocation gives a balancing loss of 10·4 per cent. Notice that there is unassigned time at each station, the largest work-station time of 0·53 h occurring at station 2. In fact, we now have a situation similar to the one depicted in Figure 4.3. A flow diagram for such a procedure using the r.p.w. technique is shown in Figure 4.9.

It is not difficult to criticize this simple assembly-line-balancing procedure or to suggest improvements. Mansoor (1964) has developed an improved r.p.w. technique involving a 'backtracking' procedure which appears to provide better results in certain conditions. We can, of course, criticize the heuristic approach to the r.p.w. method, but, like all heuristic methods, proof of its efficiency can only be obtained empirically or by simulation.

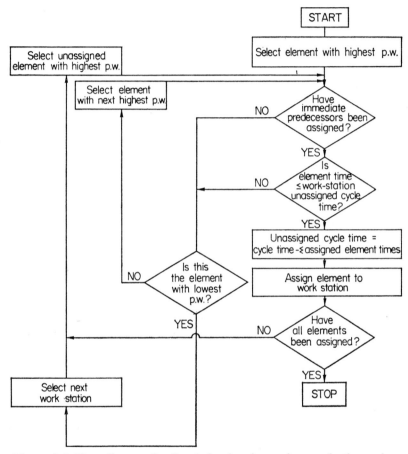

Figure 4.9 Flow diagram for line balancing for a given cycle time using r.p.w. method [reproduced from R. Wild (1971). *Techniques of Production Management*, Holt, Rinehart and Winston, London]

The positional weight of an element is a measure of its own size and its precedence position. Elements with high p.w. occur at the beginning of the job and/or have large standard times, and using the improved r.p.w. technique we attempt to allocate these first, and those with low p.w.s last.

The largest-candidate rule

Using this technique elements are allocated to stations, beginning with the first station, by selecting from those elements that are feasible in descending order of size. For example, if we consider the precedence diagram previously used in describing the r.p.w. technique (Figure 4.8), this rule would be applied as follows:

Consider station 1: Initially there are two feasible elements, i.e. 0 and 1. Since 0 has the largest time, allocate this to the first station. Now there is only one feasible element, i.e. 1, which is therefore allocated to this station. Now although both elements 2 and 3 are feasible in respect of precedence, only 3 is feasible for allocation, since there is only 0·13 h unassigned cycle time remaining. This element is therefore allocated to station 1. This completes station 1.

Now consider station 2: There are two feasible elements, i.e. 2 and 4. The former, being the largest, is allocated to the station. Elements 5 and 4 are now feasible, and the former is allocated as it is the largest. Elements 4 and 7 are now feasible (element 6 is too large) and 4, being the largest, is allocated to complete this station.

If this procedure is followed an assignment identical to that obtained by the r.p.w. technique would be obtained. For this small problem, balancing using the largest-candidate rule offers a quicker solution than r.p.w. However, the heuristic approach used is less sophisticated than that adopted in the r.p.w. technique; hence the latter may provide better balances in more complex situations.

One other technique is worth brief examination, not only because of its own particular merit, but because it represents a somewhat different approach to the line-balancing problem.

Comsoal

An interesting method of assembly-line balancing called Comsoal (computer method of sequencing operations for assembly lines) was developed around 1965 by Arcus (1966). Comsoal uses a digital computer to sample data and *simulate* possible assembly-line balances. The simulation follows the following comparatively simple, basic procedure:

(1) Consider the job in terms of a precedence diagram of minimum rational work elements of the type shown in Figure 4.8. Construct a list (List A) showing, in one column, all the work elements and, in an adjacent column, the total number of elements which *immediately*

Table 4.8 Comsoal List A

Element number	Number of immediate predecessors
0	0
1	0
2	2
3	1
4	1
5	1
6	1
7	1
8	2
9	2
10	1

Table 4.9 Comsoal List B

Elements without immediate predecessors
0
1

precede them in the precedence diagram. (Such a list based on Figure 4.8 is shown in Table 4.8.)

(2) Construct a list (List B) showing all elements which have *no* immediate predecessors, i.e. elements having a zero in the second column of List A (Table 4.9).

(3) Select at random one element from List B, say element 0.

(4) Eliminate the selected element from List B and move all elements below the selected element up one position.

(5) Eliminate the selected element from the precedence diagram and update List A.

(6) Add to List B those elements which immediately follow the selected element and now have no immediate predecessors.

This simple procedure is then repeated until a sequence containing all elements has been constructed. The elements (in this order) are then assigned to station 1, 2, 3, etc., the cycle time at each station being diminished until no further elements can be accommodated, at which stage the next element is assigned to the next station. The number of stations used in the balance is counted and compared to the previous best balance.

If there is an improvement, the new balance is stored in the computer and the previous best discarded. Thus, by generating a fairly large set of possible solutions, a good flow-line balance can be obtained.

Arcus improved this basic procedure by extracting from List B a further list, C, consisting of those elements whose times did not exceed the time available at the station under consideration, and by selecting elements randomly from this new list. A further improvement was achieved by using a biased or weighted sampling procedure to select elements from List C, in place of purely random selection. Arcus also incorporated a procedure whereby a solution could be aborted before completion, if the total station idle time of the incomplete solution exceeded that of the previous best solution.

Comparison of methods

The line-balancing techniques that have been described are perhaps the most straightforward and simplest of those available. They should be found to be readily applicable in most situations, and their use is not dependent on the availability of electronic computing facilities (although computer programs are likely to be of value in practice no matter what techniques are adopted). Many more complex procedures are available, but there is little evidence to suggest that these are substantially and generally more effective than the simpler techniques presented here. Only one large comparative study has been made (Mastor, 1970) in which ten balancing methods* were compared. The criterion of effectiveness adopted was the output rate from lines of given length, while the computing time required was taken as the measure of cost.

It was found that, although there were consistent differences between the effectiveness of these rules when applied to lines of various lengths with jobs with different numbers of work elements and different 'strengths' of precedence orderings, these differences were not large. The best results were consistently obtained using a dynamic programming method proposed by Held, Karp and Shareshian (1963). However this method was found to require substantially more computing time than the Arcus method, which consistently provided second-best results, and very considerably more computing time than the other simple heuristic procedures (ten and fifty times as much computing time, respectively, for a forty-station problem). Although more effective techniques are doubtless

---

* The methods developed by Arcus; Held, Karp and Shareshian; Hoffman; Helgeson and Birnie; Jackson; an adaptation of Kilbridge and Wester; the largest-candidate rule and three 'bench-mark' heuristic methods.

available at increased cost, the simpler methods, such as those presented here, are likely to be adequate for the majority of situations.

Modification of cycle time

The methods that have been described can be used to obtain a line balance for a given cycle time. In general the minimization of balancing loss will involve the minimization of the number of stations, but this approach to line balancing often results in the design of lines with comparatively high losses. For example, the balance shown in Table 4.7 has been obtained for a given cycle time of 0·55. For this cycle time the minimum number of stations is four, and the balancing loss = 10·4 per cent. Notice that each station incurs loss, since there is unassigned cycle time at each station. In fact the largest service time occurring at station 2 is only 0·53, compared to the cycle time of 0·55. It is immediately obvious, therefore, that, for this balance, i.e. for this allocation of elements to the four stations, the cycle time could be reduced to 0·53, thus reducing the balancing loss for the line to 7 per cent. In this case any further reduction in the cycle time would necessitate the use of five stations.

Although in this section we are explicitly concerned with the balancing of flow lines at a given cycle time to obtain a desired output, it is important to recognize the possibility of modifying the initial cycle-time requirements in the light of the line balance achieved. For the balance shown in Table 4.7, there would seem to be little merit in using a cycle time of 0·55, since to do so appears to add unnecessarily to the inefficiency of the line. However, reduction of the cycle time to improve the balance would, of course, mean that either a greater output is achieved, or that the time worked by the line is reduced to obtain the required output. The merit of these alternative policies depends on the various costs involved (e.g. the costs of inventory, idle time, etc.). We could, of course, continue this argument. For example, in certain circumstances it might be desirable to increase the cycle time to obtain a superior line balance, perhaps with fewer stations, but at the cost of reduced output.

LINE BALANCING FOR A GIVEN NUMBER OF STATIONS

Obtainment of the best line balance for a line with a given number of stations will normally involve minimizing the cycle time, since this will imply a reduction in balancing loss. As we have already seen, a reduction in cycle time involves an increase in output, and thus in this method of line balancing the output is not fixed. In the previous discussion we indicated that, in certain circumstances, it might be beneficial to change the cycle time and output, despite the fact that originally these had been stipulated to improve the line balance.

In this case we are, from the outset, accepting cycle time as a variable quantity. Such a situation is likely to occur infrequently, but on occasions it may be necessary to design a line to utilize a given number of stations. For example, an assembly department in a particular plant may be required to work on several products. Thus, when a new product is to be made, the number of facilities (i.e. work stations) is essentially fixed, and work must be allocated to them. Such a situation might also occur on a multimodel flow line. If a batch of new items is to be made, it may not be possible or justifiable to rearrange the line, and, consequently, all existing stations must be occupied by the production of the new item. Furthermore, in such situations, since we are concerned essentially with batch production, output is often for stock. The production rate is determined after line balancing and is not too important, since here the purpose of the line is to produce a particular quantity of products, an objective which is, of course, a function of production-run length as well as cycle time.

In this approach to the line-balancing problem, the cycle time T_C is determined by the maximum service time, $\max T_{Sj}$ ($j = 1, 2, \ldots, N$). Thus the objective of line balancing is the minimization of total balancing loss

$$
\begin{aligned}
L &= \frac{NT_C - \sum_{i=1}^{m} T_{Ei}}{NT_C} \times 100 \text{ per cent} \\
&= \frac{N(\max T_{Sj}) - \sum_{i=1}^{m} T_{Ei}}{N(\max T_{Sj})} \times 100 \text{ per cent.}
\end{aligned}
$$

None of the line-balancing procedures currently available take the minimization of cycle time and balancing loss for a given number of stations as their primary objective. However, it is, nevertheless, possible to use certain of the procedures in pursuit of this objective.

One approach to this problem is as follows:

(1) Calculate minimum cycle time for a given work content and number of stations, i.e.

$$
T_{C\min} = \frac{\sum_{i=1}^{m} T_{Ei}}{N}.
$$

This is the cycle time that would be obtained if a perfect balance were possible.

(2) Attempt to obtain an N-station balance for this cycle time.

(3) If an N-station balance is not available, increase T_C and try again to obtain an N-station balance.

(4) Continue increasing T_C in *relatively large* increments until a balance with the requisite number of stations N is obtained.

(5) Now reduce T_C by *small* increments until the smallest T_C consistent with an N-station balance is obtained.

Of course, in certain circumstances it may be possible to 'short circuit' this procedure by first establishing a cycle time for which an N-station balance can be achieved and then reducing the cycle time to obtain the best balance.

For example, it might have been possible to establish by observation that, for the precedence diagram shown in Figure 4.8, a four-station balance could be achieved with a cycle time of $T_C = 0.55$. Had this been the case, the use of the r.p.w. technique would have given the balance shown in Table 4.7. We could now use an extension of the r.p.w. procedure (Figure 4.10) to obtain the minimum-cycle-time, minimum-balancing-loss assignment for a four-station line. A similar approach can be adopted with some of the other line-balancing techniques; indeed, two of these specifically provide for this. Phase III of Tonge's (1960) technique, in which a heuristic is used to improve the balance for a certain number of stations, is an attempt to provide a means of obtaining the best balance for a certain number of stations. This procedure is similar to the extended r.p.w. method described above. A further heuristic line-balancing technique developed by Moodie and Young (1965) provides a similar facility. Since this technique is also capable of accommodating variable work-element times, it is particularly relevant to the next chapter, where it will be discussed in more detail.

AIDS TO LINE BALANCING

Occasionally minor engineering or methods changes enable better line balances to be obtained. While such changes are obviously no substitute for thorough line balancing, it is nevertheless worthwhile to remember that aids such as those that follow might, on occasions, facilitate significant improvements in line design.

(1) *Improved work methods:* This is perhaps the first possibility to investigate, although, of course, work measurement to obtain element times for use in line design should normally follow work-method design. By changes in work methods, improved or extra tooling, work-

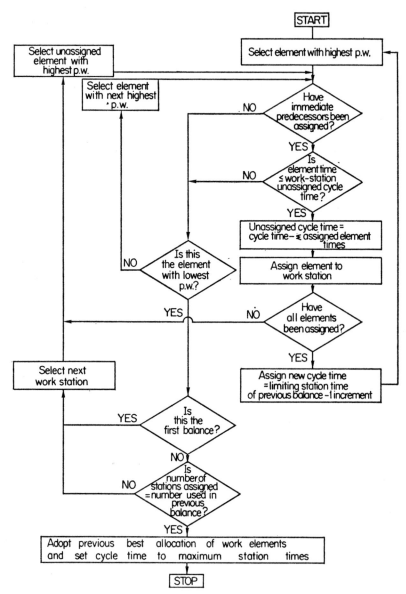

Figure 4.10 Flow diagram for r.p.w. technique used to establish balance for a given cycle time and then reduce the cycle time obtained in that balance [reproduced from R. Wild (1971). *Techniques of Production Management,* Holt, Rinehart and Winston, London]

holding devices, work-place layout, etc., it may be possible to reduce element and service times and to obtain a superior line balance.

(2) *Changed machining speeds:* On transfer lines, and to a lesser extent on manual flow lines, it may be possible to reduce element and service times by changing machine or tool feedrates and speeds. Such changes may be obtained through the use of different types of tools, material, etc. Not only may it be possible to increase machine speeds to obtain a better balance, but the possibility of 'utilizing' idle time at stations by reducing machine speeds to increase tool life should also be explored.

(3) *Increased operator performance*: Occasionally a line balance can be improved through increasing the performance of the worker(s) at 'bottleneck stations'. Normally, equal effort will be expected from all workers, and, consequently, in standard conditions, equal performance levels would be obtained. This concept is one of the foundations of work-measurement practice. It should be recognized, however, that, because of physiological, psychological, situational and skill differences, some workers may be both capable and prepared to provide higher-than-average performance levels. Recognition of such differential performance levels may facilitate improved line efficiency, and in such circumstances some differential method of remuneration will normally be adopted. Alternatively, performances at stations may be increased through the provision of permanent or intermittent skilled or unskilled assistance at stations.

(4) *Diversion of excess items:* It may, on occasions, be possible and beneficial to provide a system whereby occasional items are taken from in front of bottleneck stations, to be completed on separate lines.

(5) *The movement of workers:* It may be possible, on occasions, to arrange for those workers with relatively less work to do to assist those working at bottleneck stations. This cannot usually be accomplished, however, without the need to introduce some sort of buffer stocking arrangement on the line. Additionally, workers at stations with low service times might be able to work at several stations, or even on more than one line. This cannot usually be achieved without the use of buffer stocks, except perhaps when cycle times are very high.

It is often possible to obtain an improved line balance by avoiding or ignoring some of the restrictions implicit in the formal line-balancing algorithms (Mariotti, 1970). Some of the methods by which such improved balanced lines may be pursued are summarized below:

Parallel and multiple-manned stations

If the sum of the work-element times allocated to a station is in excess of the cycle time, it will be necessary to adopt one of the following policies:

(a) To provide extra working at such stations during overtime, extra shifts, etc.
(b) To *duplicate* or parallel such stations.
(c) To assign more than one operator to such stations, i.e. *multiple* manning.

For example, if a line is being balanced to a cycle time of 10 and one of the minimum rational elements has a duration of 15, this element could be

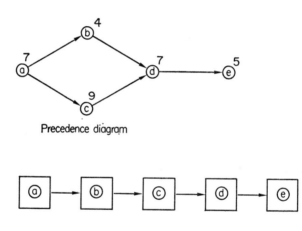

Precedence diagram

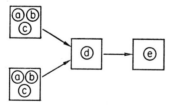

Five-station line

Four-station line with two paralleled stations

Figure 4.11. Use of parallel work stations

allocated with other elements to a station with cycle time 20, two such stations being provided in parallel on the line. This type of situation can be accommodated without undue difficulty when balancing lines using one of the available procedures, as also can the alternative solution of providing double manning at a single station with a service time in excess of the cycle time.

In contrast, a second type of station paralleling cannot be accommodated so readily. Consider the following example (Freeman and Jucker, 1967):

Required cycle time = 10 units. There are five work elements with precedence relationships and durations as shown in Figure 4.11.

A. Balance *without* paralleling or multiple manning of stations requires five stations and results in a balancing loss of 36 per cent.
B. Balance *with* paralleling of stations requires four stations and results in a balancing loss of 20 per cent. Alternatively, a three-station design might have been adopted, with double manning of the first station.

Question

Which line design should be used? A has five operators but no duplication of facilities, whereas B has four operators, but duplicates facilities required for work elements a, b and c.

The possibility of obtaining a superior line design through paralleling of this type cannot easily be identified or accommodated by the techniques currently available, and consequently such possibilities can only be dealt with by separate investigation following initial line balancing. This is one of the major shortcomings of current flow-line-balancing procedures.

Cycle times less than largest element time

If we accept the possibility of using multiple manning, it becomes possible to assign elements to stations against a cycle time which is less than the largest element time. The argument is, of course, that the multiple resources allocated to the stations with 'excess' work will enable such work to be executed within the allowed time. Such an arrangement often permits a better balance to be obtained, and often has an added advantage in that a desired output which was not available at a higher cycle time may be achieved at the lower cycle time. Such an arrangement is more appropriate for lines with large cycle times, where work at stations can conveniently be shared, and where some workers are permitted to move along the line [see (5) on p. 79].

Dividing minimum rational work elements

There may be occasions when the division of work beyond the rational level enables an improved balance to be achieved. For example, normally one might consider the drilling of two identical and adjacent holes in an item to constitute one work element. However, it may be possible to improve a line balance be allocating each hole to separate stations, even though this subdivision of the rational element adds to the total amount of work to be done.

LINE-BALANCING PRACTICE

At the beginning of this chapter we commented on the general lack of definition of objectives for line balancing. Subsequently we examined the two most usual and realistic approaches to balancing, and noted that in both cases the balance obtained may be unsatisfactory. The design of a line for a given cycle time, if pursued inflexibly, may result in a line with substantial balancing loss, whereas the design of a line with a given number of stations may result in a cycle time and output rate substantially different to that required.

Often the objective in line balancing will fall between the two approaches discussed in this chapter. For example, the objective of simple line balancing may be stated as follows:

'Assign work elements to stations to obtain an output rate in the range $X-Y$ and to minimize the balancing loss and hence the number of stations on the line.'

Alternatively, using financial terms, one objective for simple line balancing might be expressed as follows:

'Assign work elements to stations to obtain the least-cost cycle time for the line.'

None of the line-balancing techniques currently available can be relied on to fulfil either of these objectives. Consequently, a 'trial-and-error' approach must be adopted. For the first objective, one of the techniques would be used to obtain balances for several cycle times within the desired range, from which the balance incurring least loss would be chosen. In the second case, a similar approach would be adopted, the choice of line in this case being dependent on an examination of such costs as labour, inventory, facilities, etc., for each of the alternatives. In practice, therefore, line balancing often involves numerous sets of calculations to assess the merits of several alternative designs.

To add further perspectives to the preceding discussion, it may be worth noting some of the results of a survey of line-design practice conducted in America (Lehman, 1969). The results suggest that approximately one-third of cycle times are of 1 min or less (the median cycle time is 3·5 min) and that the median number of stations on lines is approximately ten. The survey also indicated that over 80 per cent of lines were balanced using manual methods, compared with approximately 15 per cent balanced using computer-based procedures. It is not, of course, suggested that these figures indicate best line-balancing practice, but merely that they reflect standard practice. While they derive from a study in one country, there is little reason to believe that practice in the U.K. would differ substantially.

LOCATION OF QUALITY INSPECTION IN FLOW LINES

Inspection is the key to the operation of an effective quality-control system. Materials bought into the plant must be inspected to ensure that they conform to the requisite specifications, and, in general, it will also be beneficial to inspect items during manufacture. The question therefore arises as to where this inspection shall take place.

In the flow-line situation, inspection may take place *at*, or more normally *after*, a production station. Indeed, we can consider inspection work to be a part of the non-productive work content of the job, and hence we can consider *inspection stations* to be much the same as the other stations, needing to be incorporated into the line, balanced against the cycle time of the line, etc.

It may be possible to build inspection requirements into the precedence diagram, in which case inspection elements will be allocated to stations in the same manner that other elements are allocated. In this case, if inspection tasks are to be grouped at stations (in the normal manner) this requirement will be specified by the use of appropriate zoning constraints. Normally, however, the location of inspection stations will be determined after line balancing, location being influenced by considerations such as the cost of inspection and the cost of defective parts.

In practice, decisions concerning the location of inspection stations are often based on empirical and qualitative rules. These may require that inspections should be made:

(1) Before a costly operation (station) to avoid the high processing cost for defective items.
(2) Before a series of operations during which inspection is impossible or difficult.

(3) After operations which generally cause a high defective-part rate.
(4) Before operations which would conceal defects caused at previous stations, e.g. painting or assembly.
(5) Before a point of no return, after which rectification is impossible.
(6) Before points at which potential damage can occur, e.g. prior to equipment that might be damaged by a defective item.
(7) Before a change in quality responsibility, e.g. between sections, groups or items.

A simple approach to the location of inspection stations is illustrated by means of the following example:

Consider a six-station line ($N = 6$) where the expected proportion of defective items created at each station and the processing cost per item for each station are given in Table 4.10.

Table 4.10

Station number (j)	1	2	3	4	5	6
Proportion of defective parts created at station	0·010	0·015	0·005	0·010	0·002	0·005
Number of defective parts for a production run of 10,000 items	100	150	50	100	20	50
Processing cost/item for station (£)	1·00	0·50	1·00	1·00	0·60	1·10

Table 4.11

Station number (j)	Number of defective parts	Cost of processing defective parts created at station j through subsequent stations (£)					
		1	2	3	4	5	6
1	100		420	370	270	170	110
2	150			555	405	255	165
3	50				135	85	55
4	100					170	110
5	20						22
6	50						
Column sums (£)			420	925	810	680	462

Table 4.11 shows the processing cost of the defective items created at a station through subsequent stations. For example, processing the 100 defective items created at station 4 through stations 5 and 6 incurs a cost of £0·60 × 100 + £1·10 × 100, i.e. £60 for station 5 and £110 for station 6, a total of £170. Thus if an inspection station capable of identifying *all*

passing defective items were located after station 4, it would lead to the saving of this £170, but, in addition, it would save the remaining processing costs for defective items created at earlier stations, i.e. a total saving of £680.

Thus the processing cost saving given by the location of a single inspection station after station j is given by the total of the figures in the column for station $j+1$ in Table 4.11. If we know the cost of inspection, we can use this method to assist in determining the location of inspection stations. For example, the best location of *two* inspection stations is after stations 2 and 4, i.e.

Inspection after station 2 saves   = £925
Inspection after station 4 saves £680 − (170 + 255) = £255
                                                       £1180

This method of analysis relies on two basic assumptions. First, it is assumed that 100 per cent inspection is used, and all defective items are identified. Secondly, no account is taken of the accumulation of defects in items; for example, it is assumed that the 150 defective items created at station 2 do not include any of the 100 created at station 1, and thus that the total number of defective items produced by the line is equal to the sum of those produced at each station. This is unlikely to happen in practice. The technique can be modified to take account of this fact, but the distortion of the results occasioned by this assumption is unlikely to be high, unless the proportion of defects produced at the stations is high.

Several more complex approaches to the problem of locating inspection facilities have been developed, many depending on the use of dynamic programming. However, description of these is beyond the scope of this section (see L. S. White, 1966, 1969, and Lindsay and Bishop, 1964).

References

Review articles
Freeman, D. R., and Jucker, J. V. (1967). 'The line balancing problem', *J. Ind. Eng.*, **XVIII**, No. 6, 361–364.
Ignall, E. J. (1965). 'A review of assembly line balancing', *J. Ind. Eng.*, **XVI**, No. 4, 244–254.
Sawyer, J. H. F. (1970). *Line Balancing*, Machinery Publishing Co., Brighton.

Specific balancing techniques for simple single-model lines
Arcus, A. L. (1966). 'COMSOAL—a computer method of sequencing operations for assembly lines', *Int. J. Prod. Res.*, **4**, No. 4, 259–277.

Bowman, E. H. (1960). 'Assembly line balancing by linear programming', *Operat. Res.*, **8**, No. 3, 385–389.

Held, M., Karp, R. M., and Shareshian, R. (1963). 'Assembly line balancing— dynamic programming with precedence constraints', *Operat. Res.*, **11**, No. 3, 442–459.

Helgeson, W. B., and Birnie, D. P. (1961). 'Assembly line balancing using ranked positional weight technique', *J. Ind. Eng.*, **XII**, No. 6, 394–398.

Hoffman, T. R. (1963). 'Assembly line balancing with a precedence matrix', *Mgt. Sci.*, **9**, No. 4, 551–563.

Jackson, J. R. (1956). 'A computing procedure for a line balancing problem', *Mgt. Sci.*, **2**, No. 3, 261–271.

Kilbridge, M. D., and Wester, L. (1961). 'A heuristic method of assembly line balancing', *J. Ind. Eng.*, **XII**, No. 4, 292–298.

Kilbridge, M. D., and Wester, L. (1962). 'The balance delay problem', *Mgt. Sci.*, **8**, No. 1, 69–84.

Klein, M. (1963). 'On assembly line balancing', *Operat. Res.*, **11**, No. 2, 274–281.

Mariotti, J. (1970). 'Four approaches to manual assembly line balancing', *Ind. Eng.*, June, 35–40.

Salveson, M. E. (1955). 'The assembly line balancing problem', *J. Ind. Eng.*, **VI**, No. 3, 18–25.

Tonge, F. M. (1960). 'Summary of a heuristic line balancing procedure', *Mgt. Sci.*, **7**, No. 1, 21–42.

Further references

Kilbridge, M. D. (1961). 'Non-productive work as a factor in the economic division of labour', *J. Ind. Eng.*, **XII**, No. 3, 155–159.

Lehman, M. (1969). 'What's going on in product assembly', *Ind. Eng.*, April, 41–45.

Lindsay, G. F., and Bishop, A. B. (1964). 'Allocation of screening inspection— a dynamic programming approach', *Mgt. Sci.*, **10**, No. 1, 342–352.

Mansoor, E. M. (1964). 'Assembly line balancing—an improvement on the ranked positional weight technique', *J. Ind. Eng.*, **XII**, No. 2, 73–77.

Mastor, A. A. (1970). 'An experimental investigation and comparative evaluation of production line balancing techniques', *Mgt. Sci. (Theory)*, **16**, No. 11, 728–746.

White, L. S. (1966). 'An analysis of a sample class of multistage inspection. plans', *Mgt. Sci.*, **12**, No. 5, 685–693.

White, L. S. (1969). 'Shortest route inspection models for the allocation of inspection effort on a production line', *Mgt. Sci.*, **15**, No. 5, 249–259.

White, W. W. (1961). 'Comments on a paper by Bowman' [*Operat. Res.*, **8**, No. 3 (1960)], *Operat. Res.*, **9**, No. 2, 274–276.

Other balancing techniques are listed after Chapter 5 and in the Bibliography.

CHAPTER 5

The Design of Complex Lines—1

The simple flow-line balancing discussed in the previous chapter was based on one fundamental assumption, namely that elements of work require a given constant time for their execution. The fact that the time required for the completion of elements of work might be variable rather than constant was not considered. To assess the validity of this assumption, it is worth looking briefly at work-method design.

One of the classic assumptions of traditional work study is that there is a single best method of performing a particular task, and that it is possible to calculate a standard time for this (and indeed any other) work method.

It is now generally accepted, however, that the best method for a job will depend on the person doing that job, and it is acknowledged that a person doing a job may change his work method from time to time. It is also suggested that the standard time, i.e. the time to be allowed for a job, must also be a function of the characteristics of the person charged with performing the job, and thus that not only is there no such thing as the single best method for a job, but there is also no justification for attempting to establish a single standard time. Work methods and the time required to perform tasks are likely not only to be different for different individuals, but also to vary for the same worker over a period of time. Even if a worker consistently uses the specified method in performing a task, factors such as faulty materials, wrongly assembled items, slips or errors in handling as well as fatigue, distractions and interruptions may all affect the time required to perform the task. If we add to this the possibility of the worker either deliberately or unwittingly changing his method of working, it becomes clear that for any worker and for any task the time required may vary.

This phenomenon of variability is the fundamental operating difference between manual flow lines and transfer lines. The stations on a transfer line each perform an automatic work cycle, and it is not unreasonable to assume that both work-element times and service times are constant. In contrast, variability is a characteristic of human work; hence it is un-reasonable to assume that work elements and service time on manual flow lines are constant.

The lack of variability in work elements and service times considerably facilitates the design of transfer lines, since, for these lines, the concept of line balance is viable. However, the variability of service times for manual flow lines means that line balance is only a notional concept. Indeed, it is virtually impossible to achieve a balanced state for a manual flow line. It may be possible, of course, to balance the standard times for work stations, or, alternatively, one might attempt to balance mean service times, although this would require a knowledge of the nature of the distribution of element and service times which might, in practice, prove difficult to obtain. However, even if such a notional balance of standard or mean times was obtained, it would not indicate that the line was operating in a balanced fashion, since at any one time it is extremely unlikely that all service times would be the same.

Thus we can see that line balancing is a viable and sufficient objective in the design of single-model transfer lines, but an insufficient objective of single-model manual-flow-line design. Some attempt to obtain notional balance must be made in the design of manual flow lines, but this attempt must be accompanied by further design objectives. When referring to line balancing with respect to manual flow lines, we shall use the notation 'balance' and 'balancing' to indicate that we are concerned with a *notional* concept. Line 'balancing' is a necessary, but insufficient, objective in manual-flow-line design.

Because of the variability of work-element and work-station times, the design of manual flow lines is considerably more complex than the design of simple lines. In the latter only three decisions are required (see p. 53), but in the former there are five problems to be solved. We shall look at each of these problems after examining the nature and consequences of operator variability and the methods of operation of manual flow lines.

OPERATOR VARIABILITY

The possibility that workers engaged on manual tasks may change or vary their work methods and may require different and varying times to perform their tasks has been recognized for many years. It is only comparatively recently, however, that the recognition of this possibility has begun to influence either practice or research in production. This recent interest has stemmed largely from the continuing sophistication of method-study and work-measurement practice. In particular, much research work has been undertaken in attempts to refine methods of performance rating, procedures for determining relaxation allowances and to examine the validity of predetermined-motion-time systems. Much of the work undertaken in the U.K. prior to 1968 has been reviewed by Dudley (1968), and many of the studies that will now be examined with respect to flow-line design derive from his book.

Unpaced tasks

The nature and types of work pacing will be discussed in some detail later. For the time being we shall consider an unpaced task as being one in which a worker is free to work at his own pace, being completely free of any imposition of a maximum, minimum or average work pace.

Research relating to the nature and causes of operator variability on unpaced tasks has dealt mainly with the nature of so called *work-time distributions*. The term was first used by Wiberg (1947) who suggested that the shape of such distributions might provide an indication of the skill, motivation and general level of performance of workers.

Because of the vast range of jobs and types of workers that might be studied, it is not surprising that the research conducted during the past twenty years has not yet led to any general, irrefutable conclusions. Nevertheless, the evidence now available does point rather convincingly to one, seemingly general, characteristic, namely that unpaced work-time distributions appear to be positively skewed. Dudley (1968), discussing the results of a series of studies conducted between 1952 and 1955, comments as follows:

'The operations studied covered a wide range of tasks and were performed by trained and experienced workers, male and female, who were free to work at their own pace, that is, they excluded operations in which a significant part of the work cycle was automatically controlled or in which the worker was paced by some external agency. In every case, the resultant frequency distribution of operation times recorded throughout the day was positively skewed.'

A typical unpaced work time and distribution for an experienced operator is given in Figure 5.1. This example demonstrates characteristics which Murrell (1962) has summarized and discussed as follows:

'When engaged in repetitive work, an operator will not work at a constant rate. . . . The characteristics (of the work-time distribution of such operators) are a minimum time, faster than which it unlikely that an individual will be able to perform and a marked skewness

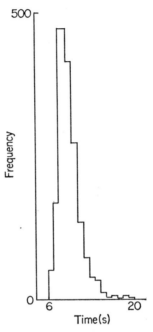

Figure 5.1 Work-time dis-
tribution for female operator
[reproduced from N. A.
Dudley (1968). *Work Man-
surement: Some Research
Studies*, Macmillan, London
and Basingstoke]

towards the shorter times. Approximately 66 per cent of the . . .
times will be at or shorter than the mean (Conrad, 1955). This variability is a perfectly normal human characteristic and it cannot be
prevented by an individual however hard he tries; it does not therefore necessarily reflect a change in the rate at which an individual is
working. . . .'

Unpaced versus paced work

A paced working condition exists when workers, for whatever reason,
are constrained or obliged to perform their tasks within a certain period
of time. Such a situation occurs when workers are fed by a conveyor or a
machine. The extent of the pacing effect is determined by the conditions
and methods of operation used, and may range from a very rigorous

situation, in which workers are permitted only a given time to perform every task, to a situation in which workers, while retaining some control of the length of the time period available for each task, must nevertheless complete tasks, on average, within a given time period.

This latter type of pacing, referred to as *pacing with margin*, is a common feature of the manual-flow-line type of work. *Rigorous pacing*, in which workers are allowed only a specific time, and neither more nor less, for their task, is rare in practice. [A very detailed classification of types of pacing has been given by Murrell (1965).] The types of work pacing and their characteristics are discussed in a later section. Most workers engaged on flow-line work are subject to some form of work pacing, and we must examine the nature of operator variability in such conditions.

Again, it is impossible to state any irrefutable conclusions concerning the nature of operator variability in paced working, but the quite considerable work which has been undertaken in this area has led Dudley (1968) to conclude that:

'Although the distribution of operation cycle and element times of trained and experienced operatives is positively skewed when workers are free to work at their own pace, there is a marked tendency for paced performances to yield a much more nearly normal distribution of operation times. . . . This was found to occur in a series of experiments, even when workers were paced on a conveyor belt at speeds based on their mean unpaced performance and when the work was designed so as to provide what appeared to be an adequate tolerance on the mean cycle time.'

More will be said about the effects of work pacing on work times when the operating characteristics of paced flow lines are discussed in Chapter 6.

Further aspects of operator variability

An area of research which attracted considerable interest several years ago relates to the variability of operator performance over a period of time. Less research work in this area has been undertaken recently, and the conclusions currently available can only be considered as tentative. The situation, however, merits our attention, since any variability is clearly of importance in the design and operation of manual flow lines. The nature of the work-time distribution of a worker at different periods in the working day is of interest because several research workers have identified a 'saddle-backed' relationship between output and time of work, i.e. low output at the beginning of the working period, rising and finally falling again at the end of the period.

There is some evidence to suggest that the variance of the work-time distribution is affected by the working period, and increases towards the end of the period. However, the consensus of opinion is that variations in output derive not so much from a change in the nature of the worker's work-time distribution, but rather from variations in the time that the worker spends working.

Labour turnover is often a problem of considerable importance in flow-line production. Turnover rates as high as 75 per cent per annum are not unusual in companies engaged in this type of production, and hence the associated tasks of labour recruitment and the training of new labour are matters of some significance. Such a situation often results in a high proportion of the labour force being comparatively new and inexperienced. Furthermore, because of the skill and speed required of operators on flow-line work, training tends to be lengthy. Flow lines are often fully or partly manned by people who are not completely trained, and it is worth examining the operating characteristics of trainee workers.

Several of the studies of the type referred to previously have been conducted among trainee workers (i.e. workers who have been taught the correct work method, but who have not achieved the required work speed), and the general consensus of the results is that the work-time distribution of the unpaced trainee worker tends towards normality. It would seem that continued practice enables operators more frequently to be able to perform their operations in shorter rather than longer times. Thus the work-time distributions for trainee workers tend to be more symmetrical, becoming positively skewed with continued task practice.

Level of training is only one of several potential sources of differences between workers. Other than the occasional observation that differences between the work-time distributions of workers may be caused by different inherent worker characteristics, this source of variation has not been investigated. It has been suggested that temperament may affect the influence of pacing on work-time distribution, but as yet little evidence is available concerning such possible effects of personality differences. It has been found, during studies of the variation of work-time distribution over a period of time, that differences between workers are greater than the differences caused by the passage of time, but such apparent effects have not been pursued in any detail. It is not unreasonable to suppose that, if the differences in skill and experience that are manifest in different levels of training affect the nature of the work-time distribution, such differences existing between fully trained operators might also have a significant effect on operation variability. Finally, it should also be recognized that operators are also likely to be characterized by differing needs and motivations, and that such differences might also affect their absolute and relative variability.

Clearly the present state of knowledge on the various aspects of operator variability is by no means complete; however, despite numerous shortcomings, there appears to be general agreement that *fundamentally* the work-time distribution of experienced operators working in an unpaced condition are positively skewed, whereas the introduction of a pacing effect tends to lead to a more normally distributed work time. Work-time distributions play an important part in the flow-line-design research that we shall be discussing later, and the limitations of present knowledge should be borne in mind. In particular, three factors appear most important:

(1) The influence of individual differences, not only on the nature of the distribution, but also on the effect of pacing on the work-time distribution.
(2) The influence of various levels or types of pacing on the work-time distribution.
(3) The possible time-dependent nature of operator variability.

TYPES OF MANUAL FLOW LINE

When discussing simple deterministic lines in Chapter 4, it was unnecessary to attempt to distinguish between different methods of operation or various line types, since, in the simple case, there is really only one logical operating method, i.e. all stations have the same fixed cycle time, and work flow along the line is regular, since the transfer or movement of items between all stations takes place at the same time. The use of buffer stocks of items is unnecessary (except to insure against the effects of line breakdowns), and idle time or station underutilization results only from inadequate line balance, or breakdown.

It is certainly possible to design simple lines to operate slightly differently to this, especially if one considers the paralleling of stations, etc., but, fundamentally, all such lines operate according to the principle given. Not only is the manner in which manual flow lines operate somewhat more complex than that described above, because of the characteristic work-element and service-time variability, but also there are many possible methods of operation. To discuss the design of manual flow lines, it is necessary to be aware of these alternative operating methods. However, any attempt to catalogue such alternatives is fraught with problems, since there are so many possible methods of classification. Rather than attempt to list all possible types and operating methods, we have attempted to identify the basic types of line, and to describe all the others as derivatives or hybrids of these basic types. Furthermore, we have adopted a normative approach by selecting basic types which are in widespread use rather than using theoretical types as the basis of our classification.

Adopting this rather pragmatic approach, we can first identify two basic types of manual flow line:

(1) *Non-mechanical lines*, consisting of lines which do not utilize a moving belt or conveyor for the transfer of work along the line or between stations. Such lines, although probably making use of power and hand tools, are, essentially, manually operated.

(2) *Moving-belt lines*, consisting of all those types of line which utilize a continually moving belt or conveyor for the transfer of items along the line and/or between stations.

Moving-belt lines can be broken down into two further categories:

(a) Items are removable from the belt.
(b) Items are fixed to the belt.

and the latter of these two categories can be further divided to give a total of five types of line. The five types are described briefly below, and their characteristics are summarized in Table 5.1.

The survey referred to in Chapter 4 (Lehman, 1969) indicated that non-mechanical lines were in more widespread use than 'moving-belt' lines—representing 34 per cent compared with 22 per cent of all methods of assembly adopted by the companies in the sample. (The remaining 44 per cent was accounted for by non-flow-line-type assembly work.)

Non-mechanical lines

If all of the stations on the flow lines are able to retain items until they have been completed and are able to pass items to the next station on completion, a variable-cycle-time situation exists in which, because there is no maximum limit, incomplete items should not be produced. Further-more, if such a method of operation were used, there should be no under-utilization of stations or idle time, since the cycle time would always be equal to the service time. In practice, it is not normally possible to operate a line in this manner because of the interdependence of stations. While

Table 5.1 Types of manual flow line and their characteristics

		Moving-belt lines			
		Items removed from line	Items fixed to line		
			Station overlap possible	No station overlap possible	
	Non-mechanical lines			More than one item available to station ($T_F < T_T$)	Only one item available to station ($T_F \geq T_T$)
Cycle time	Variable	Variable	Variable	Variable	Fixed (determined by station length and feed rate)
Work flow	Irregular	Irregular	Regular	Regular	Regular
Buffer stocks	Would reduce idle time	Would reduce number of incomplete items and idle time	Physical stocks not possible	Physical stocks not possible	Physical stocks not possible
Feed rate (interval = T_F)	None, except perhaps for first station	Fixed for first station only	Fixed	Fixed	Fixed
Limits on maximum service time	None	None	Determined by station length, feed rate and previous station	Determined by station length and feed rate	Maximum service time = cycle time
Tolerance time (T_T)	Does not apply	Yes	Yes	Yes	Yes
Mechanical pacing	None	With margin	With margin	With margin	With margin
Incomplete items	None	Possible	Possible	Possible	Possible
Station idle time { through blocking	Possible	Not possible	Not possible	Not possible	Possible because of fixed cycle time (can be considered as either 'blocking or starving')
{ through starving	Possible	Possible	Possible	Possible	

it is possible to avoid the production of incomplete items, idle time cannot be avoided, and will occur for two reasons:

(1) Because, on occasions, stations will be *starved* of work, i.e. having passed an item to the next station, a delay will follow before an item becomes available from the previous station.
(2) Because, on occasions, a worker will be prevented from passing a completed item to the next station because that station is still engaged on its work on the previous item, i.e. the station which has completed its work is *blocked* by the subsequent station.

In practice, if stations operating in this manner are not decoupled by the provision of space for *buffer stocks* of items between stations, idle time caused by both starving and blocking will be considerable. Thus, in practice, it is normal for this type of line to incorporate buffer stocks. A *buffer stock* can be defined, therefore as 'items located between stations to reduce the probability of station starving or blocking'.

This method of line operation involves no work pacing, since there is no maximum cycle time, nor, theoretically, is there a limit to the minimum cycle time.

Since the cycle time on this type of line is variable, the flow of work along the line is irregular. Since this type of line does not depend on the use of a moving belt or conveyor, a fixed feed rate does not exist, except perhaps at the first station. Again, because of the absence of a moving belt, the concept of a tolerance time does not apply.

Moving-belt lines

Items removed from line

There are several methods of operating lines in which item movement is by means of moving belts. Perhaps the most complex type of line is the one in which workers at stations remove an item from the line to perform their work, placing it back on the line on completion of the work prior to picking up the next item. If we consider any one station on such a line, we can identify the following possibilities:

(1) Idle time or station underutilization may occur if, on completion of one item, the subsequent item is not available to the operator, i.e. idle time may occur because of *starvation* at the station. The possibility of blocking does not arise because of the continuous movement of the belt and because:
(2) Items may pass a station without being worked on at the station. If a worker finds it necessary to spend considerably more time than usual

working on a particular item, it is possible that, during this time, the moving line may carry the next item past the station. Thus on this type of line, the production of *incomplete items* is a possibility.

On such lines there is likely to be a fixed *feed rate* for the first station, since items will probably be fed to the moving line at regular intervals. However, for subsequent stations, the fixed rate is likely to be irregular and dependent on the service time of preceding stations. *Work flow* therefore is irregular, and line output is determined by the average feed rate or the fixed feed rate of the first station. The *cycle time* on these lines is variable, and since there is (theoretically, at least) no maximum cycle time, there is no *work pacing*, at least not in a mechanical sense. (Notice, however, that on both this and the previous type of line there may be a psychological pacing factor, since excess time spent on one item will result in either the accumulation of large buffer stocks or the production of incomplete items.)

Buffer stocks may be introduced into these lines if workers at stations remove items from the line rather than letting them pass by while completing work on a previous item. Even so, station blocking will not occur, since, when such buffer stocks reach the maximum level, *provided the stock is off the line*, it will always be possible for the previous station to place items on the line.

On such lines the *tolerance time* is an important concept. The tolerance time is the time period during which an item is available to be taken from the line, and therefore it is determined by the belt speed and the length of the station through which it passes.

Items fixed to line

Station overlap possible

Very often, on a flow line in which a moving belt is used, the items on which work is to be performed are, in effect, fixed to the line. By this we mean that they are attached to the line, or, by virtue of their weight or other characteristics, cannot be removed from the line. The latter situation exists in motor-vehicle assembly lines. In this type of line the work must be performed at each station while the item is in motion. This requires workers at stations to either reach up and down the line, or to move with the line to complete their work. In such cases, depending on the physical nature of the line, it is possible for some *overlapping of stations* to occur, the extent of the possible overlap being determined by the spacing, reach or permitted movement of workers.

On lines of this type the *work flow* is regular, and the *cycle time* is variable.

Since there will be a limit to either the reach or the permitted movement of workers in either direction, the cycle time is subject to a maximum limit, and thus the work is *paced with margin*. The maximum cycle time available for an item at a station will be determined by the time at which it is completed by the previous station, the line speed, and the maximum permitted reach or movement of the station down the line. It will be possible for incomplete items to pass from stations because of the limit on cycle times. *Idle time* may also occur because of work *starvation* at stations, but blocking is not normally possible, and neither is it possible to introduce physical stocks of items (i.e. buffer stocks) onto such lines. Notice that the term *tolerance time* is useful in describing this type of line.

No station overlap possible

On occasions, the class of line described above is used without the facility for station overlap, although this is perhaps less usual than the previous case. Depending on the spacing of the items on the belt and the length of work stations, two alternatives are available:

(1) Lines on which more than one item is available to the station.
(2) Lines on which only one item is available to each station.

Alternative (1) is the more usual case, and we shall examine this first. The characteristics of such lines are very similar to fixed-item/station-overlap lines in that:

(a) The *cycle time* is variable with a maximum determined by the length of the station and the line speed and item spacing. Thus:
(b) Work is *paced with margin*.
(c) *Work flow*, as in all lines with fixed items, is regular, and
(d) The *feed rate* is fixed.
(e) The production of *incomplete* items is possible because of the limit on the maximum cycle time, and
(f) *Idle time* is possible because of *starving*, but blocking is not possible.
(g) The use of physical buffer stocks of items is not possible.

This type of line is not, perhaps, in widespread use, although frequently individual stations on other types of line are obliged to operate in this mode. The best example of this is the case of a spray booth on a flow line. This is a 'closed' station, and overlap with the stations on either side of it is normally impossible.

The fundamental difference between this type of line and the type described previously concerns the influence of preceding stations. Since the preceding station cannot encroach on the subsequent station, the cycle time is limited only by station length and feed rate, and is independent of the service time or completion time of the previous station.

Alternative (2), in which only one item is available to non-overlapping stations, is a more abstract case, and here we are departing from our principle of defining basic types of line according to their practical usage. The reason for the inclusion of this type will become clear shortly. In this type of line, the *cycle time* is fixed and is determined by the station length and the feed rate (line speed and item spacing). As before, *work flow* is regular and the *feed rate* fixed. Again, it is possible for *incomplete items* to be produced because of the limited cycle time, and, furthermore, it is possible for station *idle time* or underutilization to occur, but in this case the cause of idle time differs from that described previously. Here idle time or underutilization can and will occur because, irrespective of the time required for work at a station (the service time), the item remains at the station for a fixed time (the cycle time). The obligation for a worker at a station to take a fixed time for each item and the resultant idle time which may occur can be likened to either starving or blocking, but, strictly speaking, it is quite a different phenomenon. On such lines, *pacing* is with *margin*, and again it is, strictly speaking, different from the pacing experienced by workers on the other types of line because the maximum service time available for any station is the same for each cycle.

This type of *moving-belt flow line* is rarely found in practice. However, its operating characteristics are identical to those of a type of line which does not incorporate the moving-belt principle. Rather than add a further category to our classification to accommodate this type of line, it is more convenient to describe it in terms of our existing class. In practice, therefore, fixed-cycle-time lines of this type often take the form described below.

Visual or audible signals are often used to enforce this method of line operation, i.e. to prompt the passage of items between stations. For example, in suitably arranged lines in which all workers are facing in one direction, a 'traffic-light' type arrangement at the head of the line is sometimes used. These lights flash or change colour at cycle-time intervals, at which times workers are required to pass the item on which they have been working to the next station. Alternatively, an audible signal such as a bell or buzzer may be used if more convenient, workers being required to pass their work down the line on hearing the signal. In lines operating in this manner all stations have the same maximum time in which to complete their work, i.e. the cycle time, which is determined by the line output requirement. This is the maximum time available, but the work could be completed in less than this cycle time. Thus pacing with margin applies, the time available ranging in theory from zero time to the cycle time. Because items remain at each station for the cycle time, irrespective of the work-station time for the particular item, the work flow on this type of line is regular, idle time may occur and incomplete items may be produced.

Hybrids and variations

These are the five basic methods of operation of manual flow lines. However, there are, in addition, numerous hybrids of these basic themes, two of which are now discussed.

In one hybrid, the 'signalled' line described above is sometimes modified to prevent the possibility of producing incomplete items. For example, if an operation cannot be completed within the given cycle time, the entire line is delayed until the operation is complete. Alternatively, it is possible to accommodate the same situation by providing space between stations for work in progress or buffer stocks. When work on an item is not completed within the cycle time, the item from the preceding station is passed into temporary stock, from where it is taken by the operator when work on the original item is completed. Notice, however, that the extensive use of buffer stocks in this manner would, in effect, convert this type of operation to the type of line first described, i.e. *non-mechanical.*

In another type of hybrid, it is possible (although not usual) to operate a flow line so that the cycle time at all stations is determined directly by the actions of one operator through a type of 'shunting' arrangement. In the simplest case, the cycle time is determined by the worker at the first station on the line, i.e. completion of work at the first station is followed immediately by the passage of all items to their next station. (In practice, lines are often designed so that the output and pace of working is influenced by the first station. However provision is normally made for buffer stocks between stations, and the influence of the first station is not direct.) It is also possible for the cycle time at all stations to be determined by workers at any station on the line. In such a design the passage of an item from a station not only displaces items at all subsequent stations, but also those at preceding stations. Such a situation is, in practice, rare. Notice, however, that a similar principle sometimes applies on lines using buffer stocks, i.e. when the stock before a station has reached its capacity, the completion of an item at a previous station leads to the displacement of one of the buffer-stock items, which, in turn, necessitates the displacement of the item currently being worked on at the station, in an incomplete form. Alternatively, a full buffer stock will lead to blocking of the preceding station.

Apart from these hybrid versions of the basic line types, various modified methods of operation are possible. The *station-grouped line* is one derivative of the basic line types. In this method of operation there are fewer operators than stations, operators being required to move about the line undertaking work at several stations. Such a line must therefore make extensive use of buffer stocks and a *non-mechanical* method of line operation, and work will be unpaced. In addition, various devices may be introduced to overcome problems of incomplete items, idle time, etc. Operators may be required to conduct rectification work, service two lines, work double shifts, etc.

Despite the vast scope for the modification and extension of the types of line described above, these five basic types will provide a sufficient foundation for our subsequent discussion of line design.

On reflection, we can see that one or both of two types of operating inefficiency apply to all five basic line types; these are the production of incomplete items and idle time. (In the interests of brevity, we shall continue to refer to *idle time*, taking the term to also mean station underutilization.) Idle time can occur on one type of line (p. 95) for the same reason that it occurred on deterministic lines, i.e. because of balance delay. However, more frequently idle time on manual flow lines will be caused directly by 'blocking' or 'starving' (more usually the latter). These inefficiencies or losses are sometimes referred to collectively as *system loss* to distinguish it from balancing loss. A third source of inefficiency peculiar to this type of line might be considered to derive from the use of buffer stocks, i.e. the cost of capital tied up in work in progress. Certainly buffer stocks represent tied-up capital, but stocks are themselves helping to overcome one or both of the sources of inefficiency mentioned above. The problem, therefore, is to balance such costs.

THE DESIGN OF MANUAL LINES

The design of manual flow lines is a fairly complex problem because of the characteristics and problems that have been discussed. The following points must be considered:

(1) How are work elements to be allocated to work stations, and against what 'cycle time'?
(2) Should any work stations be paralleled, i.e. duplicated?
(3) What will be the method of operation of the line (and should buffer stocks be used)?

Any attempt to answer these questions objectively is bound to be confused by the present lack of knowledge. Much research has been conducted in this area during the past ten years, but even so there is still comparatively little useful information available. Furthermore the information that is available is in many cases conflicting, and, in general, suffers from the fact that it derives from research based on rather abstract models or restricting assumptions. For these reasons we can do no more than survey some of what appear to be the more relevant findings in an attempt to summarize the information and principles available for use in the design of this type of flow line. Questions (1) and (2) will be dealt with in the next section, while Chapter 6 will be devoted entirely to a discussion of question (3), which, because of its importance and the large amount of research which has been undertaken, merits close attention.

LINE 'BALANCING' WITH VARIABLE ELEMENT TIMES

The classical or traditional line-balancing techniques, some of which were described in the previous chapter, deal only with a rather abstract type of production flow line. With the exception of the transfer line, no flow lines operate with constant element or service times, yet the need to develop a different approach to line balancing has only recently been recognized. During the last six years some attempts have been made to develop procedures for 'balancing' flow lines in which element and station times are variable, but, not surprisingly in view of the complexity of the problem, comparatively little progress has been made. Rather than begin by discussing the various approaches that might be made, or objectives that might be adopted, we shall first discuss the few available techniques and later evaluate them within this broader framework.

Throughout this section we shall continue to refer to cycle time in line 'balancing', despite the fact that we have previously recognized that, on most types of manual flow line, a constant cycle time does not exist. However, that such lines operate in an irregular, stochastic manner does not alter the fact that the objective of the first stage of line design is to allocate work elements to stations to minimize loss while satisfying certain output requirements, the latter being best described by the average time interval of deliveries from the line. In certain types of manual line this time interval could be referred to as the feed rate or average feed rate, but since this term does not apply to all types of line, it is convenient to retain the term cycle time for the purposes of manual flow-line 'balancing'.

The first 'balancing' technique capable of dealing with the problem of element and service-time variability was developed by Moodie and

Young (1965). Theirs is a two-phase heuristic procedure, the first phase of which consists of the application of the 'largest-candidate rule'. They assume that work-element times are independently normally distributed with known means and variances. They argue that, if the objective of 'balancing' for lines with constant element times is the minimization of balance delay, i.e.

$$\min \sum_{j=1}^{N} (T_C - T_{Sj})$$

then for variable element times the objective can be represented by

$$\min \sum_{j=1}^{N} \left[T_C - \sum_{i \epsilon j} \bar{T}_{Ei} - z \sqrt{\left(\sum_{i \epsilon j} \sigma_{Ei}^2 \right)} \right]$$

where $\sum_{i \epsilon j} \bar{T}_{Ei}$ = the sum of the mean times for the elements i allocated to station j, σ_{Ei}^2 = variance of element time i and hence $\sqrt{\left(\sum_{i \epsilon j} \sigma_{Ei}^2 \right)}$ = standard deviation of service time for station j. z is a constant.

In other words, this statement involves the minimization of balance delay subject to a certain probability of the station time exceeding the cycle time. This probability is represented by z, values of which can be obtained from tables of areas under the normal curve. For example, if we were required to assign work elements to stations, subject to the requirement that on a minimum of 97·5 per cent of occasions work assigned to stations would be completed within the cycle time provided, a factor $z = 1\cdot96$ would be required. This would imply that the sum of the mean times for elements assigned to each station would be equal to or less than the given cycle time minus a quantity equal to 1·96 times the standard deviation of the distribution of the service time for the station.

Reference to normal-distribution tables provides values of z for different probability levels (see Table 5.2).

In the second phase of the 'balancing' procedure, several heuristic techniques are used to move elements between stations in an attempt to

Table 5.2

z	Probability of $T_{Sj} \leqslant T_C$
1·00	0·85
1·28	0·90
1·65	0·95
1·96	0·975
2·33	0·99

equalize not only the mean, but also the variance of service times at stations.

This technique has limitations. First, since it assumes a given fixed cycle time, it cannot be used directly for the 'balancing' of lines with a given number of stations. Neither does the technique provide explicitly for the possibility of paralleling stations or for the inclusion of buffer stocks. The latter does not imply that it cannot be used for 'balancing' lines on which buffer stocks are to be included. It does, however, mean that for such lines the technique can only be considered as a first step in line design. As with the 'balancing' techniques discussed in the previous chapter, this technique does not provide a means of obtaining the optimum cycle time. Finally, while the criterion of allocating elements to stations subject to a certain limiting probability that service time should not exceed cycle time is of merit, it raises the problem of establishing what this probability should be.

A computer program for line 'balancing' with variable element times has been described briefly by Ramsing and Downing (1970). The program uses the r.p.w. procedure and allocates elements to stations against a given cycle time. After this first balance has been obtained, the cycle time is decremented by any given quantity for any number of trials, the balances obtained for each cycle time being printed out together with the number of stations required and the balancing loss or efficiency for the line. The program therefore provides a certain flexibility for line-design decision making, and indicates not only the best balance—against the criterion of balancing loss—but also indicates the efficiency of line designs for different output levels. To obtain these balances, management is required to specify a significance level, which is used in a manner similar to that already described, in that the given significance level determines the element times used in the program Thus the higher the level of significance, the larger the number of standard deviations included in the element times used in the balancing procedure.

The problem of line 'balancing' assuming element and service times to be independently normally distributed has also been studied by Brennecke (1968). He discusses the two approaches to the line 'balancing' problem identified in the previous chapter, i.e.

(1) Given the cycle time, minimize the number of stations and the balancing loss.

(2) Given the number of stations, minimize the cycle time and the balancing loss.

The method suggested for both formulations of the problem is iterative. For example, in the case of approach (2) above, it is suggested that the procedure to be adopted is one of 'balancing' the line, initially in terms of element mean time plus one standard deviation. This should be undertaken with the objective of satisfying all element precedence constraints. Having assigned elements to stations in this manner, the cycle time for the line would be established to provide a maximum acceptable probability of service times exceeding cycle time. Here the iterative procedure is applied as follows:

(1) Identify the 'controlling station'. This is considered to be the station with the highest value of 'mean service time plus one standard deviation.'

(2) To begin, set the cycle time so that the probability that the service time for this station exceeds the cycle time is equal to the stipulated value. This is accomplished by reference to standard probability tables, e.g. for a probability of $0 \cdot 10$, the cycle time must be equal to the mean, plus $1 \cdot 28 \times$ the standard deviation, etc.

(3) For each of the other stations calculate the probability of service time exceeding cycle time (i.e. calculate the ordinate of the standardized normal distribution $z = (T_S - T_C)/\sigma_{Sj}$, and determine the probability from standard probability tables).

(4) Add these probabilities for all stations.

(5) If necessary, increase the cycle time in increments until the sum of the probabilities is equal to, or just less than, the required value.

The procedure suggested for 'balancing' lines for a given cycle time is somewhat more involved and appears to offer no advantage over the simpler procedure devised by Moodie and Young.

At the time of writing, these procedures are the only ones available capable of dealing with the variable-element line 'balancing' problem. Other procedures are available for dealing with associated aspects of this type of line 'balancing', but these are not intended as means of 'balancing' lines. For example, Mansoor and Ben-Tuvia (1966) have attempted to develop a method to establish the best cycle time for a perfectly balanced line in which element-time distributions are independently normally distributed. Their approach, however, seeks only to minimize labour costs, and it is unlikely that the method will provide a cycle time which provides the minimum total operating cost. Mansoor (1968) has also examined another aspect of variability in flow lines, i.e. the effect of different average-performance levels of operators at stations. Here again the objective was not specifically the 'balancing' of variable-service-time lines.

As for simple lines, the techniques of line 'balancing' available are not capable of dealing directly with the possibility of using paralleled or duplicated stations. For this reason this aspect of line design must be dealt with as a separate issue in the manner suggested in Chapter 4.

The procedures discussed above each involve the concept of an acceptable probability of the service time exceeding the cycle time. The objective determination of this probability requires a knowledge of the costs associated with incomplete items and station idle time, and, in more complex lines on which buffer stocks exist, a knowledge of the costs of such storage. The measurement of these costs is difficult, and, furthermore, the need to balance such costs adds to the already complex problem of 'balancing' this type of flow line.

Another problem area is that of establishing the variability of element times. If direct work measurement is used to establish time standards, a large number of measurements will need to be taken to provide a reliable estimate of element-time variability. If a predetermined-motion-time system (p.m.t.s.) is used, it will be necessary either to estimate or calculate element-time variability by reference to the nature of the element, or to have previously built up a library of work-element-time variance data to complement the p.m.t.s. element.

The line 'balancing' procedures we have discussed in this section, like those discussed in Chapter 4, have assumed that a situation in which the cycle time at each station is equal exists. We have seen, however, that such a situation does not necessarily apply on manual flow lines. This does not invalidate these line 'balancing' procedures, since, irrespective of the method of operation, 'balance' is an objective of line design. A line may be designed to operate with buffer stocks between stations and the extent of these stocks is likely to affect a management's willingness to permit service times occasionally to exceed the intended cycle time, but not to affect its desire to achieve 'balance'.

We have previously pointed out that, because of element-time variability, the concept of 'balance' on a manual flow line is a notional one. The achievement of notional 'balance' is, however, an important objective, and thus line 'balancing' is one essential procedure in manual-flow-line design. The fact that such 'balancing' procedures make use of concepts such as a line cycle time which do not necessarily have any real or useful existence on some types of lines, is, therefore, unimportant. The concept of a fixed cycle time for a line, although often an abstraction in practice, enables a notional line 'balancing' procedure to be followed.

Finally, it will be seen that, because of the variability of element and service times, if a line is 'balanced' so that the mean service time is equal to the required cycle time as determined from output requirements, the output obtained will be less than that required. Thus, to obtain the required output, it is inadequate to determine the cycle time in the manner that it was determined in the simple case, i.e. $T_C = T/Q$. A value of T_C less than T/Q must be used.

References

Operator variability

Conrad, R. (1954). 'The rate of paced man–machine systems', *J. Inst. Prod. Eng.*, **33**, No. 10, 562.

Conrad, R. (1955). 'Setting the pace', Report 232/55, Medical Research Council (A.P.U.), Cambridge.

Conrad, R. (1955). 'Setting the pace', *The Manager*, **23**, September, 664–667.

Conrad, R., and Hille, B. A. (1955). 'Comparison of paced and unpaced performance at a packing task', *Occ. Psy.*, **29**, No. 1, 15–28.

Dudley, N. A. (1958). 'Output patterns in repetitive tasks. Parts I, II, III and IV', *Prod. Eng.*, **37**, Nos. 3, 4 and 5, 187–206, 257–264, 303–331 and 382–384.

Dudley, N. A. (1962). 'The effect of pacing on worker performance', *Int. J. Prod. Res.*, **1**, No. 2, 60–72.

Dudley, N. A. (1963). 'Work time distributions', *Int. J. Prod. Res.*, **2**, No. 2, 137–144.

Dudley, N. A. (1968). *Work Measurement: Some Research Studies*, Macmillan, London.

Murrell, K. F. H. (1962). 'Operator variability and its industrial consequences', *Int. J. Prod. Res.*, **1**, No. 2, 39–55.

Murrell, K. F. H. (1963). 'Laboratory studies of repetitive work—I: paced work and its relationship to unpaced work', *Int. J. Prod. Res.*, **2**, No. 3, 169–185.

Murrell, K. F. H., and Forsaith, B. (1963). 'Laboratory studies of repetitive work—II: progress work on results from two subjects', *Int. J. Prod. Res.*, **2**, No. 4, 247–264.

Murrell, K. F. H. (1965). 'A classification of pacing', *Int. J. Prod. Res.*, **4**, No. 1, 69–74.

Wiberg, M. (1947). *Work-Time Distribution*, McClure, Haddon and Ortman, Chicago.

Line balancing

Brennecke, D. (1968). 'Two parameter assembly line balancing problem'. In M. P. Hottenstein (Ed.), *Models and Analysis in Production Management*, International Textbook Co., Scranton, Penn.

Mansoor, E. M., and Ben-Tuvia, S. (1966). 'Optimizing balanced assembly lines', *J. Ind. Eng.*, **XVII**, No. 3., 126–132.

Mansoor, E. M. (1968). 'Assembly line balancing—a heuristic algorithm for variable operator performance levels', *J. Ind. Eng.* **XIX**, No. 12, 618–629.

Moodie, C. L., and Young, H. H. (1965). 'A heuristic method of assembly line balancing for assumptions of constant and variable work element times', *J. Ind. Eng.*, **XVI**, No. 1, 23–29.

Ramsing, K., and Downing, R. (1970). 'Assembly line balancing with variable element times', *Ind. Eng.*, January, 41–43.

CHAPTER 6

The Design of Complex Lines—2

In this chapter we shall deal largely with the nature and the operating characteristics of the five basic types of flow line.

We shall look, essentially, at past research, which is of two varieties— analytical and computer simulation. In general, the analytical research studies predate the simulation research and rely heavily on the use of statistical queueing theory. Such studies, while providing exact and rigorous treatment of problems, are, in general, confined to simple cases, for example flow lines with few stations. In contrast, simulative studies do not provide a means of rigorous examination, but are, nevertheless, capable of providing quite considerable insight into problems whose size or complexity place them beyond the scope of analytical examination.

We shall make no attempt to provide an exhaustive study of all available research, but will concentrate on those studies whose results appear to have most relevance to our purpose, which is to develop principles for flow-line design. Neither shall we attempt to describe, other than briefly, the nature of the analysis or simulation adopted in these studies.

Before studying manual flow lines, we will look briefly at one problem associated with the design of single-model transfer lines.

TRANSFER LINES

The previous two chapters have demonstrated the comparative simplicity of the design requirements of deterministic flow lines, i.e. transfer lines. The absence of station-service-time variability means, of course, that problems of pacing do not arise. Hence, ostensibly, there is no need to consider the use of interstation buffer stocks. However, buffer stocks of items are frequently found between the stations of transfer lines—to insure against line disruption caused by the breakdown of equipment.

Buffer stocks

All equipment, however well designed and maintained, is liable to failure, such failure often occurring without warning.

The existence of a buffer stock after the station which is out of service will ensure that the subsequent stations are not immediately 'starved' of work. Likewise, the existence of unused buffer capacity between the stations prior to the failed station will ensure that these stations are not immediately 'blocked'. Theoretically, these two types of provision are, to some extent, conflicting, since maximum protection against 'starving' will be obtained from maximum buffer stocks (i.e. full buffer capacities), while maximum protection against 'blocking' will be afforded by maximum unused buffer capacity (i.e. minimum buffer stocks). Since the failure of stations is, essentially, random, it will be necessary to attempt to provide both maximum stock and maximum capacity between each pair of stations.

Such a conflict of requirements does not normally occur, since, in practice, buffer capacity and buffer stock are physically separate entities. Transfer lines are normally designed so that partially completed items can be taken from the line at certain points to be placed in intermediate storage until the line is free for subsequent processing. In theory, this buffer capacity, being remote from the line, is unlimited, but, in fact, the complete line will normally be halted if a failed station is not rectified within a certain time. Provision of such capacity is not normally difficult. However, the provision of sufficient stock to ensure against 'starving' is a more complex problem, since here such stock physically exists *until* required, whereas in the previous case stock exists only *when* required. Since machine failures are probably comparatively infrequent, capital tied up in large buffer stocks may represent more of a financial loss than would be incurred through the halting of part of the line following station failure. The problem, therefore, is to determine the optimum buffer-stock size, and also the position(s) of the buffers.

As yet, comparatively little research has been directed to this problem, and there is a shortage of definitive information to assist the transfer-line designer. One of the earliest studies, reported by Koenigsberg (1956), is attributed to Finch, who examined the case of a 'balanced' two-station line, i.e. a line with equal, constant, station service times and equal breakdown characteristics at both stations. This work was extended by Freeman (1964), who, as well as examining Finch's analytical results, also simulated three-station lines. Since such short lines are rather abstract, we do not propose to present detailed research results; however, brief comment is necessary.

Freeman assumed infinite stock prior to the first station and infinite capacity after the last station, together with exponentially distributed times between station breakdowns and similarly distributed station-breakdown times. He found that, for balanced lines, the buffers required to provide a given line efficiency in terms of station idle time were a linear function of the ratio of the mean station-breakdown duration to the cycle time. The buffer required for a given line effectiveness increases as the mean downtime increases, and increases as the cycle time decreases. Freeman, who also simulated unbalanced three-station lines, recognized that the available research results provided inadequate information, but nevertheless developed the following generalizations to assist in transfer-line design:

(1) Avoid extreme allocations, i.e. no buffer capacity between some pairs of stages and a great deal between other pairs. Even with large disparities between the good and bad stages, this extreme allocation is poor.

(2) The worse a bad stage is, relative to the good stages, the greater the buffer capacity that should be allocated to it.

(3) More buffer capacity should be allocated between a bad stage and a mediocre stage (or two bad stages) than between a bad stage and a good stage. The worse the two bad stages are and the larger the total buffer capacity, the poorer are the results of misallocation.

(4) The optimum relative allocation is substantially invariant to changes in the total buffer capacity.

(5) The end of a line is more critical than the beginning. If a bad stage occurs toward the end of a line, it should be allocated an even larger share of the total buffer capacity.

NON-MECHANICAL MANUAL LINES

Unless interstation buffer stocks are provided on non-mechanical lines, considerable idle time due to both blocking and starving will occur. The provision of very large buffer stocks will ensure that station and line utilization is high. However, this is achieved only at the cost of considerable work in progress. Small stocks will minimize the cost of work in progress, but will, for the same service-time distributions, increase the probability of station idle time. A compromise must be obtained and finite buffer capacities provided which minimize the sum of the costs of idle time and work in progress.

Before looking at research undertaken with the objective of determining the optimum buffer-stock capacity, we will look at the operating character-istics of this type of line, paying particular attention to the influence of interstation stocks.

Work performed on this type of flow line is, essentially, unpaced, and, as we have previously noted, the unpaced work-time distributions of trained workers tend to be positively skewed. For this reason research should be based on the use of positively skewed service-time distributions. For statistical reasons, most of the analytical work that has been under-taken has made use of such distributions, but some of the simulation work, for reasons of expedience, has incorporated normally distributed (i.e. symmetrical) distributions. Fortunately, where studies have been under-taken using both types of distributions, the results obtained have been found to differ only marginally (e.g. Davis, 1966). Consequently, we are justified in considering simulation studies based on normally distributed service times, especially as many such studies are only exploratory and do not purport to offer incontrovertible results.

Line characteristics

One of the earliest and most important studies in this area was under-taken by Hunt (1956), who used a statistical queueing-theory approach to examine the operating characteristics of the situation characterized by the non-mechanical flow line.

In his analysis, Hunt, like many of those who followed, assumed service times to be distributed exponentially, each with the same mean and vari-ance. He further assumed that the arrival of items at the first station was random, and that there was no restriction on the delivery of items from the last station. The analysis was confined largely to the rather abstract case of the two-station line. The results of the research, while, perhaps, indicative of the characteristics of larger lines, are not of direct practical value.

Eleven years later Hunt's pioneer work was extended considerably by Hillier and Boling (1967) to enable analytical results to be obtained for longer lines. The results summarized in Figure 6.1 (Hillier and Boling, 1966) derive from the use of this procedure, which again assumed balanced, exponentially distributed, station service times. The curves show the output rate of lines with up to four stations with equal buffer capacities (X) between stations to a maximum of four. The flow lines described by these curves were designed so that if service times were constant and equal to the mean values of the distributions used, the line output would be one unit per time unit. Thus we see that the effect of the service-time variability is to

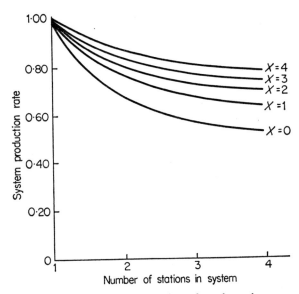

Figure 6.1 Effect of the number of work stations on
the production rate of a system [reproduced from F. S.
Hillier and R. W. Boling (1966). 'The effect of some
design factors on the efficiency of production lines with
variable operation times', *J. Ind. Eng.*, **XVII**, No. 12,
651–658]

reduce line output, the reduction or loss being greatest for lines with most
stations and least buffer capacity. This loss in output is due to station idle
time caused by both starving and blocking. Clearly the greater the number
of stations, the greater is the opportunity for both blocking and starving;
the smaller the buffer capacities between stations, the less is the protection
against such occurrences. These curves demonstrate the significant effect
that even comparatively small buffer stocks can have on line output. For
example, for a four-station line, the output of a line with buffer capacities
of four items is approximately 50 per cent higher than for a line in which
no provision is made for buffer stocks. Furthermore, we can see that, if
the total average work time required for one unit were to remain the same,
the output of two two-station lines would be greater than that of one
four-station line.

This result might be taken to suggest that the division of work and the
use of long manual flow lines does not necessarily result in increased
productivity. However, this may not be the case, since greater specialization of work may facilitate a reduction in the average time required for the

completion of an item. Indeed, were this not the case, the results demon-strated in Figure 6.1 would encourage the use of single operators, since it is evident that if the work content were to remain the same, the output from four one-station lines would be greater than that of one four-station line.

The first major simulation of a non-mechanical line was published by Barten (1962), who experimented with 'balanced' lines of up to ten stations, the service times being assumed to be normally distributed, the first station being preceded by an infinite store (i.e. never being starved) and the last station never being blocked. To assess the effect of the variability of service times on line performance, a six-station line was simulated with various equal buffer capacities between stations. Figure 6.2 shows the mean delay time per item for three lines having different service-time means ($\bar{T}_S$) and standard deviations (σ_S). This family of curves indicates that greater average delay time is incurred on lines with smaller buffer capacities and greater service-time variability, the former characteristic confirming the results shown in Figure 6.1. The importance of service-time variability is readily explained, since the greater the variance, the greater the possibility of different service times occurring simultaneously at adjacent stations, and the greater the use of the buffer items in an attempt to avoid delay or idle time. All three curves appear to flatten out at around a buffer capacity

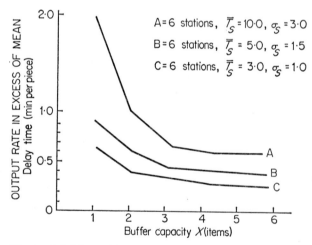

Figure 6.2 Mean delay for various service-time distribu-tions and buffer capacities [modified from K. A. Barten (1962). 'A queueing simulator for determining optimum inventory levels in a sequential process', *J. Ind. Eng.*, **XIII**, No. 4, 245–252]

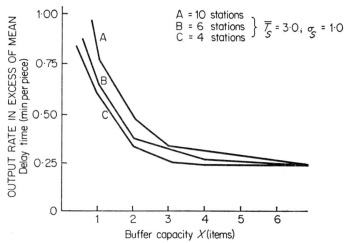

Figure 6.3 Mean delay for various line lengths and buffer capacities [modified from K. A. Barten (1962). 'A queueing simulator for determining optimum inventory levels in a sequential process', *J. Ind. Eng.*, **XIII**, No. 4, 245–252]

of four, thus indicating that, irrespective of buffer capacity, the line output will be less than that of an equivalent balanced deterministic line. In these cases provision of buffer capacities greater than four would appear to provide rapidly diminishing returns in terms of increased line output. The curves in Figure 6.3 show the effect of buffer capacity on delay time, and thus output, for lines of various lengths. It is clear that, as in the analytical results shown in Figure 6.1, line efficiency decreases as length increases, and that the number of stations has less effect on line performance as the buffer capacity increases. Again, these characteristics are readily explained as before.

Many other analytical and simulation studies, most of which are listed in the references at the end of this chapter, have been undertaken in this area. However, those described here are sufficient to identify the principal characteristics of 'balanced' non-mechanical flow lines. In retrospect, we can summarize these characteristics as follows:

(1) Line inefficiency, as measured by average idle time or output, is a function of (a) line length, (b) service-time variability and (c) buffer capacity. Other things being equal, line inefficiency increases with increased line length, increased service-time variability and reduced buffer capacity.

(2) Manual line output is less than that of an equivalent deterministic line (i.e. a line balanced to a cycle time equal to the mean service times of the manual stations).

These characteristics imply that, for a given work content and output requirement, the number of stations required on a manual flow line will exceed the number required by a deterministic line. The extent of these differences will depend, as we have seen, on the variability of service time, and on the buffer capacities used. The determination of the optimum buffer capacity for lines is dealt with in the next section, and knowledge of this capacity, together with knowledge of the service-time variability, is essential if manual lines are to be designed for a specific output.

Optimum buffer capacity

For the reasons mentioned previously, the study of flow lines with more than two or three stations requires the use of a simulation approach. Barten (1962), who dealt with lines of up to ten 'balanced' stations, each with normally distributed service times, used a simulation approach to develop a simple formula later validated by Young (1967). More recently a formula has been developed by Anderson and Moodie (1969) for lines with buffer capacities of up to 20, with two, three, four and five stations having 'balanced' normally distributed service times with means of $1 \cdot 0$ and coefficients of variation of $0 \cdot 3$. Their formula is:

$$X^* = p \sqrt{(y - \alpha_2)}$$

where
$$p = \sqrt{\left[\frac{\alpha_1}{(1 \cdot 45N - 1 \cdot 32)} \right]} \text{ and } y = \frac{C_3}{C}$$

X^* = economic buffer capacity
N = number of stations on line
C_3 = delay cost per unit time
C = effective inventory cost per unit time

and where α_1 and α_2 are parameters determined by line length, i.e.

$$\alpha_1 = 0 \cdot 22 - 0 \cdot 22 \, (N)^{-0 \cdot 76}$$
$$\alpha_2 = 0 \cdot 81 - 0 \cdot 28 \, (N)^{-0 \cdot 51}.$$

Anderson and Moodie also used the results of Hillier and Boling (1967) to develop a similar expression for 'balanced' lines with exponentially distributed service times, the only difference between the two expressions being that the values of p and α_2 are dependent on the nature of the service-time distribution. For exponentially distributed service times, these parameters are given as follows:

$$p = \sqrt{\left[\frac{1}{(1 \cdot 54N - 1 \cdot 57)}\right]}$$

$$\alpha_1 = 2 \cdot 07 - 2 \cdot 36\,(N)^{-1 \cdot 16}$$

$$\alpha_2 = 3 \cdot 74 - 1 \cdot 10\,(N)^{-0 \cdot 75}.$$

There are important limitations on the use of the formulae developed by Barten and Anderson and Moodie. Barten's formula for X^* includes a constant whose value varies with line length and which was determined only for values of $N = 2, 4, 6$ and 10, while the formulae of Anderson and Moodie apply only to lines with service-time coefficient of variations of $0 \cdot 3$. Recently Knott (1970) has pointed out that a consistent mathematical structure exists in the numerics of service-time delay occurring on non-mechanical-type lines, and that it should, consequently, be possible to develop formulae for predicting delay in which line length, service-time variability and buffer size are variables. In fact, such formulae have been reported by Knott and Freeman (1968). We shall deal with the former— the more recent approach. Knott constructed a theoretical expression for determining the efficiency of lines in terms of delay times, and explored the validity of this expression for various cases, using simulation and, where possible, analytical investigation. The expression, which was found to be satisfactory for its purpose, was of the following form:

$$D \text{ or } T = \frac{C_v{}^2 V}{(X+J)}$$

where
C_v = coefficient of variation of service times
X = buffer capacity
V = $2\,(N-1)/N$ where N is the number of stations
J = constant, depending on the nature of the service-time distribution, i.e. $J = 1 \cdot 773\,(C_v)$ for *normal* distribution, $J = 3$ for *exponential* distribution.

In this expression D applies when service times are *normally* distributed, and is the mean delay occurring at stations, i.e. the proportion of extra time required at a station over and above the mean service time. For example, Table 6.1 shows the mean delay D for stations on lines of various lengths with various buffer capacities. A two-station line with zero buffer capacity would be expected to incur a mean delay of $0 \cdot 167$, i.e. for a mean

Table 6.1 Delay D for stations with normally distributed service times with $C_v = 0\cdot3$; comparison of results from expressions developed by Knott (1970) and Anderson and Moodie (1969)—the latter are shown in brackets [based on A. D. Knott (1970). 'The inefficiency of a series of work stations—a simple formula', *Int. J. Prod. Res.*, **8**, No. 2, 109–119]

Number of stations (N)	Buffer capacity (X)				
	0	1	2	3	4
2	0·167	0·059	0·036	0·026	0·020
	(0·147)	(0·056)	(0·035)	(0·026)	(0·020)
4	0·254	0·088	0·053	0·038	0·030
	(0·213)	(0·086)	(0·054)	(0·039)	(0·031)
6	0·282	0·097	0·059	0·043	0·033
	(0·235)	(0·096)	(0·061)	(0·044)	(0·035)
8	0·296	0·103	0·062	0·045	0·035
	(0·245)	(0·102)	(0·064)	(0·047)	(0·037)
10	0·305	0·106	0·064	0·046	0·036
	(0·251)	(0·106)	(0·067)	(0·049)	(0·039)
12	0·310	0·108	0·065	0·047	0·036
	(0·255)	(0·108)	(0·068)	(0·050)	(0·040)

service time of 1·0, a further 0·167 time units of delay will be incurred on average for each unit at each station. When service times are exponentially distributed, T applies, and this is the long-term probability of system idleness, i.e.

$$T = 1 - \text{efficiency}$$

$$= \frac{D}{1+D}.$$

The figures outside brackets in Table 6.1 show the average delay for various lines with normally distributed service times. These figures are calculated using the formula developed by Knott, while those in brackets have been calculated using the expression used by Anderson and Moodie in developing the expressions shown previously.

Similar, favourable, comparisons with the expressions developed by other research workers demonstrate the usefulness of Knott's simple formula. The formula does not provide directly figures for optimal buffer capacities. However, it may be used to calculate line inefficiencies in terms of delay times, the cost of which may be compared with the costs of providing for buffer storage. This is currently perhaps the most satisfactory approach available for establishing buffer capacities, because of the general validity and simplicity of the formula. Knott also used his expression for cases of binomial and Erlang service times.

Finally, returning to Table 6.1, the provision of limited buffer stocks drastically reduces delay time. For example, on an eight-station line with no buffers, mean delay time is approximately one-quarter of the total 'running' time. This falls to about one-tenth when one buffer is introduced, and about one-twentieth when two buffers are used. Improvement follows with more buffers, but at a much reduced rate. Notice that the purpose of buffer stocks is to accommodate short-term differences between input and output rates. Consequently, the extent to which the buffer stock varies over a period of time is a good measure of the effectiveness of a buffer stock. Lack of variation of the quantity held would indicate that the stock was not serving its intended purpose.

Unbalanced and non-steady-state lines

All of the foregoing discussion has related to 'balanced' non-mechanical-type manual flow lines operating in a *steady-state condition*. By this we mean that the lines studied were notionally 'balanced', i.e. had equal station-service-time means, and that they were operating in a stable manner, being unaffected by model changes, breakdowns, etc. In practice, it is possible that neither of these conditions may apply, and consequently we must look at the implications of 'unbalance' and 'instability' on line design.

The majority of the analytical and simulated flow-line research work that has been undertaken has dealt with line, as opposed to station, characteristics. For example, researchers have tended to concentrate on the average idle time for complete lines, rather than for individual stations on the lines. Hillier and Boling (1966) considered the possibility of unbalancing non-mechanical lines with the object of obtaining higher production per unit time. They considered the rather abstract case of two-, three- and, to a lesser extent, four-station lines with limited buffer capacities up to $X = 4$. They concluded that:

(1) The production rate of a two-station line is maximized by balancing the stations.
(2) The production rate of a three-station line is increased by assigning proportionately lower average service time to the middle station—a characteristic which they called the 'bowl phenomenon'.
(3) There is some evidence to indicate that this phenomenon also leads to improvements when applied to lines with more than three stations.

More recently a small simulation study (Payne, Slack and Wild, 1971) has shed some further light on this subject. In this study, 'balanced' twenty-

E

station lines with unlimited buffer-stock capacities and normally distributed service times were simulated, the effect of service-time variability on the idle time at stations and the maximum stock occurring before stations being examined. Figure 6.4 shows the percentage idle time occurrence at each of the stations on three lines during the period of operation. Although the lines were 'balanced', the stations towards the end of the line incurred more idle time than those at the beginning, the

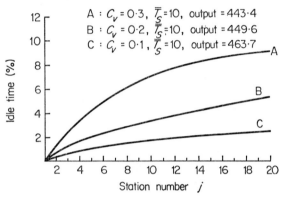

Figure 6.4 [Reproduced from S. Payne, N. Slack and R. Wild (1972). 'A note on the operating characteristics of "balanced" and "unbalanced" production flow lines', *Int. J. Prod. Res.*, **10**, No. 1, 93–98]

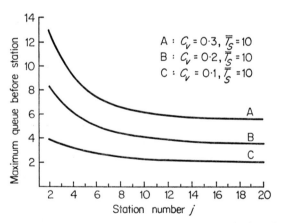

Figure 6.5 [Reproduced from S. Payne, N. Slack and R. Wild (1972). 'A note on the operating characteristics of "balanced" and "unbalanced" production flow lines', *Int. J. Prod. Res.*, **10**, No. 1, 93–98]

idle time at all stations being greater for lines with greater service-time variability. Line output is also seen to be adversely affected by increasing the service-time variability. Figure 6.5 shows that the maximum queue occurring before stations towards the end of the line was less than at the beginning of the line, the difference, as well as the size of the maximum queue for all stations, being affected by the service-time variability.

These results are associated with *non-steady-state* operation of the line. Although the results presented relate only to the latter part of a long simulated-line operating period (500 times the mean service time), the line clearly had not reached a stable condition; indeed, steady-state operation of such an unlimited queue situation is theoretically achieved only after an infinite run period. The results presented therefore relate only to the conditions that apply during a specific and substantial time period, and describe a non-steady-state condition.

The differing idle-time situations at stations occurs because each station is dependent on all predecessors for the supply of work; hence the more predecessors, the greater is the probability of a station being starved of work. Furthermore, because the supply of work is also dependent on the variability of the service times of preceding stations, an increase in variability leads to an increase in idle time and a reduction in output. The queue occurring before a station is a function of the utilization of that station; hence smaller queues occur before stations with greater idle time.

In practice, it is unlikely that the means and variances of the station service times on manual flow lines will be equal, since, despite the concept of a standard time for operations, it is likely that, because of the nature of the work and the capabilities of the workers, the means and/or variances of station service times will differ. The designer of a flow line, therefore, wants to know how to allocate workers with different capabilities, to the stations on a line. Figures 6.4 and 6.5 provide some indication of the solutions of this problem for *limitless or large-buffer-capacity* lines operating under non-steady-state conditions, since they suggest that, to reduce the total idle time, the line should be designed and manned so that stations towards the end of the line have greater service-time means. An alternative policy might involve the use of 'balanced' mean times, with the allocation of workers or operations to stations so as to provide greater service-time variability towards the end of the line.

These results not only suggest that under certain conditions the design of 'unbalanced' flow lines or the selective distribution of service-time variance on otherwise 'balanced' lines might give rise to higher utilization and output, but also indicate that the buffer capacity required between stations on balanced lines may depend on the position of the stations on such lines. As yet, this latter possibility has not been reflected in research dealing with the determination of optimum buffer capacities.

Non-steady-state operating conditions will occur on lines not only when they first begin operation, but also after breakdowns, model changes and other disruptions. There is good cause to believe that, in practice, many flow lines, even single-model lines, spend a significant portion of their time engaged in unstable operation. If this belief is well founded, this characteristic is of considerable importance in line design, since the implication is that many of the results of present research are of limited value, since, almost without exception, they have relied on the assumption of steady-state operation.

The problems of designing lines for efficient non-steady-state operation are considerable, and research is only now beginning to be undertaken in this area; consequently there is little material available to review.

Anderson and Moodie (1969) have shown that, for a four-station 'balanced' normal- or exponential-service-time line, minimum-cost operation is obtained by initially setting buffer capacities at the steady-state level, rather than attempting to build up buffer capacities to this level during the transient non-steady-state period following line 'start up'. In contrast, Young (1967), while attempting to determine economic buffer capacities for lines, established that the economic buffer capacity for use on 'balanced' normally distributed service-time lines during non-steady-state conditions was less than that for steady-state operation. He suggests that to establish the economic capacity, several simulation 'runs' should be made with the different buffer capacities. These two sets of results shed little light on this particular problem, although Young does suggest a procedure for establishing economic transient non-steady-state buffer capacities. However, it remains to be demonstrated how factors such as the comparative length of the transient period affect economic transient buffer capacities, and how the manipulation of such capacities affects the length of this period for practical-sized flow lines.

Multiple station manning and the 'double' line

Before concluding this review of the characteristics and design of non-mechanical lines, we will look briefly at a derivative of this type of line, which offers advantages in terms of reduced station idle time. We shall refer to this development as the 'double' line.

Figure 6.6 demonstrates the principle of this double line and compares it to the basic 'single'-operator-per-station non-mechanical line. Comparing the double line, without buffer stocks, to the equivalent basic configuration, we see that each station on the double line, other than the first two, is fed by two stations. One might reason that this type of feed arrangement provides a reduced likelihood of starving or blocking of stations, and that such a line might be expected to incur less idle time than the equivalent single configuration. Likewise when buffer stocks are introduced. For the same work-in-progress capacity, the buffer stocks on the double line may be twice the size of those on the single line. Again, it can be hypothesized that such stocks should provide better protection against starving, and thus enable double lines to operate with lower idle time.

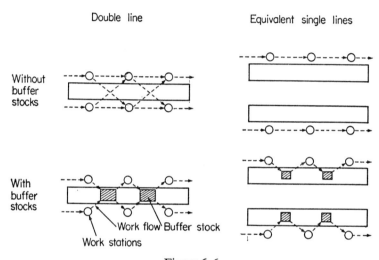

Figure 6.6

To test these hypotheses, several simulations were performed (Wild and Slack, 1972), each concerning 'balanced' lines with normally distributed service times having a coefficients of variation of 0·1, 0·2 and 0·3.

Figure 6.7 compares idle time for both types of line for $C_v = 0·2$ and for various buffer capacities. These results support the hypotheses that have been advanced, and indicate the nature of the operating advantages offered by the double line. Notice that the double line is, in effect, a 'two-operators-per-station' line where both operators perform the same work, and that, theoretically, the number of operators at stations might be increased to more than two to obtain greater operational benefits. In practice, however, physical factors are likely to place limits on the staffing levels of stations.

The inherent operating advantages of the double or multiple line might

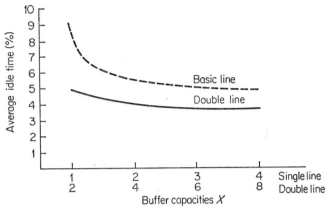

Figure 6.7 The lines are balanced; each single line has 15 stations and the double line has 30 stations; service times are normally distributed ($C_v = 0 \cdot 2$)

be utilized to provide either improved output efficiency for the same total buffer capacity or to enable lower buffer capacities to be used for the same delay or idle-time loss. The improved output efficiency afforded by the double line is influenced by X, N and C_v. Table 6.2 shows the approximate magnitude of this operating benefit.

Table 6.2 Percentage improvement in output efficiency through adoption of double line

Buffer capacity	1	2	3	1	2	3	1	2	3
Number of stations	$C_v = 0 \cdot 1$			$C_v = 0 \cdot 2$			$C_v = 0 \cdot 3$		
3	0·81	0·71	0·20	1·78	0·92	0·31	4·58	1·46	1·36
10	1·35	1·33	0·82	3·15	1·90	1·15	5·98	3·50	1·53
20	1·68	1·23	0·83	3·54	2·15	1·49	5·97	4·17	1·66
30	1·80	1·37	0·83	3·57	2·15	1·52	6·38	4·35	1·91

Practical considerations

The principal operating characteristics and requirements of non-mechanical lines are:

(1) The need to provide for buffer stocks of items between stations.
(2) Irregular item or product flow.
(3) No work pacing, and consequently:
(4) No incomplete items produced.

Various practical considerations which might well influence the suitability of this type of line are associated with these characteristics. First, because of the need to provide buffer stocks to ensure efficient operation, this type of line is perhaps inappropriate for use in the manufacture of bulky items. In such situations it may well prove impossible to provide sufficient storage space between stations to accommodate the required buffer capacity. These lines may also be less appropriate for the manufacture of expensive items because the lines will normally operate with comparatively high work-in-progress levels (and consequently with a high throughput time) which would involve high tied-up-capital costs, etc.

Secondly, because of the irregular product- or item-flow characteristic, non-mechanical lines are less suitable than moving-belt lines for the manufacture of heavy items whose movement is best accomplished by mechanical means.

It can be argued that, because of the absence of mechanical work pacing, this type of line is particularly suitable for use where the variability of service times is high. Such a condition may be caused by the nature of the work being done, and/or by the nature of the workers undertaking this work. For example, this type of line might be considered to be an appropriate facility on which to use trainee workers.

In some industries, the cost of defective output is high. For example, in the electronics industry, components assembled on flow lines often constitute one part of a complex piece of equipment, and failure of the component is expensive. Furthermore, it is often difficult to identify and locate faults in such components, and frequently the rectification of faults is both difficult and expensive. Non-mechanical lines should not produce items which, for lack of service time, are incomplete. Incomplete or defective items may be produced for other reasons, such as operator error or material faults. However, the comparatively lesser probability of producing defective items is a characteristic which perhaps renders this type of line particularly suitable for use in situations where defective-output cost is high.

The double line appears to offer certain benefits over the basic non-mechanical line—sufficient benefits to make it an attractive proposition in some circumstances despite its added physical complexities. Its use, however, depends, among other things, on the nature (especially the size) of the items being made and the layout of the work place.

MOVING-BELT LINES

The major part of the research work dealing with this class of flow line has concentrated on the pacing effect—the principal characteristic and perhaps the main determinant of the performance of moving-belt lines. Much industrial and laboratory simulation research has been undertaken to establish the effect of variables such as feed rate and tolerance time on line performance, particularly idle time and incomplete-item output. Much of the work that has been undertaken is concerned primarily with lines on which items may be removed for processing, but the results of much of the work is of relevance to all four types of moving-belt line.

The fact that moving-belt-type lines provide complex subjects for investigation, together with the fact that research in this area was only begun in the last ten years, means that much of what is available is necessarily exploratory and deals with, in some cases, rather abstract situations.

Single-station studies

The feed rate and tolerance time for the 'fixed-item' class of lines will be constant for all stations, whereas on lines where items are removed from the belt, the feed rate may only be constant at the first station. Such a characteristic complicates the problems of the research worker, and is one reason for the popularity of 'single-station' studies.

Sury and others, in a series of investigations, have been concerned with the dependence of output on feed rate and tolerance time, 'misses' (incomplete items), and delays, and with the response of workers to the pacing effect. An industrial study (Sury, 1964, 1967) undertaken in 1964 dealt with three trained operators engaged on an assembly task. Four feed rates were used for each operator, two above, one equivalent to, and one below the mean unpaced service time, and two tolerance times were chosen. Both feed rate and tolerance time were found to have a significant effect on station output, delay time and the number of 'misses'. To obtain a paced work output equal to the output from unpaced working, the feed rate must be above the unpaced mean service time. The delay time increases substantially as the tolerance time is decreased and when the feed rate is set below the mean unpaced service time. It has been argued that the effects of pacing are of two types—mechanical and psychological. The mechanical effect is manifest by the idle time, and 'misses' incurred because of the enforced work pace, while any change in a worker's unpaced service-time distribution is taken to result from a psychological effect. The latter is often referred to as *operator response*, which is measured by the extent to which operators respond to work pacing by speeding up their work rate.

Initial studies, such as the one mentioned above, were aimed at establishing the influence of the mechanical effect of work pacing, whereas more recent studies have dealt with both aspects. A laboratory study of operator response to pacing (Franks and Sury, 1966) has tended to indicate that the service time required by an operator for an item is affected by the time available before the next item to be processed is missed (i.e. the tolerance time remaining for the next item), and that operators respond to increasing feed rate by reducing their service time.

To develop principles for the design of this type of flow line, simulation studies have been undertaken which take account of this operator response. The manner in which the characteristic has been accommodated is less than satisfactory, since it has been assumed that service time is reduced if an item, when picked up, has reached a particular portion of the tolerance zone. However, this treatment is adequate for the purposes of exploratory research. The following observations are taken from a study (Sury, 1965) in which service times were generated by random sampling from an actual unpaced service-time distribution. Various levels of operator responses were tested, paced service times equal to 0·8, 0·85 and 0·9 of the unpaced service time being considered to apply when an item picked up had reached a point at which the time remaining was less than 0·5, 0·7 and 0·9 of the tolerance time. Each value of 'tolerance time remaining' and 'paced service time' was combined, and simulated station performance was compared to actual performance. The following are among the conclusions offered by the researcher:

(1) 'In order that operator response to overcoming the adverse mechanical effects of pacing be minimized, the tolerance times should be set at least equal to the range of the mean to 99 per cent of an operator's unpaced service time distribution. It would be necessary to set feed rate in the region of 10 per cent above unpaced performance for equivalent output to be achieved and delay to be at a minimum. An increasing proportion of misses would result at feed rates above this setting if no operator speed up in working occurs.'

(2) 'Reasonable agreement has been found between simulated and actual results of successes and misses in a range of feed rates up to 10 to 13 per cent above unpaced performance. The agreement rests on the assumption of a reduction in operator service time taking place if a part is picked up within an arbitrary time interval of being missed.'

Multiple-station studies

Two studies have been reported concerning the effect of pacing on multistation moving-belt lines. In the one study (Davis, 1966), a three-station line was simulated, similar results being obtained for both skewed and normally distributed service times. No operator-response effect was considered, and the line was taken to be of the removable-item type, both idle time and output being measured for various service-time means, variances, feed rates and tolerance times. The results obtained for 'balanced' lines support those discussed above in indicating that maximum output and minimum station idle time was associated with maximum tolerance time, and that the number of 'missed' items decreases and the idle time increases with decreasing feed rate.

A more recent study (Sury, 1971) has dealt with eight-station 'balanced' lines on which operators were assumed to respond to the pacing effect by reducing their service times. Line output, missed items and delay was examined for two tolerance times and for feed rates below, equivalent to and above the mean unpaced service time. As we would expect from our knowledge of the operating characteristics of balanced non-mechanical lines, the output was found to be lower, while idle time was higher for stations towards the end of the line, a characteristic which derives from the increasing feed-rate mean and variability from station to station along the line. The possible benefits to station output obtained by setting feed rate above the mean unpaced service time was found to decrease for stations towards the end of the line. The number of missed items decreased as the feed rate was reduced, the number being lower for stations towards the beginning of the line. Tolerance time was found to have an important effect on the amount of idle time occurring; a tolerance time considerably in excess of the mean service time is required if misses are to be avoided, even for a feed rate equal to the mean service time.

Design requirements and considerations

The importance of the pacing effect is clearly evident from the foregoing discussion. Tolerance time and feed rate in all cases appear as important determinants of line output, idle time and the proportion of incomplete items produced. While it is not possible to enumerate precise design requirements, it is certainly possible to identify desirable design objectives for this class of flow lines:

(1) In the interests of line utilization, the pacing effect should be minimized; more specifically:
(2) Every effort should be made to maximize the tolerance time provided.
(3) To provide an output equivalent to unpaced working, the feed rate must be set above the mean unpaced service time, but unless this is accompanied by a tolerance time of about twice the mean service

time, the output will contain a significant proportion of incomplete items.

(4) As for non-mechanical lines, other things being equal, line efficiency is greater for shorter lines, and for lines with lower service-time variability. Hence the number of stations and operator variability should be minimized where possible.

The manner in which these objectives are pursued will depend on the type of line concerned. Fixed-item lines can be provided with maximum tolerance by an appropriate selection of belt speed and item spacing. For example, if an output of 60 units per hour is required, several combinations of belt speed and item spacing are available, e.g.

(1) Belt speed = 2·5 ft/min, item spacing = 2·5 ft.
(2) Belt speed = 5 ft/min, item spacing = 5 ft.
(3) Belt speed = 10 ft/min, item spacing = 10 ft.

For a station length of 5 ft, the tolerance times for these three cases are 2 min, 1 min and 0·5 min, respectively. Hence the first arrangement clearly fulfils design objectives more satisfactorily. For this reason fixed-item lines in which more than one item is made available to the work station either by providing for station overlap and/or by an appropriate choice of belt parameters provide more satisfactory line design, although at the expense of high work-in-progress costs. It follows, therefore, that lines of the type described on p. 99 (see Table 5.1) in which only one item is available to a station and in which station length is fixed, are inefficient with respect to idle time and incomplete items. In practice such conditions normally obtain when operators at stations are given the same fixed time in which to complete operations, all stations being required to pass items to the next station at the same time. Such lines are in quite widespread use.

In situations where items may be removed from the line, it is possible to introduce buffer stocks to reduce the effect of pacing. In such cases operators often remove items from the line to provide a stock of items awaiting processing, and, furthermore, it is possible for stations to maintain a stock of completed items. The latter is of benefit only when there is a constraint on the manner in which completed items are to be fed back onto the line. For example, to provide a constant feed rate for all stations, operators are sometimes required to replace items at specific points on the moving belt, perhaps marked by a spot or cross. In such cases the maintenance of a stock of completed items at stations enables operators to alleviate some of their work-pacing effect. Little work has yet been undertaken to determine the size and effect of buffer stocks on this type of line. However, a recent single-station study (Franks, Gillies and Sury, 1969) has demonstrated their value. In this laboratory study, which concerned a task with a mean service time of approximately 3 s, six feed rates were used (one below, one equivalent and four above the mean unpaced service time) together with a tolerance time of 3 s. A buffer capacity of six items was provided, and measurements of buffer usage, output, and misses were taken. The following tentative recommendations for the tolerance time T_T, the feed interval T_F and the buffer capacity X were made:

(a) For feed rates less than 2·5 per cent below the mean unpaced service time
$$T_T = 2T_F$$
or if $T_T = T_F$, then $X = 1$
or if $T_T = 0$, then $X = 2$.

(b) For feed rates between the mean unpaced service time and 5 per cent above
$$T_T = 3T_F$$
or if $T_T = T_F$, then $X = 2$
or if $T_T = 0$, then $X = 3$.

(c) For feed rates more than 7·5 per cent above the mean unpaced service time
$$T_T = 4T_F$$
or if $T_T = T_F$, then $X = 3$
or if $T_T = 0$, then $X = 4$.

Practical considerations again influence whether or not moving-belt-type lines are appropriate for given situations. It is difficult, for example, to envisage how the flow-line manufacture of heavy bulk items can be accomplished except by fixed-item moving-belt lines. Even so, as we have seen, by careful selection of the feed rate and tolerance time, the inherent inefficiency of this type of line can be minimized.

Finally, as in all of our previous discussions, we must recognize that the extent of the effect of pacing on station, and hence on line, performance is likely to be a function of the characteristics of the individual worker. This in particular applies to the 'operator-response' effect, since response to pacing is likely to be associated with operator skill and motivation. Individual differences are found in the performance of workers operating in unpaced conditions. Equally, it is likely that such differences also occur in the paced situation, and, consequently, for maximum efficiency in paced working, it is likely to be necessary to establish line parameters with respect to the nature of individual stations. Furthermore, because of such differences, we must recognize the necessity to design unbalanced lines. As yet there is little evidence available to indicate how such unbalance should be arranged. [Two studies refer to the unbalanced situation, i.e. Davis (1966) and Sury (1970). The results shed little light on the subject and provide less agreement.] However, it seems reasonable to suppose that the conclusions obtained for nonmechanical lines might provide the basis of intuitively viable design objectives.

References

Transfer lines

Buzacott, J. A. (1966). 'Automatic transfer lines with buffer stocks', *Int. J. Prod. Res.*, **5**, No. 3, 183–220.

Freeman, M. C. (1964). 'The effects of breakdowns and interstage storage on production line capacity', *J. Ind. Eng.*, **XV**, No. 4, 194–200.

Koenigsberg, E. (1959). 'Production lines and internal storage—a review', *Mgt. Sci.*, **5**, No. 4, 410–433.

Non-mechanical lines

Anderson, D. R., and Moodie, C. L. (1969). 'Optimal buffer storage capacity in production line systems', *Int. J. Prod. Res.*, **7**, No. 3, 233–240.

Barten, K. A. (1962). 'A queueing simulator for determining optimum inventory levels in a sequential process', *J. Ind. Eng.*, **XIII**, No. 4, 245–252.

Van Beek, H. G. (1964). 'The influence of assembly line organization on output, quality and morale', *Occ. Psy.*, **38**, 161–172.

Freeman, D. R. (1968). 'A general line balancing model', *Proceedings of the 19th conference of A.I.E.E.*, New York, 1968, 230–235.

Hillier, F. S., and Boling, R. W. (1966). 'The effect of some design factors on the efficiency of production lines with variable operation times', *J. Ind. Eng.*, **XVII**, No. 12, 651–658.

Hillier, F. S., and Boling, R. W. (1967). 'Finite queues in series with exponential or Erlang service times—a numerical approach', *Operat. Res.*, **15**, No. 2, 286–303.

Hunt, G. C. (1956). 'Sequential arrays of waiting lines', *Operat. Res.*, **4**, No. 6, 674–683.

Knott, A. D. (1970). 'The inefficiency of a series of work stations—a simple formula', *Int. J. Prod. Res.*, **8**, No. 2, 109–119.

Patterson, R. L. (1964). 'Markov processes occurring in the theory of traffic flow through an N-stage statistic service system', *J. Ind. Eng.*, **XV**, No. 4, 188–193.

Payne, S., Slack, N., and Wild, R. (1972). 'A note on the operating characteristics of "balanced" and "unbalanced" production flow lines', *Int. J. Prod. Res.*, **10**, No. 1, 93–98.

Richman, E., and Elmaghraby, S. (1957). 'The design of in-process storage facilities', *J. Ind. Eng.*, **8**, No. 1, 7–9.

Wild, R., and Slack, N. (1972). 'The operating characteristics of "single" and "double" non-mechanical flow line systems', *Int. J. Prod. Res.* (forthcoming).

Young, H. H. (1967). 'Optimization models for production lines', *J. Ind. Eng.*, **XVIII**, No. 1, 70–78.

See also E. Koenisberg.

Moving-belt lines

Buffa, E. S. (1961). 'Pacing effects in production lines', *J. Ind. Eng.*, **XII**, No. 6, 383–386.

Davis, L. E. (1966). 'Pacing effects on manned assembly lines', *Int. J. Prod. Res.*, **4**, No. 3, 171–184.

Franks, I. T., Gillies, G. J., and Sury, R. J. (1969). 'Buffer stocks in conveyor based work', *Work Study Mgt. Serv.*, February, 78–82.

Franks, I. T., and Sury, R. J. (1966). 'Operator response in conveyor based work', *Int. J. Prod. Res.*, **5**, No. 2, 97–112.

Sury, R. J. (1964). 'An industrial study of paced and unpaced operator performance in a single stage work task', *Int. J. Prod. Res.*, **3**, No. 2, 91–102.

Sury, R. J. (1965). 'The simulation of a paced single stage work task', *Int. J. Prod. Res.*, **4**, No. 2, 125–140.

Sury, R. J. (1967). 'Operator performance in conveyor based working', *Work Study Mgt. Serv.*, January, 12–15.

Sury, R. J. (1971). 'Aspects of assembly line balancing', *Int. J. Prod. Res.*, **9**, No. 4, 501–512.

Part 3

Multimodel and Mixed-model Production Flow Lines

CHAPTER 7

The Design and Operation of Multimodel and Mixed-model Flow Lines

In 1909 the Ford company decided to concentrate exclusively on the 'Model T'. The chassis was to be the same for all cars built, and Henry Ford announced: 'Any customer can have a car painted any colour that he wants so long as it is black'. Such were the circumstances in which flow-line technology was born. Sixty years ago, for most people, cars were luxury items and there were comparatively few companies making them. It was a manufacturer's market, and companies were able to make what they wanted how they wanted, and yet still remain in business—a situation which does not exist today.

The use of flow-line techniques certainly leads to highly efficient production when product variety is small or non-existent, but any increase in the variety of the product not only leads to more complex design and management problems, but also results inevitably in reduced production efficiency. The increasing affluence and discretion of consumers and increasing competition from other manufacturers restrict a company's ability to rationalize production, and few, if any, motor-vehicle assembly lines are now devoted to the continuous production of single uniform products. A similar situation exists in many other industries.

Consider the case of the Ford 'Capri', introduced by the Ford company of England in January 1969, and manufactured at their Halewood plant near Liverpool. Five different engine builds were available. Additionally, five 'custom plans' were available. If extras such as inertia-reel safety belts, rear seat belts, a radio, cloth trim and radial-ply tyres, which are available on each of the basic derivatives, are included, the total model range is in excess of 800, and this without consideration of options such as an automatic gearbox, an electric clock, servo-assisted brakes and a range of body-shell colours. In fact, the company claimed that they could build $1\frac{1}{4}$ million Capris without any two being precisely the same.

A similar situation is described by Kilbridge and Wester (1964), who refer to a truck manufacturer producing 700 different variations or models of one type of truck. There were said to be about 43 types of front axle, 42 basic engine types, 63 transmission types, and 162 rear-axle types plus different ratios. Every truck had about 2000 major parts, and 130,000 trucks per year were produced on a mixed-model line.

Of course, variety of product and part designs is not, in itself, a factor affecting line design, except in so much as such variety complicates materials management. The variety of work content which is often associated with design variety is more important in this context.

The net result of situations such as those that have been described is that the design of efficient flow lines becomes a problem of considerable complexity. Many of the problems identified in previous chapters still apply (for example, the problems associated with operator variability, different methods of line operation, the determination of buffer capacities, etc.) and, in addition, several other problems arise. In this chapter we shall concentrate largely on the problems peculiar to multimodel and mixed-model lines. To provide a framework, we can identify the decisions necessary in the design and operation of both types of line, i.e.

For multimodel lines

(1) Which models are to be made on each line?
(2) How are work elements to be allocated to stations?
(3) Should any station be paralleled or duplicated?
(4) What will be the method of operation of the line, and will buffer stocks be used?
(5) In what order will the batches of each model be manufactured (the *batch-sequencing* problem)?
(6) What will be the batch size for each model?

For mixed-model lines

(a) Which models are to be made on each line?
(b) How are work elements to be allocated to stations?
(c) Should any station be paralleled or duplicated?
(d) What will be the method of operation of the line and will buffer stocks be used?
(e) How, and in what order, will the different models be fed or launched onto the line? (The *model-launching* problem.)

We shall look first at problems of design, and secondly at problems of operation. Decisions (3) and (4) and (c) and (d) have been discussed in the previous chapters. Consequently here we shall be concerned only with

decisions (1), (2), (5), (6) and (a), (b) and (e). Problem (e)—*model launching*
—is concerned essentially with the operation of mixed-model lines, and
will be discussed later in the chapter.

MULTIMODEL LINE DESIGN

The design of flow lines for multimodel operation is a good deal simpler
that the design of lines for mixed-model operation. The multiple models
may either be different products or different versions of the same product,
but in either case the different models or products will have similar,
although not identical, manufacturing requirements, since otherwise
there would be little justification in manufacturing them on the same basic
line. In practice, the line is 'set up' for one model, and then adjustments
are made to the line prior to the manufacture of a batch of the second
model, and so on. We can therefore consider the problem as being a
succession of separate flow-line design problems; hence decisions (2),
(3) and (4) above may be treated in the manner outlined previously.

The multimodel method of operation may be used on either transfer
lines or manual flow lines. However, because of the comparative lack of
flexibility of the former, multimodel operation of transfer lines is normally
associated with the production of very similar models so that only small
set-up changes are required, or with very large batches incurring very
few set-up changes. Multimodel operation of manual lines is common,
since the reallocation of work and equipment between stations is often
accomplished without undue difficulty.

Before looking at some of the specific problems associated with multimodel line design, we shall look more closely at the nature of this type of
line. In particular, let us look first at the nature of the family of products
to be manufactured on the line, and secondly at the nature of final inventories.

The 'family' of products or models being manufactured on the line may
be 'finite' and known—as in the case of most motor-vehicle manufacture—
or alternatively the range may be 'infinite' and unknown. The latter possibility is uncommon, and implies a situation in which the general nature
of the product is known, but the precise specification of the items to be
ordered by customers is unknown. Such a case might arise when 'custom-
built' cars using a basic body shell and chassis are built on a flow line.
It is, of course, conceivable that an intermediate situation may exist in
which some models are known and produced regularly while others are
produced only once.

The production plan for a multimodel line can be conceived along two broad lines. Production of a particular model may only occur on receipt of an order, or a line may produce finished stock from which specific customer orders are satisfied.

It should now be clear that four basic possible multimodel production situations exist, i.e.

(1) Finite and known product range:
    (a) Manufacture to demand.
    (b) Manufacture to stock.
(2) Infinite and unknown product range:
    (a) Manufacture to demand.
    (b) Manufacture to stock.

If we examine each of these situations with respect to the design decisions identified previously, we can observe the following:

(1) (a) Batch size and sequence decisions do not *normally* occur.
    (b) All decisions occur.
(2) (a) Batch size and sequence decisions do not *normally* occur.
    (b) The situation is impossible in practice.

The multimodel situation in which models or products from a finite and known range are to be manufactured to stock thus represents possibly the most comprehensive case of the line-design problem, and it is largely with this situation that we shall be concerned throughout this section.

Allocation of models to lines

If we were to be concerned with the use of a single line for the production of several similar models, the model-allocation problem would not arise. In practice, however, we are often concerned with more than one line. For example, taking the situation that we have previously identified (finite model range/production to stock) we might view the design problem as follows:

'Design one or more lines for the efficient production of a given number of models to satisfy a forecast demand pattern for each.'

Thus we must decide how many lines to employ, how long such lines must be, and which models are to be made on each line. As yet there are no satisfactory quantitative procedures for dealing with these interrelated problems, except, of course, through simulation, and, in practice, the design of such multimodel production systems will owe a great deal to the demands of the particular situation, the experience of the designer and to trial and error (i.e. the examination of various alternative designs and the adoption of successive improvements). A central feature of this design problem is that of allocating models to lines, and this problem, if treated in a sufficiently comprehensive manner (i.e. the allocation of models to an unknown number of lines of an unknown length to satisfy certain production and design objectives) might be considered to provide the key to this problem area. However, not only has model allocation yet to be examined in this manner, but also very little attention has yet been paid to more narrowly defined problems of this type. In fact, at the present time, only two papers relating to this subject are available. Since both of these were developed explicitly for the allocation of models to mixed-model lines, they will be discussed in a later section. However, one in particular—the similarity-index method—also applies to the multimodel line-design problem.

Line balancing

The nature of the line-balancing problem depends to a very large extent on the model batch sizes. For very large batches it is probably adequate to consider multimodel line balancing as a series of single-model balancing problems. In such a situation, given a number of models to be produced, the following procedure might be adopted:

(1) Select the model with the largest production-output requirement.
(2) Allocate the work elements of this model to stations using the balancing methods discussed in Chapters 5 and 6. Since production is likely to be for stock, it is not essential that the line be balanced for a precise cycle time. A cycle time within a given range is probably sufficient; consequently, by manipulation of both the cycle time and the number of stations, it should be possible to minimize balancing loss.
(3) For each remaining model, allocate the work elements to the number of stations obtained during step (2) so as to:
   (a) Minimize balancing loss.
   (b) Ensure that similar elements for each model are allocated to the same stations, thus ensuring that minimum setting up and reallocation of labour and equipment is necessary when model changes take place.
(4) Assess the efficiency of the line design by calculating the weighted average balancing loss (i.e. the average loss for all models weighted according to their relative production-run lengths).
(5) Repeat steps (1), (2), (3) and (4). In step (1), select the remaining model with the largest production requirement. Repeat until either all

models have been selected in step (1) or until a satisfactory solution is obtained.

(6) Select the line design which provides the lowest weighted average balancing loss.

This heuristic procedure provides an appropriate means of *approaching* the multimodel line-balancing problem. However, since it lacks rigour, it can only be considered as a means of assisting in the search for an adequate design. Clearly, as model sizes reduce, the multimodel line-balancing problem approaches that of the mixed-model line. Hence, for small batch sizes (and, additionally, when the allocation of similar types of work to the same station is of paramount importance) multimodel lines might best be balanced using the method described for mixed-model lines.

Batch sequencing

The optimum manufacturing sequence for the batches of different models is clearly influenced by the cost of setting up the assembly line. The total cost of setting up the line comprises the cost of tool and machine change-overs, tool and machine resetting, machine and labour idle time, etc., and is clearly influenced by the nature of the preceding and succeeding models. The problem, therefore, is to determine the sequence order of the model batches to minimize the total setting-up cost over a given period of

Cost		Succeeding model			
		A	B	C	D
Preceding model	A	0	100	150	80
	B	50	0	100	75
	C	80	40	0	110
	D	115	100	60	0

Figure 7.1 Setting-up cost associated with pairs of models [reproduced from R. Wild (1971). *Techniques of Production Management*, Holt, Rinehart and Winston, London]

Cost	Succeeding model			
	A	B	C	D
Preceding model A	920	20	70	⓪
Preceding model B	⓪	950	50	25
Preceding model C	40	⓪	960	70
Preceding model D	55	40	⓪	940

Figure 7.2 Least-cost solution to the assignment problem (a cost of 1000 was allocated to the diagonal elements) [reproduced from R. Wild (1971). *Techniques of Production Management*, Holt, Rinehart and Winston, London]

time. It is highly unlikely that line 'set-up' costs will be constant, but, of course, if this were the case, the sequence order of the model batches would be immaterial.

One attractive and simple technique, which *may* provide a solution to batch-sequencing problems, is the *assignment* method of *linear programming*. The matrix shown in Figure 7.1 shows the setting-up cost associated with pairs of models, i.e. the figures in the matrix are the cost of changing the assembly line from a set up suitable for production of the 'preceding' model to one suitable for production of the 'succeeding' model. The zeros appear in the diagonal of this matrix because these batch sequences involve no changes in the line set up. However, since our objective is to determine the least-cost sequence of changes, we must ensure that the diagonal elements do not feature in the solution by attaching very high cost values to them.

The solution to this assignment problem which is shown in Figure 7.2 indicates that, for minimum setting-up cost, model D must follow model A, model A must follow model B, B must follow C and C must follow D. These minimum cost assignments are given by the cells with zero values. In other words, starting with model A, the model batch sequence would be as follows:

A D C B A D C and so on.

The assignment algorithm will not, however, always produce a sequence which includes all models. Consequently it is an inadequate method of dealing with batch sequencing. A more satisfactory method of dealing with the problem involves considering it as a *travelling-salesman* problem, which is normally formulated as follows:

'A salesman must travel from his base or office and visit each of several locations once only before returning to base, the sequence of visits being designed to minimize either distance travelled or travelling time'.

The batch-sequencing problem is directly analogous to this, the objective being the minimization of cost. Several methods and algorithms are available for solving the classic travelling-salesmen problem (see any comprehensive book on operations research), and, furthermore, this approach to the model-sequencing problem can also be extended to cover the situation in which the initial state of the line is important. Such a situation may occur when a line is being set up 'from scratch' or where the existing set up reflects the requirements of a model which is no longer to be manufactured.

In such cases there are two aspects to the model-sequencing problem. These are, first, the determination of the optimum sequence of models to be produced, and, secondly, the determination of which model to produce first to minimize the cost of changing the line set up from its existing state. The first part of the problem can be approached using the assignment algorithm or, should that fail, using the travelling-salesman formulation. The second part of the problem is solved merely by identifying the cost of changing the present line set up to that required for each of the models and by starting the manufacturing sequence with the model which incurs least initial set-up cost.

This discussion assumes a situation in which the same number of batches of each model is to be produced, each model being produced once before the second batch of any model is produced. A further method of sequencing under such conditions is also provided by use of the model 'similarity index' discussed later in this chapter.

Batch sizes

If it were sufficient to determine individually production batch sizes of each product to be manufactured on a multimodel line, the batch-size problem could be easily solved by the application of one of the many economic-batch-quantity formulae. However, such an approach to the problem would be inadequate. How, for example, could we be certain that the manufacture of models in batches whose size had been determined in such a manner could be accomplished on the line? It could be that, if the batch sizes were large, and hence the production cycles long, each model could only be produced infrequently. Indeed, it might be that the frequency of production of any model (i.e. the time between successive batches) was too large, and that, during this interval, stock of the model would fall to zero. In other words, if such optimal or economic batches are to be produced, how are they to be fitted into a production schedule which itself imposes certain limitations on batch sizes and production cycle times?

Clearly such a problem can only be overcome if the batch sizes and production cycles are established having regard to the requirements of all models, i.e. their production and consumption rates and production costs. There are several methods of establishing such batch-production schedules (Maxwell, 1964), and we shall look briefly at two of these.

When a number of models are to be manufactured successively on a flow line, the following formulae can be used to establish first the total number of complete cycles required, where one complete cycle consists of the manufacture of one batch of each model, and secondly the production batch size for each model, to minimize total set-up and holding costs.

$$N' = \sqrt{\left[\frac{\sum_k C_{1k}\, r_k \left(1 - \dfrac{r_k}{q_k}\right)}{2\sum_k C_{2k}}\right]}$$

where N' = number of complete production cycles
  r_k = consumption rate for model k
  q_k = production rate for model k
  C_{1k} = holding cost per unit of model k per unit of time
  C_{2k} = line set-up cost for model k.
Since Q = batch quantity for the product = r_k/N'

$$Q_k = \sqrt{\left[\frac{2r_k^2 \sum C_{2k}}{\sum_k C_{1k}\, r_k \left(1 - \dfrac{r_k}{q_k}\right)}\right]}.$$

These formulae are derived from one of the simple economic-batch-quantity formulae (Magee and Boodman, 1967), i.e.

$$Q = \sqrt{\left[\frac{2C_2\, r}{C_1 \left(1 - r/q\right)}\right]}.$$

One problem which is apparent in attempting to apply such formulae to the mixed-model flow line is the determination of C_{2k}, since, for any model, the line set-up cost will depend on the nature of the preceding model. Consequently, solution of the batch-sequencing problem must precede the solution of the batch-size problem.

The use of these formulae is best illustrated by means of a simple example.

Example

Four models are to be manufactured on a single mixed-model flow line. The consumption and production rates, as well as all relevant costs, are shown in Table 7.1. Notice that, since all the models are basically

Table 7.1

Model	Consumption per year	Production rate per day	Holding cost per item per year (£)	Line set-up cost for product
A	10,000	160	0·005	100
B	6000	192	0·005	50
C	4000	128	0·010	80
D	20,000	160	0·008	60

similar, the line production rate for each model is similar, and, since the line has been specifically designed for the manufacture of these four products, it is intended to be capable, when fully utilized, of producing all four in the quantities required. For our purposes we shall assume a 100 per cent line utilization rate when working, and 250 working days per year.

To use the above formulae, the production and consumption rates for all products must be expressed in common units, which in our case will be 'days of production per year'. Notice also that the holding cost per item must also be related to 'days of production' and that the production rate for each product is the same since in each case it requires one day to produce one 'unit' of each.

Table 7.2 gives all data in the new units. For example, the consumption

Table 7.2

Model	r_k	q_k	C_{1k}	C_{2k}
A	62·50	250	0·80	100
B	31·25	250	0·96	50
C	31·25	250	1·28	80
D	125·00	250	1·28	60
	250·00 days			

rate r_A for model A is 62·5 in the new units, because 62·5 days at 160 per day are required to produce 10,000 units. Similarly

$$r_B = \frac{6000}{192} = 31\cdot25$$

and so on.

Now we can proceed with the calculation necessary for the determination of N, as shown in Table 7.3, from which we find

$$N' = \sqrt{\left(\frac{178\cdot75}{2\times290}\right)} = 0\cdot556 \text{ cycles/year}$$

Consequently 0·556 production cycles per year should be made.

Table 7.3

Model	$\dfrac{r_k}{q_k}$	$1-\dfrac{r_k}{q_k}$	$C_{1k}\,r_k$	$C_{1k}r_k\left(1-\dfrac{r_k}{q_k}\right)$	C_{2k}
A	0·25	0·75	50	37·5	100
B	0·125	0·875	30	26·25	50
C	0·125	0·875	40	35	80
D	0·50	0·50	160	80	60
				178·75	**290**

The production batch sizes for each model are established as follows:

$$Q_A = 10,000/0\cdot556 = 18,000$$
$$Q_B = 6000/0\cdot556 = 10,000$$
$$Q_C = 4000/0\cdot556 = 7200$$
$$Q_D = 20,0/000\cdot556 = 36,000$$

The procedure provides the model batch sizes which lead to minimum-cost operation, i.e. the production schedule which minimizes total set-up and holding costs. Because the objective was the minimization of such costs over the entire schedule, the batch sizes obtained differ significantly from those that would have been found had each product been considered individually.

Eilon (1962) provides a more comprehensive approach to this batch-scheduling problem, which, while requiring greater computational effort, might be worthwhile in certain cases. He derives formulae for establishing multimodel batch sizes for the optimization of objectives such as cost per unit and rate of return. He points out, however, that it is risky to consider (as we did above) the production schedule and forget about the require-ments of the individual products, and consequently he outlines a procedure designed to satisfy the requirements of both individual models and the total schedule. This procedure is basically as follows:

(1) *Compute the production range* (p) or the economic production range (depending on the selected criterion) for *each* model individually. The production range is the tolerance about the calculated economic batch quantity which is acceptable to management. Because the total-cost curve is usually fairly flat about the economic batch quantity (i.e. its lowest point), a small acceptable increase in total costs is normally associated with a large production range.

(2) *Find the ideal optimal solution* for a multiproduct *schedule*, using one of the procedures developed by Eilon.

(3) *Test the solution by:*

    (i) Subjecting it to what may be termed the *p test*, which simply implies that it is necessary to ascertain that the batches included in the ideal *schedule* solution lie within the limits of the production range of the respective models.

    (ii) Subjecting it to the *cycle test*. Since the proposed schedule involves a certain production cycle time (which can be computed when the rates of production are known), it is necessary to examine whether this time matches the consumption cycle.

If by any chance the ideal schedule solution passes the two tests, the individual approach and the schedule approach are evidently not incompatible, and the ideal solution can therefore be adopted. If, however, the schedule solution does not pass either test, it may be modified as follows:

Failure to pass the p test

When the batch size for a certain product lies beyond the limits of the production range, there are two possibilities:

(1) The batch is too large (i.e. above the upper limits of the range), in which case it can be divided into two or more subbatches. Each subbatch should lie within the range. This means that the model will be produced more than once in the cycle.

(2) The batch is too small (i.e. below the lower limit of the range), in which case the quantity can be doubled or trebled and produced only once every two or three cycles, the idea being that the new quantity thereby derived would fall within the range and pass the *p test*. In this way, non-identical production cycles are formed: long cycles, which include all the models on the schedule, and short cycles, which include only some of them. This will necessitate reconsidering each

cycle on its own, and the batch size of the product that is not produced every cycle will have to be modified accordingly.

Failure to pass the cycle test

Since we will normally have designed the flow line specifically for the production of the models being investigated, it is likely that the schedule solution obtained will be feasible, as in the above case. However, for completeness, we will outline Eilon's procedures for dealing with schedules that do not satisfy this requirement.

We may have either of the following two alternatives:

(1) The production cycle is shorter than the consumption period, i.e. when the nth model is completed, there is still extra time left before the first one is due again for manufacture. If this time is to be utilized to advantage, we have to seek methods to step up the rate of consumption of some of the models and use the available time to produce more of these, or we have to consider the introduction of an additional model into the schedule.

(2) The production cycle is larger than the consumption period, i.e. the schedule presents too heavy a load compared with the available facilities. In a purpose-designed multimodel line such a situation is unlikely. However, possible courses of action would be:

   (i) Increase the plant capacity by use of overtime, by purchase of new or additional machines, or by subcontracting some of the orders.

  (ii) Reduce the commitments either by dropping certain models from the schedule or by relaxing the restriction that all the models must always be available.

MIXED-MODEL LINE DESIGN

The advantage of this type of production is that, unlike multimodel lines, a steady flow of models is produced to meet customer requirements, theoretically without the need for large stocks of finished goods. The major disadvantages arise from the differing work contents of the models, resulting in the uneven flow of work and consequent station idle time and/or congestion of semifinished products.

This type of assembly line undoubtedly presents the most complex design and operating problems. Indeed, some of these problems are so complex that adequate analytical solutions have not yet been developed.

A certain amount of research has been undertaken, but a great deal more has yet to be learned before fully satisfactory management techniques are developed. We can therefore only attempt to summarize the issues involved and describe briefly some of the solutions that have been suggested. We will deal mainly with the line-balancing and the model-sequencing problems, the latter being the more complex. Some computer programs have been developed by companies to deal with their own particular balancing and sequencing problems (e.g. 'This is line balancing', *Factory*, April 1963, pp. 84–90), but none of these are available for general use.

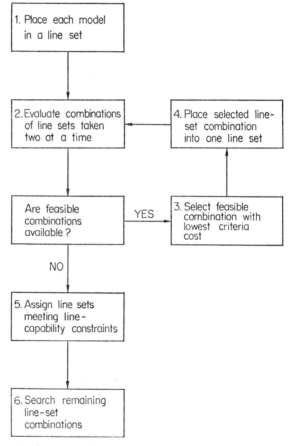

Figure 7.3 Flow chart of assignment methodology [reproduced from M. Lehman (1969). 'On criteria for for assigning models to assembly lines', *Int. J. Prod. Res.*, **7**, No. 4, 269–285]

First we must look at the *allocation of models to lines*. If we visualize a situation in which several mixed-model lines are to be used in the manufacture of a large range of similar models, the number of groupings of models on lines—or *line sets*—is probably quite large. There will, of course, be certain restrictions in that each line will probably have a minimum economical and maximum production capacity, but, even within such restrictions, it will often be possible to minimize total production costs by the effective allocation of models to lines.

This model/line-allocation problem has been studied by Lehman (1969), who devised a heuristic procedure for obtaining line sets which, in addition to meeting line-capacity requirements, minimized the costs associated with balance delay, sequence delay and learning (learning is discussed in Chapter 9). Sequence delay was used as a measure of idle time or time loss due to the sequencing of models on the line, while learning was a measure of the improvement in operator productivity as tasks were repeated. Lehman's assignment procedure is described by the flow diagram shown in Figure 7.3.

Initially each model is placed in a different line set (block 1 of Figure 7.3), and then (block 2) all combinations of these sets are taken two at a time. Of the feasible combinations (i.e. those pairs for which the output requirements do not exceed the line capacity), the pair providing least total balance, sequence and learning costs is selected (block 3). These two sets are combined, thus reducing the total number of sets by one (block 4). This process is then repeated until no further feasible combinations remain, at which point those sets which satisfy both upper and lower line capacities are assigned to lines while the remainder require further examination, for which purpose an exhaustive search procedure is provided.

An alternative approach to the model/line-allocation problem involves examining the nature of models to identify those line sets which contain models which are most alike or similar from a manufacturing point of view. If a measure of model similarity is to be used in allocating models to lines, the measure must obviously be associated with the work content of models. Such a measure, or *similarity index*, has been developed by Thomopoulos (forthcoming). The index, which takes values from zero to unity, is based on the association of work elements and their processing times on each model. The index is calculated using the formula:

$$S_{k^*} = \left(U_{k^*} - \frac{1}{N_{k^*}} \right) \Big/ \left(1 - \frac{1}{N_{k^*}} \right)$$

where S_{k^*} = similarity index for models in line set k^*

N_{k^*} = the number of models included in line set k^*

U_{k^*} = the utilization index for work elements in the models, i.e.

$$\left(\sum_{i=1}^{m} \sum_{k^*} T_{Eik} \right) \Big/ \left(\sum_{i=1}^{m} \sum_{k^*} \hat{T}_{Eik} \right)$$

Note that T_{Eik} = time required for element i ($i = 1, \ldots, m$) for model k.

Hence $\sum_{i}^{m} \sum_{k^*} T_{Eik}$ is the sum of all element times for all models in set k^*.

$\hat{T}_{Eik}$ = maximum time required for element i for the models in line set k^*. Hence $\sum_{i}^{m} \sum_{k^*} \hat{T}_{Eik}$ is taken to be the sum of all element times for all models in the set, the maximum of each element time being assumed to apply for each model.

The determination of these values and the calculation of the index is best illustrated by reference to the simple example provided by Thomopoulos.

Table 7.4 Element times T_{Eik} for models

Element i	Model k					
	1	2	3	4	5	6
1	2	2	0	2	2	2
2	0	1	1	1	1	1
3	4	0	4	0	4	0
4	3	3	0	3	3	3
5	2	0	2	2	2	0
6	1	1	1	0	0	1
7	0	1	1	1	1	1
8	0	4	4	0	4	0
9	2	2	0	2	2	2
10	1	0	1	0	1	0
$\sum_{i=1}^{m} T_{Eik}$	15	14	14	11	20	10

Suppose six models are to be made in equal quantities using mixed-model lines. Further, assume that three models are to be allocated to each line, i.e. line sets = 3. Table 7.4 gives the element times for each model. Now consider the line set consisting of models 1, 2 and 3. S_{k^*} can be calculated as follows:

$$U_{k^*} = \frac{43}{63} = 0 \cdot 68$$

$$N_{k^*} = 3$$

$$S_{k^*} = \frac{0 \cdot 68 - 0 \cdot 33}{0 \cdot 67} = 0 \cdot 52.$$

Similarly, S_{k^*} can be calculated for each of the other 19 possible sets of three models. Table 7.5 lists the ten possible pairs of three-model sets, together with the similarity index for each line set, and the mean index for each pair. For this table it can be seen that $k^* = (1, 3, 5)$ with $k^* = (2, 4, 6)$ gives the highest mean index, thus suggesting that the models should be allocated to the two lines in this manner.

Table 7.5 Similarity indices for line sets

Line 1		Line 2		$\bar{S}_{k^*}$
k^*	S_{k^*}	k^*	S_{k^*}	
123	0·52	456	0·50	0·51
124	0·45	356	0·55	0·50
125	0·65	346	0·33	0·49
126	0·43	345	0·56	0·49
134	0·45	256	0·55	0·50
135	0·65	246	0·58	0·62
136	0·43	245	0·56	0·49
145	0·37	236	0·40	0·39
146	0·55	235	0·64	0·60
156	0·56	234	0·43	0·49

This type of similarity index has other possible uses; for example, it could be used to assess the similarity of units produced on one line. In such cases, as well as in the allocation of models to lines, it may be necessary to take account of the number of each model produced. This can be done using a modified but similar formula for S_{k^*}.

The index might also be used in the sequencing of batches of models on multimodel lines. If the similarity of all pairs of models is determined, a sequence of models could be established to maximize the sum of the similarity indices.

Line balancing

Line balancing for mixed-model lines might be considered merely as several single-model balancing problems, i.e. each model could be considered separately and the total work content divided as equally as possible between the work stations. Consider a case where a line is built for the assembly of two similar models A and B of a product. The work elements of model A are allocated to the work stations so that during the periods in which A is being assembled, balancing loss is minimized. Similarly, the work elements of B are allocated to work stations to minimize balancing loss during the assembly of model B. Such a procedure is often adopted and is fairly satisfactory when the models to be produced are of a similar nature, i.e. when the production of each model involves similar work elements to be undertaken in a similar order or when the production of all models merely involves the repetition of similar work elements. When such circumstances apply, the workers at each station will be required to do the same type of work irrespective of which model is being produced. If, on the other hand, dissimilar models are to be produced, independent line balancing for each will often result in dissimilar work elements, e.g. work involving different skills, necessitating different training, etc., being allocated to each station. In circumstances such as these, balancing should be undertaken so as to ensure that similar work elements are allocated to the same work stations or groups of stations, irrespective of which model is being produced. A method by which this might be achieved is to assign elements to stations on a *total time* rather than *cycle time* basis.

Consider the case already mentioned. Two models A and B are to be assembled on the same line. Model A is the product we have considered previously (Figure 4.8); model B is dissimilar, but, nevertheless, has several work elements in common with model A.

The precedence relationship of the elements of both models are shown

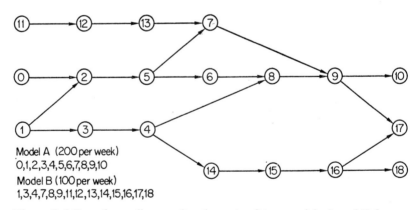

Figure 7.4 Precedence diagram for elements of two models A and B [reproduced from R. Wild (1971). *Techniques of Production Management*, Holt, Rinehart and Winston, London]

in Figure 7.4 (elements 1, 3, 4, 7, 8 and 9 are common to both models). The production requirements are: model A, 200 per week; model B, 100 per week. Table 7.6 gives all the data that we shall require for balancing the line. Column (b) gives the element duration. Column (e) shows the number of times that the work element must be performed during the week to satisfy the output requirements of both models. The total time required for each work element per week is given in column (f) [total time per week = (b) × (e)].

Table 7.6 Date for the two-model line-balancing problem [reproduced from R. Wild (1971). *Techniques of Production Management*, Holt, Rinehart and Winston, London]

(a)	(b)	(c)	(d)	(e)	(f)	(g)
		Number of times per week				
	Element	elements must be performed			Total	Positional
Element	duration				time (h)	weight (using
number	(h)	A	B	Total	Σ = 569	total times)
0	0·32	200	0	200	64	411
1	0·10	200	100	300	30	463
2	0·2	200	0	200	40	347
3	0·05	200	100	300	15	292
4	0·1	200	100	300	30	277
5	0·23	200	0	200	46	307
6	0·2	200	0	200	40	246
7	0·05	200	100	300	15	125
8	0·32	200	100	300	96	206
9	0·1	200	100	300	30	110
10	0·3	200	0	200	60	60
11	0·1	0	100	100	10	167
12	0·15	0	100	100	15	157
13	0·17	0	100	100	17	142
14	0·08	0	100	100	8	61
15	0·07	0	100	100	7	53
16	0·13	0	100	100	13	46
17	0·20	0	100	100	20	20
18	0·13	0	100	100	13	14

The line balance is obtained using the ranked-positional-weights technique, but, instead of calculating positional weights by summing element times, they are found by summing total times. All that now remains is to allocate elements to work stations. The available time per station per week is considered to be 40 h (five 8 h days) and the element allocation is shown in Table 7.7. Balancing loss is 5·1 per cent, but it has been necessary to parallel or duplicate several work stations because the total time for four elements (0, 5, 8 and 10) is greater than the available 40 h.

These figures indicate that, for one week's production, we have achieved quite a respectable line balance (a 5·1 per cent balancing loss is very good). Such a method of line balancing is justified *only* when production is truly *mixed*-model. Had there been a tendency to send models through the line in batches rather than individually, a quite unsatisfactory situations would have resulted. If a batch of model A is being assembled, stations 1, 8, 9, 10, 11, 13, 14 and 15 will be underutilized and incur a great deal of balancing loss, and, while the batch of model B is being assembled, stations

Table 7.7 Two-model line balance [reproduced from R. Wild (1971). *Techniques of Production Management*, Holt, Rinehart and Wilson, London]

Station number	Element number	Total time per week for element (h)	Time remaining from 40 h week (h)
1	1	30	10
	11	10	0
2 and 3ᵃ	0	64	16
	3	15	1
4	2	40	0
5 and 6ᵃ	5	46	34
	4	30	4
7	6	40	0
8, 9 and 10ᵃ	8	96	24
	12	15	9
	14	8	1
11	13	17	23
	7	15	8
	15	7	1
12	9	30	10
13 and 14ᵃ	10	60	20
	16	13	7
15	17	20	20
	18	13	7

ᵃ Stations paralleled

2, 3, 4, 5, 6, 7, 13 and 14 will be underutilized. Only if model A and model B are produced concurrently on the line will a satisfactory situation result from the allocation shown in Table 7.5. In other words, this method of 'combined' line balancing for a shift's or a week's production of all models is beneficial where:

(a) Models are to be produced concurrently on the line and not in batches.

(b) Dissimilar work elements are involved and it is desirable to ensure that work of a similar nature is allocated to separate stations or groups of stations.

In other words, this method of balancing is effective in attempting to minimize differences in the *total* work allocated to each station for *all* models. However, a further requirement of mixed-model line balancing is not satisfied, i.e. the minimization of the differences between station service times for *each* model.

An extension of this method, which also seeks to smooth the differences in station service times for each model, has been developed by Thomopoulos (1970). The method which is proposed works in an iterative manner, evaluating the possible allocations of work to stations to provide for maximum 'smoothness' of times for each model. The procedure is also shown to be of value in the balancing of lines for multimodel production, where the allocation and balance requirements are similar to those of mixed-model lines.

Service-time variability on mixed-model lines derives from two sources: the inherent operator variability of the type discussed in Chapter 6, and the different station-service-time requirements of different models. Such service-time variability is no less important in the design of mixed-model line than it is for the design of single-model lines, and the manner in which the phenomenon is accommodated in this situation is identical to that discussed previously. In other words, the efficient operation of mixed-model lines depends on the reduction or elimination of the pacing effect through the decoupling of stations, such decoupling being obtained by the use of buffer stock or through the provision of station-length flexibility.

THE OPERATION OF MULTIMODEL AND MIXED-MODEL LINES

Assuming that the sequence of batches has been determined, the problems associated with the operation of multimodel lines will resemble those occurring on single-model lines, and there is no need for any further discussion of the subject here. Our discussion in this section will, therefore, relate entirely to the mixed-model situation. Certain clerical procedures have been developed to assist in flow-line production (Nissen, Kallem and Christianson, 1968), and such situations may in certain cases benefit from the use of control techniques such as Line of Balance (Turban, 1968).

MIXED-MODEL LINES

The principal operating problem peculiar to mixed-model flow-line production relates to the feeding or launching of models onto the line. This launching problem has two components which can be summarized in the following manner:

(1) In what manner will models be fed or launched onto the line, i.e. what is to be the *launch discipline*? For example, will models be launched at equal time intervals?
(2) What should be the *sequence* of models launched onto the line?

One might, of course, consider these to be design problems, in that a discipline and sequence for the launching of models onto the line might be established during line design prior to line operation. Given a knowledge of the required model mix, it should be possible to establish such operating principles during line design. In practice, launch discipline is often established prior to line operation. Indeed, it might be argued that it is unnecessary or impractical to attempt to establish a complete model sequence during line design, and that what is required is a principle or rule for model sequencing to be applied during line operation. We shall examine attempts to devise methods of establishing such a principle after looking briefly at model-launch disciplines.

Model-launch discipline

This problem relates to the time interval between the starting or feeding of items onto the line. There are two fundamental launch disciplines— *variable-rate launching* and *fixed-rate launching*. In variable-rate launching the time interval between the starting of successive items down the line is equal to the first station service time of the leading item. For example, if three models C, D and E whose station service times are $T_{Sk} = 4, 2$ and 1 min, respectively, are to be assembled on a line, a variable-rate launching system as shown in Figure 7.5 might be used. Here a model C is launched first, and remains at station 1 for 4 min before passing to station 2. A model D is launched 4 min after the preceding unit and it remains at station 1 for 2 min only. Thus after 6 min of line operation the second unit is available to be worked upon at station 2. However station 2 has not yet completed the preceding unit, hence the second one must remain idle, either in interstation storage or on the moving line, depending on the type of line operation being used. If we continue to look at the second unit launched, we see that the second station begins work on it after 8 min has elapsed. It is worked on at this station for 2 min, then remains idle for a further 2 min before being worked on by station 3 for 2 min. Consequently it is completed 10 min after launching,

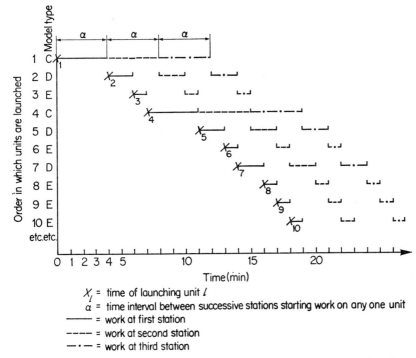

X_l = time of launching unit l
α = time interval between successive stations starting work on any one unit
—— = work at first station
---- = work at second station
—·— = work at third station

Figure 7.5 Variable-rate launching of three models onto a three-station flow line [reproduced from R. Wild (1971). *Techniques of Production Management*, Holt, Rinehart and Winston, London]

the unit idle time (or difference between this 10 min and the total work content of 6 min) being caused by the fact that it was launched after a model with greater work content.

For the same reason the third unit launched—model E—requires 9 min for completion at all three stations, although its work content is only 3 min. It is quite clear from this description and from Figure 7.5 that the time interval α between successive stations starting work on any one unit is equal to the largest model service time and, when models with shorter service times are being assembled, a considerable amount of unit idle time results. Notice also that this same idle time results even when none of the models with longer service time are present on the line (after the nineteenth minute there are no model Cs on the line, yet the time interval is still 4 min). This launching discipline ensures that stations are kept busy, but only at the expense of high work in progress.

There is little that can be done by way of model sequencing to minimize

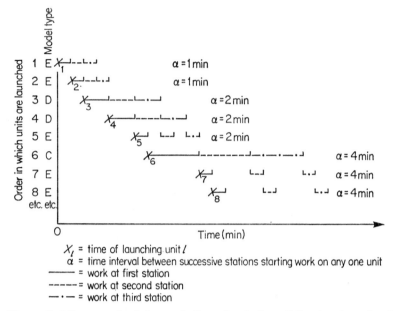

X_l = time of launching unit l
α = time interval between successive stations starting work on any one unit
——— = work at first station
– – – – = work at second station
—·— = work at third station

Figure 7.6 Increase in delay and throughput time following launch of model C [reproduced from R. Wild (1971). *Techniques of Production Management*, Holt, Rinehart and Winston, London]

this delay or work in progress, since, assuming that for each model the service time remains constant, and is equal at each station, the delay will always be determined by the difference in model service times. A reduction in delay would be obtained by launching models with shorter service times first, but unless complete batching of models were possible, i.e. assembly of all model Es, then all model Ds, and finally model Cs, the improvement would last only until it was necessary to launch one model C (see Figure 7.6). Variable-rate launching is used extensively on manual flow lines, especially on non-mechanical lines. Here the operator at the first station is often required to take units from a container at the beginning of the line to keep himself supplied with work. This launching discipline is, perhaps, more appropriate for non-mechanical lines with interstation buffer facilities than for moving-belt lines, since, in the latter, many of the units may be carried some way past a station before being worked on at the station. This feature may not be unduly disadvantageous if items can be removed from the line, but, when items are fixed to the line, variable-rate launching can lead to considerable movement of operators along the line.

A further important practical disadvantage of variable-rate launching occurs where there is a need for related activities to be synchronized with the main flow line, e.g. the supply of materials at points along the line, or the merging of two or more lines (such as the merging of chassis and body assembly lines in automobile manufacture). In such a case these related activities must be carefully planned and controlled to synchronize with the variable launching on the assembly line. In such circumstances,

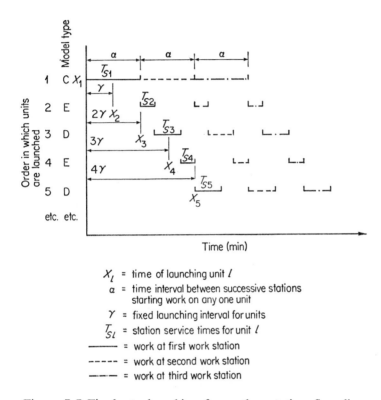

X_l = time of launching unit l
a = time interval between successive stations starting work on any one unit
γ = fixed launching interval for units
T_{Sl} = station service times for unit l
——— = work at first work station
----- = work at second work station
—·—·— = work at third work station

Figure 7.7 Fixed-rate launching for a three-station flow line [reproduced from R. Wild (1971). *Techniques of Production Management*, Holt, Rinehart and Winston, London]

a system of fixed-rate launching in which units are launched or started on the line at regular intervals γ may be preferable.

Fixed-rate launching involves the starting or feeding of units onto the flow line at regular time intervals. Such a system is depicted in Figure 7.7 for a three-station line. Here units are launched at equal intervals γ, the launching interval. It is clear from Figure 7.7 that to avoid station idle time

$$\gamma \leq T_{S1}$$

similarly $2\gamma \leq T_{S1} + T_{S2}$ or $\gamma \leq \dfrac{T_{S1} + T_{S2}}{2}$

$$. \qquad .$$
$$. \qquad .$$
$$. \qquad .$$

$$\gamma \leq \frac{T_{S1} + T_{S2+} \ldots + T_{SQ}}{Q}$$

where Q = total number of units to be produced.

Each of this series of requirements must be satisfied simultaneously if station idle time is to be avoided, and this can only be achieved through careful selection of T_{Sl} ($l = 1, \ldots, Q$). It is therefore clear that the model sequence employed is an important parameter when this launching discipline is used. Consequently, to fully understand this method of launching, we must look more closely at sequencing. Notice that the last relationship specified above implies that the fixed launching interval

$$\gamma \leq \frac{\sum\limits_{k} Q_k T_{Sk}}{\sum\limits_{k} Q_k}.$$

However, if γ is less than this quantity, items will be launched prematurely and congestion will occur. Hence, to avoid both station idle time and congestion,

$$\gamma_{\text{optimal}} = \frac{\sum\limits_{k} Q_k T_{Sk}}{\sum\limits_{k} Q_k}.$$

Before looking at the sequencing problem, it is worth noting the principal advantages and disadvantages of this launching discipline.

Fixed-rate launching is more easily 'mechanized' than variable-rate launching. It is, therefore, perhaps a more appropriate method for feeding moving-belt lines, especially where heavy items are involved. It is also more appropriate for moving-belt lines because of the more regular flow pattern it creates. It also facilitates the merging of lines, etc.

Model sequencing for fixed-rate launching

Clearly, if a series of models whose station service times are less than the launching interval are launched onto a line, station idle time will result. Alternatively, if a series of models with longer service times were launched, congestion would occur, and/or incomplete items might be produced (depending on the operating method employed).

We shall look briefly at two approaches to the model sequencing problem, and first at that provided by Wester and Kilbridge (1964).

We have shown that to avoid station idle time and congestion

$$\gamma_{\text{optimal}} = \frac{\sum\limits_{k} Q_k T_{Sk}}{\sum\limits_{k} Q_k}.$$

In addition, it can be shown that, as for variable-rate launching

$$\alpha_{\text{optimal}} = \max T_{Sk}.$$

We have already shown that, if station idle time is to be avoided,

$$\sum_{h=1}^{l} T_{Sh} - \gamma \geq 0.$$

Furthermore, to prevent congestion of units or the forcing of operations out of their stations

$$\alpha \geq T_{S1}$$

$$\alpha + \gamma \geq T_{S1} + T_{S2}$$

.

.

.

$$\alpha + (Q-1)\gamma \geq T_{S1} + T_{S2} + \ldots + T_{SQ}.$$

Again, these requirements must be satisfied simultaneously, and this can only be done if the T_{Sl} are properly chosen each time a unit is launched onto the line.

Therefore to avoid both station idle time and congestion, T_{Sl} should be chosen as each unit is launched, so that:

$$\sum_{h=1}^{l} T_{Sh} - l\gamma \geq 0$$

and
$$\alpha + (l-1)\gamma \geq \sum_{h=1}^{l} T_{Sh}.$$

In other words, at each launch the following expression should be satisfied:

$$0 \leq \sum_{h=1}^{l} T_{Sh} - l\gamma \leq \alpha - \gamma.$$

It is usually impossible, unless both models and service times are very carefully chosen, to avoid both station idle time and work congestion, but, by careful ordering of the models, both of these inefficiencies can be minimized. To select the correct order, a decision must be made every time a unit is launched onto the line, i.e. at every step l. For example, to avoid station idle time and minimize work congestion, models should be launched onto the line so that, for every launching or step l,

$$\sum_{h=1}^{l} T_{Sh} - l\gamma$$

is minimized.

Example

Three models A, B and C of a particular product are assembled concurrently on an assembly line. The quantities required over a given period and the model cycle times are as follows:

Table 7.8

Model k	Number of units required Q_k	Model cycle time T_{Sk}
A	60	0·5
B	110	0·6
C	55	0·8

Calculate the fixed interval at which units must be launched onto the line, and show how the sequence of models might be determined to avoid station idle time.

$$\gamma = \frac{\sum_k Q_k T_{Sk}}{\sum_k Q_k} = \frac{30+66+44}{60+110+55}$$

$$= 0·62.$$

Units must be launched onto the line so that multiples of the launching interval ($l\gamma$) are less than, but as nearly equal as possible to, the sum of the model cycle times

$$\sum_{h=1}^{l} T_{Sh}.$$

Such a method of launching is illustrated in Table 7.9.

In this example the optimum sequence of models results from the repeated launching of models in the order:

C A B B B

Table 7.9

Unit l	$l\gamma$	Model k	T_{Sl}	$\sum\limits_{h=1}^{l} T_{Sh}$	$\sum\limits_{h=1}^{l} T_{Sh} - l\gamma$
1	0·62	C	0·8	0·8	0·18
2	1·24	A	0·5	1·3	0·06
3	1·86	B	0·6	1·9	0·04
4	2·48	B	0·6	2·5	0·02
5	3·10	B	0·6	3·1	0·00
6	3·12	C	0·8	3·9	0·18
7	4·34	A	0·5	4·4	0·06
8	4·96	B	0·6	5·0	0·04
9	5·58	B	0·6	5·6	0·02
10	6·20	B	0·6	6·2	0·00
11	6·82	C	0·8	7·0	0·18
12	7·44	A	0·5	7·5	0·06
13	8·06	B	0·6	8·1	0·04
14	8·68	B	0·6	8·7	0·02
15	9·30	B	0·6	9·3	0·00
16	9·92	C	0·8	10·1	0·18
17	10·54	A	0·5	10·6	0·06
18	11·16	B	0·6	11·2	0·04
19	11·78	B	0·6	11·8	0·02
20	12·40	B	0·6	12·4	0·00
21	13·02	C	0·8	13·2	0·18
22	13·64	A	0·5	13·7	0·07
.	.	.	.	.	.
.	.	.	.	.	.
.	.	.	.	.	.

but notice also that the continual launching of units in this order would not lead to the assembly of the requisite number of each model in the given time period (too many of model B and too few of models A and C would be completed). Consequently, in practice, it would be necessary to depart from this optimal procedure to some extent to satisfy manufacturing requirements. Had the figure in the final column ($\sum T_{Sh} - l\gamma$) have been greater than $\alpha - \gamma$ ($= 0\cdot18$) at any time, this would have indicated that the operator would have been forced out of his work on the particular unit, or alternatively that the unit would continue to the next station incomplete.

A somewhat more complex method of model sequencing developed by Thomopoulos (1967, 1968) applies primarily to moving-belt type lines to which items are fixed and on which station length are variable, i.e. a line of the type described on p. 97. Thomopoulos describes stations on such lines in terms of the three 'regions' shown in Figure 7.8.

Four sources of inefficiency are identified, and these can also be described in terms of the regions shown on Figure 7.8, i.e.

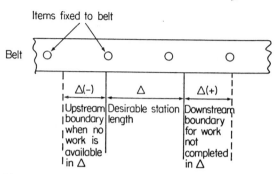

Figure 7.8 Regions of a variable-length station on a
moving-belt-type line

(1) *Idle time:* occurs when an operator has no work to perform in any of the three regions.

(2) *Work-deficiency time:* occurs when an operator has to move into region $\Delta(-)$ to get work.

(3) *Work-congestion time:* occurs when an operator is forced into region $\Delta(+)$ to complete a unit.

(4) *Utility work or incomplete items:* occurs when an operator cannot complete an item, even by working in the $\Delta(+)$ region of a station.

Penalty costs can be attached to these four types of inefficiency—in the case of (1), (2) and (3) in terms of time, and in the case of (4) either in terms of the number of incomplete items or the amount of additional time required for their completion. The object of model sequencing is, then, to minimize the total inefficiency cost associated with the production of the required number of each model. It is assumed that a feed rate has been established after reference to the work content of the models and the output requirements, i.e.

either   the fixed launch interval $\gamma = \dfrac{\sum\limits_{k} Q_k\, T_{Sk}}{\sum\limits_{k} Q_k}$ (see p. 162)

or $\gamma = \max \gamma_k$

Hence   spacing of items on belt $= \dfrac{\text{belt speed}}{\gamma}$.

One method which might be used to determine the model sequence to be adopted is best illustrated by reference to a very simple example

(Thomopoulos, 1968). Two models, A and B, are to be produced on a four-station line. Station dimensions, limits and service times are shown in Table 7.10. The belt is to move at 1 ft/min and the inefficiency costs are £2, £1, £1 and £2 per minute for idle time, work deficiency, congestion and utility, respectively. Two units of A and one of model B are to be produced.

Table 7.10 Station parameters for sequencing example [reproduced from Thomopoulos, N. T. (1968). 'Some analytical approaches to assembly line problems', *The Prod. Eng.*, **47**, No. 7, 345–351]

	Station dimensions (ft)			Operation times per model (min)	
Stations	$\Delta(-)$	Δ	$\Delta(+)$	A	B
1	0	5	1	5	2
2	2	4	2	3	6
3	2	5	0	4	4
4	0	5	0	5	2

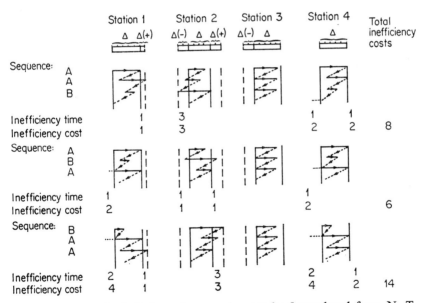

Figure 7.9 Graphical display of sequencing results [reproduced from N. T. Thomopoulos (1968). 'Some analytical approaches to assembly line problems', *The Prod Eng.*, **47**, No. 7, 345–351]

The three possible sequences AAB, ABA and BAA are simulated in Figure 7.9 which shows the movement of the operators at the stations. It can be seen from this figure that sequence ABA provides the best operating strategy.

Where a larger number of different models are to be produced on a line consisting of many stations, it would, of course, be impractical to evaluate all possible model sequences in this manner. In such cases a simulation method for obtaining a 'suboptimal' sequence can be employed. Unit 1 is considered first. All models in turn are processed along the line, and the total inefficiency cost is determined for each model in the manner described. The model with least total cost is placed first in the sequence. The second unit in the sequence is established by again simulating the processing of all models in turn. The model which, when launched after the chosen unit 1, provides least total cost is adopted as the second unit in the sequence. Subsequent units are established in a similar manner until the requisite number of each model has been produced. A record must be maintained to show the number of each model launched, so that production requirements are not exceeded.

When a complete sequence is to be devised for the production of a large number of units, the above procedure may be impractical in terms of both time and cost. In such cases a method of *partitioning* the schedule may be found more appropriate. For example, rather than devising a sequence for an entire production schedule of 100 units consisting of say 20, 20, 12, 24 and 24 units of models A, B, C, D and E, respectively, a sequence may be devised for a schedule of 50 models (i.e. 10A, 10B, 6C, 12D, and 12E) or for a schedule of 25 units (5, 5, 3, 6 and 6), such sequences then being repeated two or four times to provide the requisite output.

Although this simulation-based method of establishing a sequence of models is intended primarily for moving-belt lines with variable station lengths, it can, of course, be used for lines with 'closed' stations if the station regions are appropriately described (see, for example, station 4 in Figure 7.9.) Furthermore, although the technique described by Thomopoulos is not itself suitable for use in determining model sequences for other types of line, the principle employed—simulation—is, of course, appropriate in many situations. One might, for example, use a similar approach to establish model sequences for non-mechanical lines or moving-belt lines from which items can be removed, providing that operating efficiency can be formulated in appropriate terms.

Finally, the basic procedure developed by Thomopoulos does not satisfy the sequencing requirement established previously, i.e. 'a principle or rule—to be applied during line operation . . .' (p. 156), but rather attempts to establish, in advance of production, a complete sequence for all units. The technique, therefore, is applicable only where a finite and known model range with appropriate forecasts of demand for each model over some future period exists.

References

Eilon, S. (1962). *Elements of Production Planning and Control*, Macmillan, New York.

Lehman, M. (1969). 'On criteria for assigning models to assembly lines', *Int. J. Prod. Res.*, 7, No. 4, 269–285.

Magee, J. F., and Boodman, D. M. (1967). *Production Planning and Inventory Control*, McGraw Hill, London.

Maxwell, W. L. (1964). 'The scheduling of economic lot sizes', *Naval Res. Log. Quart.*, 11, 89–124.

Nissen, R., Kallem, L., and Christianson, P. (1968). 'Loading techniques for the multiproduct assembly line', *J. Ind. Eng.*, XIX, No. 5, 243–246.

Thomopoulos, N. T. (1967). 'Line balancing—sequencing for mixed model assembly', *Mgt. Sci.*, 14, No. 2, B59–B75.

Thomopoulos, N. T. (1968). 'Some analytical approaches to assembly line problems', *Prod. Eng.*, July, 345–351.

Thomopoulos, N. T. (1970). 'Mixed model line balancing with smoothed station assignments', *Mgt. Sci.*, 16, No. 9, 593–603.

Thomopoulos, N. T. (forthcoming). 'The mixed model similarity index'.

Turban, E. (1968). 'Line of balance. A management by exception tool', *J. Ind. Eng.*, XIX, No. 9, 440–448.

Wester, L., and Kilbridge, M. D. (1964). 'The assembly line model-mix sequencing problem'. In *Proceedings of the 3rd International Conference on Operations Research* (1963), Dunod, Paris, pp. 247–260.

Young, H. H. (1967). 'Optimization models for production lines', *J. Ind. Eng.*, XVIII, No. 1, 70–78.

CHAPTER 8

Multimodel and Mixed-model Production and Group Technology

Flow-line production is undoubtedly a particularly efficient method of production. It scores highly against all of the usual efficiency criteria, e.g. machine and labour utilization, throughput time, work in progress. Unfortunately, we have seen (Chapter 1) that the use of this method of production depends on the existence of a high and stable demand for a product or a standardized product range, a condition which is present in comparatively few situations. Many manufacturing companies—perhaps the majority—are obliged to manufacture products in batches to stock, to satisfy a demand which is low in comparison to the production rates available, and perhaps subject to some fluctuation. In batch production, therefore, production facilities are not, in general, engaged continually with the manufacture of components for a single product, but with the sequential manufacture of batches of, perhaps, similar components for a range of different products.

One means of improving productivity and efficiency in batch production is to minimize the total machine-setting cost. This can be achieved by reducing the number of machine set ups, which, in turn, can be achieved by increasing batch sizes. This latter, however, has the effect of increasing inventory levels; thus the cost saving on set ups must be balanced against the increased cost of inventories. This, of course, is the essence of the classic economic-batch-size problem. A further means to minimize set-up costs is to attempt to sequence component batches so that the minimum number of machine conversions is required—the batch-sequencing problem. The group-technology method of production seeks to increase the efficiency of batch production by similar means, the only novelty of the approach being the emphasis on components rather than products. Fundamentally, the objective of group technology is the application of the principles of flow production to the manufacture of families of similar

168

components required for a variety of end products. Thus batch *product* manufacture is linked with flow *component* manufacture, and some of the benefits of flow production are obtained, e.g.

reduced production lead time,
reduced work in progress,
reduced handling and
increased facilities utilization,

and, perhaps,

reduced scrap and inspection,
more predictable deliveries,
fewer control problems

and so on.

The principal application of group technology is in the field of engineering manufacture, where component-family formation is on the basis of design similarity, component geometry and machining requirements. The grouping of components into families by one of the available methods (discussed later) enables common manufacturing requirements to be identified and appropriate facilities provided, perhaps by arranging suitable equipment into groups. Each group of machines thus becomes a production unit or *cell* capable of processing a complete family of parts. The facilities available within such cells will be capable of providing both the appropriate types and levels of resources. Thus such cells or units are entirely analogous to mixed-model or multimodel flow lines. On occasions, the equipment in such units may be arranged in the manner of a flow line, if component process-routing requirements permit. Alternatively, and perhaps more usually, such an in-line flow pattern may not exist. Nevertheless, the equipment will be arranged so as to minimize transfer times, and hence, in concept, this method of manufacture approximates to that of mixed-model or multimodel flow lines, the former if components are not batched for processing, and the latter if batching is employed.

The conceptual similarity of flow-line and group-technology production is clear, but to shed more light on the problems of designing a group-technology system, it will be beneficial to look more closely at the similarities and the differences of the systems.

The two basic points of similarity are, first, that in both systems the manufacturing *facilities* used are provided for the sole purpose of producing certain items. Thus they are fully occupied with such work, being matched both as regards nature and quantity to the manufacturing requirements of the items, whether these be products or components. Secondly, minimization of the cost of movement between facilities is sought in both systems through the adoption of efficient *flow* patterns.

The principal differences between the two systems relate to the constitution of the total *work content* and the nature of the *production facilities*, both factors deriving from the nature of the *items* being manufactured. In practice, group technology is employed largely for the manufacture of engineering components and is thus concerned with metal-working operations such as turning, milling, drilling, etc. In comparison, mixed-model and multimodel flow lines are employed largely for assembly work. The importance of this practical difference in system design is best illustrated by an examination of the procedures used for the balancing and layout of facilities. Manual-flow-line balancing procedures depend on the construction of some form of precedence diagram of work *elements*. The equivalent data in group technology is presented on component-process-routing sheets. In general, each component will have one routing consisting of several sequential *operations*. There may be certain alternative routings available, but, even so, the choice will be limited. Furthermore, each operation will consist of several work elements necessarily zoned together (e.g. set up/cut/inspect) and it is unlikely that any operation will be found in precisely the same form in the process routings of other different components.

Thus the group-technology equivalent of a mixed-model flow-line precedence diagram (e.g. Figure 7.4) is likely to consist simply of several parallel paths of operations, the number of each type of path depending on the number of each component to be manufactured during the period. The manner in which the operations on these paths may be allocated to facilities is severely limited, since each type of operation requires a particular type of facility, a fact which also increases the zoning constraints on allocation. For these reasons work cannot be allocated to facilities in the manner in which elements are allocated to flow-line stations. Consequently, although some flexibility is provided by the possibility of adopting alternative component routings, not only is a certain amount of bypassing and backtracking usually inevitable, but also an acceptable balance of work on all facilities is often unobtainable except by either adding or removing components from the family grouping.

From a design point of view, the production facilities of a group-technology system, i.e. the machines and the operations which they perform, are quite unlike the stations on a flow line. In designing a flow line, the precise nature of the work to be done at each facility (i.e. each station) is not usually fixed, but is determined as a *result* of line balancing. In comparison, the type of work to be done at each facility in a group-technology system is fixed by the capabilities of the equipment, i.e. in this case each station represents a type of operation. Thus we see that several factors contrive to distinguish the design of a group-technology system from the design of flow-line systems, namely:

(1) The size of the 'pieces' of work to be allocated (i.e. operations rather than elements).
(2) The lack of precedence freedom (i.e. sequences of operations rather than logical arrangements of elements).
(3) The stringence of zoning constraints on work-content allocation (i.e. the fact that certain operations on each product are similar, e.g. drilling, milling, etc.).
(4) The fixed nature of the stations or production facilities (i.e. types of operation as opposed to 'multipurpose' stations).

It is largely because of these factors that the design of group-technology systems is more complex and constrained than flow-line design, and hence such systems are normally less efficient than conventional flow-line systems. Returning to our comparisons, it can now be seen that the type of work-allocation and balancing problems that face the flow-line designer do not occur in the design of group-technology systems, being largely replaced by two key problems, namely:

(1) *Load and facility matching*, by manipulation of component families and facilities groupings.
(2) *Facilities layout* to satisfy operation routings and provide maximum flow efficiency.

In this chapter we will look very briefly at this concept of manufacture and concentrate on the layout problem.

FORMATION OF COMPONENT FAMILIES

The grouping of components into families suitable for manufacture in a group-technology cell is equivalent to the problem of allocating models to mixed-model lines that was discussed in Chapter 7. (The concept of the 'similarity index' may also be appropriate in group-technology formation, but to our knowledge has not been used for this purpose.) Numerous methods of grouping have been adopted, but for brevity these can be categorized conveniently as follows:

Product knowledge

On occasions the selection of the components for inclusion in a family may be relatively simple; hence the use of one of the more rigorous techniques will be unnecessary. Such a situation may occur when the product range is fairly static, when there are large numbers of components with similar shapes, and when several obviously exclusive categories of components exist.

Component classification and coding

Classification in this context refers to the assignment of components into predefined groups or classes, while *coding* is the allocation of symbols to these groups. The type and amount of information contained in the code depends on the potential uses of the system. A designer may wish to retrieve designs to obtain relevant information and to utilize existing components in new products, while retrieval is also necessary in connection with costing, planning, variety reduction, etc. For this reason the design of a classification and coding system is normally a compromise that attempts to satisfy as many potential demands as possible.

The demands made on the system require not only that it should establish what types of components are being manufactured, but that it should also facilitate the arrangement of components into groups suitable for manufacture by the group method. The size of some groups formed will be such that their manufacture is not economically feasible, but by merging such groups together their group manufacture may become economic.

Various classification systems have been developed, and these fall into two main categories. The first method of classification relies on the use of codes with a fixed number of digits for recording component data. Such systems are suitable for either manual or machine processing, the most familiar examples being the Brisch monocode (Gombinski, 1967) and the Opitz (Opitz *et al.*, 1966) systems. The second category are open-ended systems where the length of the code is constrained only by the data-processing equipment used in dealing with the coded component. The disadvantage of such systems is the time required for recording and processing of such data. Examples in this category include the Brisch polycode (Gombinski, 1967), and Vuoso (Gallagher, 1969).

The Brisch systems accommodate the different classification requirements of the designer and production engineer, since the design-orientated monocode is supplemented by a recently developed polycode, which is intended to cater for the production system designed to provide unique identification of components. The type and amount of information contained within the polycode depends on individual requirements, and it is intended that it should be tailor made for each company. The types of information that can be included are detailed descriptions of shape features, material requirements, machining sequences, machining times, setting times, component usages, etc. The successful implementation of such a polycode depends to a large extent on the ability of the coding engineer to make suitable decision rules so that the final groups are both mutually exclusive and collectively exhaustive.

Production-flow analysis

This technique relies on the classification of operation or process route cards for components to identify families of components which use the same group of machines, or which can be readily rerouted to do so. A progressive form of analysis is used, consisting of three basic steps as follows:

(1) *Factory-flow analysis*, the objective of which is to identify the best division of facilities into departments. The operations routings for all components (obtained from route cards) are coded to indicate the department visited by each item and then sorted by this code to create groups of components with the same interdepartment routings.

(2) *Group analysis*. The route cards for all components produced in each department are analysed to identify the best division into groups. This is achieved by sorting cards into packs containing items with the same operations routing, these packs then being combined to form viable machine/operation groupings.

(3) *Line analysis*. The object here is to obtain the best sequence of machines in groups through study of the flow patterns within these groups. This is the *layout problem* in group technology, which will be discussed more fully in the next section.

The following list summarizes some of the factors which might influence the method adopted for the formation of component families.

Product knowledge

Mainly for pilot-scheme applications. Desirable requirements are:

(a) A large proportion of specified (named) items.
(b) The existence of several obviously exclusive categories of components.

(c) Large numbers of components which are visibly similar in shape or features.
(d) A fairly static product range.

Component classification and coding (design and production codes)

(a) Reasonably accurate forward-load information.
(b) Duplication of machine types in a factory.
(c) Good data-processing facilities.
(d) Fairly stable product design.
(e) Large numbers of similar components.
(f) Components which require small numbers of machines.
(g) A high machine-costs/materials-costs ratio.
(h) Small batch quantities.
(i) Machine tools on which setting time will be reduced if consecutive components are similar, e.g. turret lathes.

Production-flow analysis

(a) Operation cards which specify the actual machine to be used rather than just a machine section.
(b) Availability of a reasonably accurate forward load.
(c) Large numbers of components which may appear different but which have similar machining sequences.
(d) Components requiring large numbers of machines to complete their manufacture.
(e) Components having a high material-costs/machining-costs ratio.
(f) A mixture of large and small batch sizes.
(g) Components with very few natural breaks in their machining cycles.
(h) Machines whose setting times will not be very much affected simply by producing very similar consecutive components on them, e.g. copy lathes.
(i) Duplication of several types of machines in the factory.

A recent development of production-flow analysis is known as *component-flow analysis*. This system, which has been used in the layout of departments in several British plants, was developed by research workers (e.g. Crook, 1969; El Essawy, 1971) at the University of Manchester Institute of Science and Technology.

MACHINE GROUPING

The equipment necessary to perform all operations on the component family, and the expected load on each piece of equipment, can be listed for each component family identified. It may be necessary at this stage to eliminate certain components from families, or to add others to avoid low or uneven machine utilization. Rarely, however, will it prove possible to achieve full utilization of all machines in a group, and some flexibility of labour is required—a characteristic which distinguishes group technology from classic flow-line production.

Arrangement of facilities

Several techniques suitable for assisting in the determination of the arrangement of facilities in a group-technology system have been developed, some of which will shortly be described. Much of the literature in this area refers to this problem as the 'layout of multimodel lines' (Hollier, 1963). However, as we have seen, the problem of ordering facilities or machines does not occur in the true multimodel or mixed-model flow-line situation, and applies only in the context of group-technology production where each station represents a type of operation. Consequently, while authors refer to 'lines'—a convention which, for simplicity, we shall adopt—this does not imply that group-technology systems are necessarily characterized by an *in-line* arrangement of facilities.

Singleton (1962) outlined a simple method for determining a layout sequence for a number of operations or machines through which a variety of components is processed, each component having a particular route through the operations. This method involves converting the process or operation sequence for each component to a common length scale of 100 units, the spacing of operations on this scale being equal to $100/N$, where N is the number of operations for that component. Histograms are plotted for each operation, showing its placing on the percentile scale for each component, the occurrences being weighted by the production quantity for each component. These distributions are then ranked in order of their means to produce a suitable sequence of operations, i.e. the operation with the lowest mean is placed first on the line and the one with highest mean is placed last. Backtracking or bypassing of operations by components is indicated by the overlapping of the distributions, while distributions with a large spread or range might suggest that alternative operations routings for components be examined to improve component flow.

This is one of the simplest layout methods developed, and while perhaps appropriate for use in situations where the emphasis is on minimizing the total distance moved and where operations routings do not differ greatly, it is subject to certain rather severe limitations. For example, no account is taken of the extent and relative costs of components backtracking or bypassing operations. One might argue that backtracking against the general direction of flow is more costly than bypassing operations, a situation which might influence the development of the operation layout.

From \ To	Operation type 1	2	3	4	5	6	7	8	Totals
1		20	10	5	5	10			50
2	5		10	10	5			10	40
3				5	5	15			25
4	5		5		5	10			25
5						5	5		10
6		5					15	15	35
7					5			10	15
8							5		5
Totals	10	25	25	20	20	45	25	35	

Figure 8.1 Travel or cross chart

The development procedures to take account of factors such as backtracking are facilitated by the use of a device known as the *travel* or *cross chart*. Such a chart or matrix (Figure 8.1) shows the nature of interoperation movements for all components for a given period of time. The row totals on the chart show the extent of movement *from* an operation, and the column totals show movement *to* an operation. Each cell of the chart shows the relative frequency of movement between two operations; an ideal movement pattern suitable for use on a flow line is indicated when all the figures in the matrix appear in the cells immediately above the diagonal. Such travel charts can be used to help develop a sequence of operations. For example, operations with a low 'to/from' ratio (i.e. rowtotal/column-total ratio) (Hollier, 1963) receive components from relatively few sources but distribute work to a large number of destinations. Hence, if in-sequence movement is to be maximized and backtracking is to be minimized, such operations should be placed early in the sequence of operations. Conversely, operations with a high 'to/from' ratio should be placed towards the end of the sequence, since they receive work from a large number of sources but distribute to comparatively few destinations.

Using this method on the data provided in Figure 8.1 gives a sequence of operations as follows:

$$1 \quad 2 \quad 4 \quad 3 \quad 6 \quad 7 \quad 5 \quad 8.$$

This heuristic approach is simple and attractive, and clearly has considerable practical merit. However, it does suffer from some shortcomings, and, while there are, at present, no quantitative methods available to overcome such deficiencies, it is nevertheless important that these should be stated and borne in mind in designing group-technology-type layouts. First, while the 'to/from' ratio takes account of *work-flow paths*, the extent of the activity at operations is ignored. In other words, the technique described leads to the placing of all operations, despite the fact that some of these may be used by few components. Operations with low *work flow activities* might be excluded from the analysis in the first instant and later placed at the end of the sequence, thus avoiding the possibility of their being placed in a position which would disrupt the flow of the majority of components. This possibility is considered by Hollier (1963), while a different approach to the measurement of work flow is taken by Holstein and Berry (1970).

A second point relates to the topology of the layout of facilities or operations. The methods referred to above apply to *in-line* arrangements, since throughout they implicitly assume that the operation placed first in the sequence is furthest away from the operation placed last, etc. In practice, sequences of facilities in group-technology cells will conform to various configurations, and thus the possibility of several facilities being close or adjacent arises. For example, a ten-machine 'line' might be arranged in a 'U' shape, in which case what might have been the first and last operation might now be as close to one another as the first two or last two. Clearly, the use of such configurations is likely to increase the number of efficient flow patterns available, but this adds to the complexity of the layout problem. Some work is currently being undertaken in this area, but since no results are yet available, the practitioner must continue to rely heavily on his own judgement in determining the final form of more complex types of group-technology layout.

SEQUENCING

The determination of the sequence in which batches of components are loaded onto a group-technology cell or 'line' will be influenced by the desire to reduce setting cost and minimize throughput time. The problem is entirely congruent with the multimodel-line batch-sequencing problem and can be approached in the same way. If component batching is not adopted, individual components will be launched into the cell in much the same manner as in mixed-model line production. However, in this case, launch discipline and model sequence are unlikely to be important, because of the far greater throughput time, and component idle time. Whether a multimodel or a mixed-model approach is adopted, machine-setting problems might be reduced with consequent improvements in throughput time, and reduction in cost, by the adoption of the *composite-component* principle.

A composite component represents all the manufacturing requirements of a component group. It has all the geometric characteristics of the components of the group, and thus machine settings capable of producing the features of the composite can be used to produce any of the components in the family. Once created, the characteristics of the composite—which may not physically exist—can be used to assess inclusion or exclusion from a family grouping. Clearly, if the components in a family are sufficiently homogeneous, and if the machines in a cell are sufficiently versatile, the use of this composite approach virtually eliminates any need to consider batch or component sequencing.

References

Gallagher, C. C. (1969). 'Small firms benefit from group technology', *Metalworking Production*, 19th March, 55–57.

Gombinski, J. (1967). 'Group technology—an introduction', *Prod. Eng.*, **46**, No. 9, 557–564.

Hollier, R. H. (1963). 'The layout of multi-product lines', *Int. J. Prod. Res.*, **2**, No. 1, 47–57.

Holstein, W. K., and Berry, W. L. (1970). 'Work flow structure: an analysis for planning and control', *Mgt. Sci.*, **16**, 324–336.

Opitz, H., Eversheim, W., and Wiendahl, H. P. (1966). 'Workpiece classification and its industrial applications', *Inst. J. Mach. Tool Des. and Res.*, **9**, 39–50.

Singleton, W. T. (1962). 'Optimum sequencing of operations for batch production', *Work Study Ind. Eng.*, **6**, No. 3, 100–110.

General references in group technology

Durie, F. R. E. (1970). 'A survey of group technology and its potential for user application in the U.K.', *Prod. Eng.*, **49**, No. 2, 51–61.

Edwards, G. A. B. (1971). *Readings in Group Technology*, Machinery Publishing Co., Brighton.

Crook, M. A. (1969). 'The investigation and development of production flow analysis as a method of introducing group production to engineering companies', *M.Sc. Dissertation*, University of Manchester Institute of Science and Technology.

El Essawy, I. F. K. (1971). 'A computerized approach to production planning and control in the multi-product engineering environment', *Ph.D. Thesis*, University of Manchester Institute of Science and Technology.

Part 4

Human and Behavioural Aspects of Flow-line Design

CHAPTER 9

Behavioural Aspects of Flow-line Design

So far we have tended to ignore the human or behavioural problems associated with the employment of the flow-line system of production. We have dealt fairly thoroughly with the characteristics of operator variability and the problem of pacing, but, with that principal exception, we have assumed the operators on our manual flow lines to be entirely predictable, reliable, amenable, homogeneous, etc. In fact, we know that such a situation does not exist and this major omission must be rectified. In previous chapters the material presented has been fairly quantitative and objective, whereas in this chapter we must, of necessity, be fairly qualitative. Furthermore, because comparatively little is known about the nature and causes of the attitudes and behaviour of people at work, the information is rather inconclusive, and in many respects conflicting. There is, however, a considerable volume of relevant literature.

We shall, of course, be dealing with the problems that derive from the practice of employing human beings as productive resources, and consequently our discussion will not concern transfer lines. We shall examine those aspects of human behaviour, human characteristics, etc., which might influence either the design or the method of operation of manual flow lines. We shall first look briefly at some organizational problems, and later in greater depth at some of the behavioural problems associated with work design.

SOME ORGANIZATIONAL PROBLEMS

Financial and social needs are of considerable importance for most workers. Table 9.1, for example, shows the relative importance attached to five basic needs by several classes of female manual-flow-line workers (Wild and Hill, 1970). Here it can be seen that, irrespective of age and

Table 9.1 Scale values for five work needs for female flow-line workers (2159 workers consulted) [reproduced from R. Wild and A. B. Hill (1970). *Women in the Factory*, Inst. Pers. Mgrs., London]

	Single women			Married women		
Age groups (years)	<21	21–30	>30	<21	21–30	>30
Adequate wages	60·34	62·39	59·91	62·48	62·61	59·10
Working with friendly people	58·14	54·39	53·11	54·65	51·00	54·32
Security of employment	49·22	51·93	56·40	53·17	51·71	54·55
Personally satisfying work	50·51	49·24	49·29	45·95	48·36	49·78
High status	31·79	32·04	31·29	32·74	32·36	30·50

marital status, the greatest importance (highest 'scale values') is ascribed to the need for adequate wages, while the social need is ranked second or third. The needs for personally satisfying work and security of employment are ranked in fourth or third positions. In this section we will look briefly at payments and social factors which are generally recognized to be of the highest importance to most workers.

Payment systems and associated problems

Because of the nature of the work flow, and the interdependence of workers on flow lines, the use of individual incentive-payment systems is usually impossible. Where incentive payment is considered desirable, group schemes are normally employed, otherwise flat- or day-rate systems of payment are normally employed. In a group incentive system, the wages of each operative in the group will be dependent on that group's performance, i.e. the line output, in comparison to either targets or standard performance. In practice, the wages of the workers in such a group may differ because of the effects of work or job grading; for example, payment may be related to job or task grading. In theory, in conditions of perfect line balance, equal pacing and stable operation, such a method of payment is equitable, but, in practice, certain occurrencies may lead to inequity and worker dissatisfaction. Taking minor points first, it might be argued that, since the distribution of idle time or loss on balanced lines may be uneven (see Table 6.1), this fact should be reflected in the structure of the payment system. A more serious point concerns the influence of *unbalance* and *pacing*.

Absenteeism tends to be high among flow-line workers (often as high as 15 per cent) and the effect of such behaviour on the operation of manual flow lines is severe. The principal problem is the need to compensate for absentees, and basically there are only two satisfactory means of achieving this, namely:

(1) The use of 'floaters', 'key workers' or 'leading hands' to 'sit in' for absentees. Such workers must, of course, be skilled in more than one aspect of flow-line work, and must—theoretically, at least—be capable of a level of performance at least equal to that of the absentee.

Two principal problems arise in the use of this strategy. First, it is difficult to establish how many floaters are required to cover each of the types of work, and secondly it is difficult for such floaters to both acquire and maintain a proficiency on each type of job. In practice, therefore, even when such a substitute is available to take the place of an absentee, their performance is often lower than that of the other workers, with the result that either the line is unbalanced and slowed, or a certain amount of the work normally undertaken by the absentee is given to the other stations on the line. In both cases the earnings of the workers may be affected unless the standard or target is amended. In the first case they are probably reduced, and in the latter they may not reflect the effort required of workers. When no 'floater' is available to cover for an absentee, the second alternative must be adopted, i.e.

(2) The work of the absentee is distributed among the other stations. Hence, unless output targets are adjusted, earnings will fall.

The use of *trainees* or *replacement workers* on established lines provides almost identical problems. When new workers are placed straight onto an existing flow line, there is clearly a need to either provide for them to receive some assistance, perhaps from the 'floater', or for some of the work normally allocated to their stations to be allocated to other stations. Thus the situation is similar to the one described above, and some adjustments must be made to avoid inequitability or loss of earnings. A similar situation arises, although perhaps to a lesser extent, when workers are transferred between lines. The occurrence of such problems with the use of trainees might be avoided if new workers were to be placed as groups to staff entire lines; however, the opportunities for the adoption of this policy are clearly limited. The provision of 'off-the-line' training facilities, such as separate training schools, may reduce, but not overcome, the problem, since, irrespective of the extent and quality of training, individuals placed on existing lines will normally require a further period of adjustment before they are able to achieve the same performance as existing workers. Adjustment to the requirements and conditions of an existing line, after the comparative seclusion of a training school or area, has been found to be a major problem and source of dissatisfaction for many workers.

The nature of the product being manufactured, the components used, the equipment or the layout of the line often influences the extent of operator pacing. For example, a worker operating or tending a machine is likely to be subject to closer pacing than a worker engaged on largely manual work. Further, it may be impossible, for technological or practical reasons, to provide buffer stops at a certain part of a line, thus affecting the working conditions experienced by the operators at adjacent stations. Rarely are payment systems designed to account for such differences in working conditions, although, of course, differences in the complexities of the work may be reflected in job gradings built into payment systems.

Social relations

Workers in factories tend to socialize in a manner determined by the physical and auditory situation, rather than on a basis of common or complementary occupational interest. The need for adequate social relations is basic. It has been widely argued that the fulfilment of this basic need helps to compensate flow-line workers for their lack of involvement in their work, the absence of interest or challenge, etc. Indeed, it is often suggested that some workers seek this type of work because the lack of mental involvement permits them to devote their attentions to conversations with their neighbours and allows them to think of other things. Whether adequate social relations at the place of work is the primary or a secondary objective of workers need not concern us here, since, in either case, it is clear that some attention must be given to this provision.

Guest and Walker (1952), in their classic study of automobile-assembly-line workers, identify three broad categories of workers whose existence is determined by the layout of the line and the nature of the work requirements, i.e.

(1) *Isolated* workers performing functions independent of other workers.
(2) Workers performing functions essentially independent of other workers, yet working in *close proximity* with one another.
(3) Workers performing functions which are dependent on a *team* approach.

Most workers on non-mechanical flow lines fall into the second category. While a minority work as teams, (e.g. at multimanned stations), few workers operate in total isolation. On moving-belt-type lines much the same basic situation will apply, although on fixed-item, variable-station-length lines team working may be more prevalent.

The relative positions of workers on most non-mechanical lines and some moving-belt-lines will be fixed. However, this feature does not necessarily enhance the opportunities for social interaction. For example, on bench-type assembly lines, although workers may be sitting opposite one another, and only a few feet apart, the product being assembled often totally obscures other workers. Ambient noise levels often militate against conversation, and, on certain types of line (e.g. automobile assembly lines), although workers are in constant close proximity, their need to move continually to and fro prohibits any possibility of lengthy interchange.

In general, it would appear that the circumstances associated with non-mechanical bench-type flow lines, particularly double lines, are more conducive to the development of adequate social relations than those characterized by the automobile assembly line. Furthermore, it is evident that little scope exists in most situations for an improvement in the facilities for social interaction, although clearly attention must be paid to the influence of workplace layout, noise levels, movement patterns, etc.

WORK OR TASK DESIGN

Work specialization, rationalization or the division of labour implies the allocation of tasks of a particular type to specific workers. Such a principle does not necessarily give rise to short-cycle work, although this is the normal consequence of work specialization, especially in manual-flow-line work. For our purposes we can consider short-cycle work to be a corollary of work rationalization.

The specialization or rationalization of work, particularly manual work, has been a continuing trend for many years. This principle of work design was first applied perhaps four or five centuries B.C. and became common practice, firstly in Europe and later throughout the industrialized world, in the 18th and 19th centuries.

Certainly increasing mechanization has done much to eliminate some types of rationalized work. For example, the extent of rationalization observed by Smith in the manufacture of pins (Chapter 2) is rarely found today, since this type of work is easily mechanized. However, the trend continues in most types of work where mechanization is either impossible or economically unjustifiable.

Currently the practice of work specialization is epitomized in the use of manual flow lines. As we have seen, this method of production is not dependent on, but is nevertheless normally associated with, fragmentation of tasks.

Economics of work specialization

The arguments to support the division of labour are numerous, but may be summarized briefly as follows:

(1) A high degree of specialization facilitates learning.
(2) A high degree of specialization facilitates the employment of unskilled and semiskilled labour.
(3) The short work cycle associated with high work rationalization permits easy, automatic performance and repetition without undue mental effort, etc.
(4) Specialized, standardized tasks may require less supervision.

Such benefits have proved to be a powerful incentive for the adoption of this principle of work design, but, of course, these advantages are not obtained entirely without cost. The disadvantages of the use of highly rationalized work may be summarized as follows:

(1) *Non-productive work.* As tasks are reduced in size, the necessary non-productive work assumes greater comparative importance. The most important non-productive work for our purposes derives from the need to transfer items between stations. For a given total work content and output, the smaller the productive work time at stations, the greater is the number of stations and the greater is the interstation transfer time. This feature was discussed in Chapter 4.
(2) *Work imbalance.* In Chapter 4 it was also demonstrated that the degree of balance obtainable on a flow line is partly a function of the relative sizes of the work elements and the cycle time; the smaller the latter in comparison to the former, the less is the likelihood of a good balance. Thus we see that imbalance is likely to increase as the cycle time reduces, or, in other words, with the increasing division of the work content among the stations.
(3) *Indirect costs.* One argument often advanced against the policy of continued division of labour is that short-cycle, repetitive work is a source of dissatisfaction for workers. It is argued that such work does not fulfil the basic work needs of operatives, and, as a consequence, it engenders certain attitudes which in turn give rise to non-productive behaviour such as absenteeism, rapid staff turnover, etc. Such psychological effects of rationalized work give rise to indirect costs, which, although often substantial, are difficult to identify and measure.
(4) *Attainable performance.* It has also been argued that the attainable performance level of a worker, both in respect to the quantity and quality of his output, is affected by the extent of work rationalization.

It has been said that, because of the adverse psychological effects of rationalization, both the quantity and quality of work done falls. In addition, however, it is conceivable that the nature of the work done, particularly in respect of the complexity of the task, has an effect on quality and output levels for other, perhaps physical or mechanical, reasons.

Looking back on the two lists of points above, we can identify certain major cost sources which must clearly be considered if we are to try to establish the nature of the work to be undertaken by flow-line workers, i.e.

(1) Learning.
(2) Attainable performance (pace and quality).
(3) Indirect costs.
(4) Skills.
(5) Non-productive work.
(6) Imbalance of work.

In the following sections we shall look at the first four of these items; points (5) and (6) have been discussed in Chapter 4. We shall not be able to develop a procedure of work design which minimizes the sum of these cost, and our purpose therefore is simply to *identify* those factors which influence flow-line work design, to indicate the *nature* of the relationships giving rise to this influence and to indicate the *extent* to which certain factors might influence work design.

LEARNING AND ATTAINABLE PERFORMANCE

The concept of learning is a complex one, so much so that, as yet, there is little agreement among research workers as to the true nature of the mental processes which take place. This is clearly not the place in which to attempt a detailed study of this complex subject, and it will be sufficient to take a rather pragmatic approach. Since we are concerned primarily with the efficiency (i.e. productivity) of flow-line systems, it is convenient for us to consider learning as the process by means of which an individual acquires skill and proficiency at a task, which in turn has the effect of permitting increased productivity in his performance of that task. We are therefore primarily concerned with the speed at which a task can be executed, the extent to which this speed increases, and the influence of the nature of the task on these factors. Further, we are concerned essentially with the motor, rather than perceptual, memory or other aspect of learning.

The *learning curve,* i.e. the increase in performance against the number of repetitions of the task, is of importance not only in determining the optimum task length, but also in respect of the following:

(1) Training: i.e. in the design of training programmes, the measurement and evaluation of training, etc.
(2) Production planning: for example, allowance must be made for a period of reduced output prior to the achievement of standard performance.
(3) Work measurement and payment: i.e. in establishing the standard time for tasks, the learning effect must be recognized. For example, allowance for learning should be made when determining times using indirect work measurement techniques such as predeterminant motion time systems. Such allowances may be reflected in the payment system employed.
(4) Batch sizes and production runs: the learning effect should influence production-batch-size determination, the learning cost being, in effect, a set-up cost for batch production. Thus, for example, production-batch-size determination for multimodel lines will be influenced by the costs of learning.

Task learning is doubtless influenced by numerous factors, perhaps the principal among which, for our purposes, are as follows:

(1) *Task length*, i.e. using our terminology, cycle time or service time at the station.
(2) *Task complexity*.
(3) The capability or *skill* of the worker and his familiarity with the type of work to be learned.
(4) *Task similarity*, i.e. the extent to which the task being learned is similar to that undertaken previously by the worker.
(5) *Worker motivation* and personal *characteristics*.
(6) *External influences*, e.g. physical conditions, etc.

Additionally, in the case of group work on flow lines, the learning time and ultimate performance of the entire group may be affected by

(7) Group size, since, for larger groups (longer lines), the range of learning capacities or skills is likely to be greater, and the performance of the group is constrained by the slowest worker.
(8) General level of capability or skill of the work group.

Certain of these factors may be of little immediate importance in line design, since they may, in the short term be fixed by the nature of the situation. Indeed, one can argue (Kilbridge, 1962) that only task length and group size are within the control of the line designer, since, normally, a given work force will already be employed, and the nature of the work to be done will be determined by product and technological considerations. Furthermore, task length and group size are interdependent, task size (cycle time or service time) determining group size (number of stations) for a given work content and output requirement. For this reason we shall treat task length as the most important design variable, but, in the interests of thoroughness, we shall also briefly examine the two other factors which are conceivably within the control of the line designer, namely task complexity and similarity.

Task length

It has been argued (Kilbridge, 1962) that task length influences learning cost in three ways, namely through:

(1) The initial learning time.
(2) The performance ultimately available.
(3) The recurring learning time.

The *initial learning time* is the time required by a worker from the commencement of his learning a task until such time as he attains his ultimate work pace. Other things being equal, it will take longer to learn a long task than a short one, and this is not only because a longer task can be repeated fewer times in a given time period. In other words, more repetitions will be required for a longer task for a worker to attain ultimate performance. This relationship is normally in the form of a power function, although numerous formulae have been suggested to define such curves, ranging from simple expressions such as

$$\bar{y} = ax^b$$

where $\bar{y}$ = cumulative average man hours for any quantity x
       a = man hours for first unit
       x = number of completed units
       b = exponent (usually negative) representing slope of curve

to considerably more complex expressions which take account of a larger number of variables.

Figure 9.1 shows a type of learning curve for seven tasks with lengths ranging from 0·5 to 3·5 min. These curves relate to group working on manual-flow-line assembly tasks, and show the pace or performance attained as a percentage of standard performance. Thus, for any given

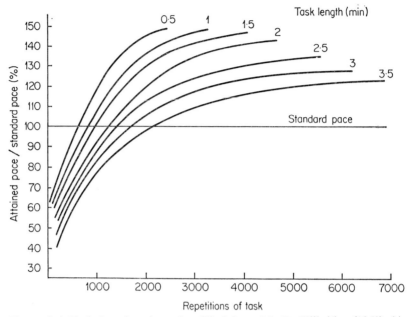

Figure 9.1 Task learning times [modified from M. D. Kilbridge (1962). 'A model for industrial learning costs', *Mgt. Sci.*, **8**, No. 4, 516–527]

number of repetitions of the task, the attained performance is higher for the shorter tasks and lower for longer tasks. It follows that more repetitions of longer tasks are required to reach a given level of performance. Several similar results have been obtained (Cochran, 1969) to support the argument that task length affects initial learning.

The suggestion that the work *pace ultimately attainable* is a function of task length is supported by the learning curves shown in Figure 9.1. Here it can be seen that the output level at which the curves flatten out is apparently dependent on task length, the ultimate work pace for tasks of length 0·5 min and 1 min being approximately equal at 145 per cent, while for longer tasks the ultimate level falls so that for 3·5 min tasks the attainable pace is only 125 per cent.

Figure 9.2, which is based on data similar to that used in constructing the previous curves, shows the pace ultimately attained as a function of task length. It suggests that, for the type of work being considered, other things being equal, higher attainable work pace is associated with tasks of length ⅓ min to 1·5 min, while both longer *and* shorter tasks are associated with lower ultimate pace. For shorter tasks this lower work pace is often attributed to 'short-task fatigue', said to derive from muscle fatigue, while

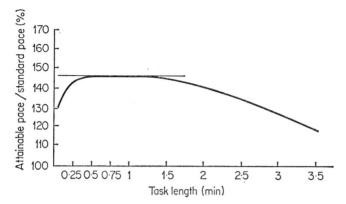

Figure 9.2 Ultimate attainable pace [modified from M. D. Kilbridge (1962). 'A model for industrial learning costs', *Mgt. Sci.*, **8**, No. 4, 516–527]

'long-task fatigue', said to derive to some extent from loss of motor skills, is sometimes given as the reason for lower work pace on longer tasks.

Because of the occurrence of worker absenteeism and turnover, it will normally be necessary to introduce new workers onto existing flow lines, either as temporary or permanent replacements. Furthermore, such replacement workers, unless they have been transferred from other identical work, will require a certain amount of learning time. Hence they will be unable initially to produce the same performance as the other workers on the line. For this reason there is a *recurring learning* cost on manual flow lines, and thus task length has a continuing effect on line operating costs. The manner in which replacement can be managed will be discussed in a later section, and it is sufficient now to note that the cost of recurrent learning will depend on the number and the timing of replacements. Clearly the substitution of a new worker into a comparatively new line consisting of workers still learning their jobs is likely to be less costly than the substitution of a new worker into a fully trained and competent line.

Task complexity

Task complexity is of importance with respect to learning, both as regards initial learning time, and ultimate attained performance. One might argue that a complex task is likely to be longer than a simpler one. However, we must distinguish between the length of a task, as regards the cycle or service time, and the number and nature of discrete motions to be performed during that time. We cannot assume that the time required to perform a motion is a measure of its complexity. For example, it might be that proficiency in the performance of two different motions was achieved by two workers after 100 repetitions. However, the proficient performance of one may take twice as long as the other, simply because the motion involves moving the hand 20 in rather than 10 in.

Several methods of measuring manual task complexity have been developed, one of the more recent (Chaffin and Hancock, 1966) being based on the association between the *cues* of information in the task and the motions that each cue requires. It is argued that a person retains basic motion patterns in his memory, all of which can be recalled by a cue received through one of his sensory channels. The number of cue–motion associations in a task is then used as a measure of task complexity. Both laboratory and industrial research has been conducted to investigate the relationship between task complexity and learning time. Some of the results are summarized in Table 9.2. These results, while by no means conclusive, are nevertheless of interest. The task length for study (d) is approximately 40 per cent greater than the longest task used in the laboratory study, yet the learning time of the longer task is only 4·4 per cent higher. The suggestion here is that learning time may only be weakly related to task length, a greater influence being exerted by task complexity [the complexity of (d) is 5·6 per cent greater than (c)]. Notice also that the result obtained for task (a) would not support the type of relationship shown by the family of curves in Figure 9.1, a fact which may also be seen as lending some support to the importance of task complexity in respect of initial learning time.

Table 9.2 Initial learning time, task length and complexity

		Task length (0·0006 min)	Task complexity (number of cue–motion associations)	Intial learning time (number of repetitions to attain standard performance)
Laboratory studies	(a)	57·2	12·5	60
	(b)	63·5	17·1	420
	(c)	68·3	19·6	460
Industrial studies	(d)	94·8	20·7	480
	(e)	130·8	35·2	1500

Little direct empirical evidence is available to associate task complexity with attainable work pace. However, there are sound reasons to suppose that a relationship might exist between these two factors. A certain amount of research has been undertaken in attempts to establish the nature of the relationship between work output and job content, particularly job variety. In general, such studies have been concerned with the content or variety evident in jobs over a period of time; for example the number of tools used and the number of different operations and tasks performed have been used as measures of content and variety.

We are concerned with the nature of work at a far more 'micro' level; nevertheless, we can, perhaps, learn something from this more 'macro' research. As one might expect in a comparatively unexplored field, the results available to date are, in some respects, conflicting. However, the concensus appears to indicate that worker output bears a relationship with job content or variety which can be described by an inverted 'U' curve. Output levels are comparatively low for jobs towards both ends of the scale of content, and highest for those in the middle. The relationship found resembles that shown in Figure 9.2, a result which might intuitively have been expected. Consequently, while at the moment it must remain little more than speculation, we might argue that such a relationship between task complexity and attainable work pace is both intuitively reasonable and indirectly supported by empirical findings. There is little or no direct evidence to relate task complexity to attainable quality levels, nor, to return to our previous topic, is there much evidence to relate task *length* to attainable quality performance.

Task similarity

The 'carryover' of learning from one task to another is known as *transfer* of learning or training. Positive transfer takes place when the learning of the old task helps the learning of the new task, and negative transfer occurs when old learning obstructs new. Transfer naturally depends upon the similarity of tasks—both perceptual and motor response similarity being important. Table 9.3 summarizes the nature of transfer for different pairs of tasks.

Table 9.3 Transfer between tasks depends on both perceptual and response similarity [reproduced with permission from D. H. Holding, *Principles of Training* (1965), Pergamon Press Ltd.]

Case	Task stimuli	Response required	Transfer
1	Same	Same	High
2	Different	Different	None
3	Different	Same	Positive
4	Same	Different (but similar)	Negative (?)

In case 1 the transfer between identical tasks is high, while in case 2 no transfer takes place because both tasks are different in all respects. In case 3 some advantage is gained through previous relevant motor or response learning. However, in the final case, previous learning is detrimental to the learning of the new task, since different responses are required to the same stimuli.

In studying these relationships, it should be pointed out that comparatively little of the research conducted in the field of learning transfer has dealt with manual work of the type found on flow lines. Nevertheless, there is little reason to suspect that the relationships shown in the exhibit do not apply to this type of work, and consequently we might reasonably use this information in the development of our principles of manual-flow-line design. The message here is clearly as follows—workers to be employed on a new flow line should, if possible, be taken from work which is similar in respect of both perceptual and motor requirements, and should not be taken from situations where similar perceptual requirements are associated with different motor requirements.

Discussion

Clearly task length and complexity are related to both task learning time and attainable pace, but the practical importance of such relationships is a matter for conjecture. It seems reasonable to conclude that, other things being equal, task length and complexity are both positively related to initial task learning time and that both bear an inverse 'U' relationship with attainable pace. However, as both length and complexity are normally interrelated, and since other factors doubtless influence both learning time and ultimate performance, it is pointless to try to generalize further. The extent to which these relationships influence task design will depend to some extent on the relative importance of the costs involved in comparison with those listed earlier in this chapter.

The evidence that has been presented suggests that, in general, flow-line operating costs may increase if a cycle time appreciably greater than 2 min or smaller than 0·5 min is used. It will be recalled from the discussion in Chapter 4 that the proportion of non-productive work increases sharply for tasks shorter than 2·5 min (Figure 4.5) and that, with the exception of one of the types of work considered (Figure 4.4), balancing loss is minimized for cycle times of over 2·5 min. Such evidence might lead one to speculate that a cycle time of around 2·5 min should be adopted. This speculation may be thought to be supported by the result of the study (Lehman, 1969) described in Chapter 4, from which it was noted that the median cycle time on lines was 3·5 min. It should be remembered, however, that the evidence presented above and in Chapter 4 with respect to imbalance of work, non-productive work and attainable pace (Figures 4.4, 4.5 and 9.1, respectively) all derive from the research conducted in a specific industry dealing with a specific type of work, and that the results obtained may not apply in other situations. These results should only be taken to indicate the general nature of the various relationships, further details of which can only be established through studies conducted in specific situations.

Perhaps the most obvious area likely to be influenced by our knowledge of learning transfer and task similarity is the design and operation of mixed-model and multimodel lines. Task similarity in models on a multimodel line is clearly desirable if performance is not to be restrained by the learning of workers. This desirability may be considered as vindication of the concept of allocating models to lines using a similarity index. However, it should be noted that the similarity index discussed previously (Chapter 7) emphasizes motor or response similarity while neglecting perceptual similarity. We have seen that, if the latter differs, no amount of motor similarity is likely to lead to positive transfer (Table 9.2). The desirability of positive transfer in respect of line operating efficiency may also influence the selection of the sequence of models on a mixed-model line, and the sequence of batches of models on a multimodel line.

In comparison with equipment set-up costs, the cost benefits associated with learning transfer may be quite small. Although conceptually such learning costs may be considered as a further component of total set-up costs, in practice they may well be ignored, unless the tasks to be performed make particularly heavy demands on learning. We have seen that model sequencing on mixed-model lines is of little value in maximizing line efficiency as far as idle time or congestion is concerned, and for this reason we might find that consideration of learning costs and learning transfer is of more practical significance. Finally, more learning time must be allowed on mixed-model lines than would be allowed on single-model lines (Thomopoulos and Lehman, 1969). Maximum performance is likely to take longer to achieve on such lines, not only because of the fewer repetitions of any one of the tasks within a given time, but also because of the increased total task complexity introduced through the allocation of a variety of tasks to at least some of the stations on the line.

SKILLS AND ABILITIES

Our discussion of learning took place on a deliberately pragmatic level, and little attention was paid to the meaning or basis of the learning process.

Table 9.4 Classification of some basic abilities [constructed from R. M. Gagne and E. A. Fleishman (1959). *Psychology and Human Performance*, Holt, Rinehart and Winston, New York, pp. 115–132; they distinguish between abilities and skills—their definition of abilities corresponds closely to our definition of skills]

Area	Type of ability	Explanation	Examples of applications in production
Discrimination	Visual discrimination (e.g. brightness, colour)		Inspection
	Auditory discrimination (e.g. volume, pitch, duration)		
Identification	Perceptual speed	Speed and accuracy of identification of differences in visual details and configurations	Inspection
	Closure abilities	Identification or recall of models, when the stimuli for these are present in incomplete form	Fault tracing
	Spatial abilities	Identification of spatial positions in two or three dimensions	
	(1) Orientation	(1) Comprehend arrangement of visual stimulus pattern	(1) Operation of equipment, assembly tasks
	(2) Visualization	(2) Imagined manipulation of visual objects	(2) Design, fault tracing
	Auditory identification	Identification of signals and patterns of signals	
Memory	Associative memory		Recall of task, instructions, etc.
	Memory span	Immediate and later recall of information	
	Visual memory	Retention of substance or content of visually presented material	
Motor abilities	Multiple-limb coordination	Simultaneous coordination of several limbs	Complex adjustments
	Fine control precision	Controlled, rapid precise positioning movements	Delicate assembly and adjustment
	Response orientation	Ability to choose correct response or direction of response	Operation of equipment

	Reaction time	Speed of reaction to a stimulus	Control of equipment
	Speed of arm movement	Speed of movement regardless of precision or accuracy	
	Rate control	Ability to make continuous anticipations and motor adjustments	Tracking and pursuit tasks
	Fine manipulative abilities		
	(1) Manual dexterity	(1) Controlled arm/hand manipulation of larger objects	(1) Assembly work, manipulation of tools
	(2) Finger dexterity	(2) Controlled manipulation with fingers	(2) Small parts assembly and adjustment
	(3) Arm/hand steadyness	(3) Precision of arm/hand positioning	(3) Assembly, stacking of small or fragile objects, disassembly, etc.
	Gross motor abilities (e.g. strength of limbs, flexibility, agility, balance)		Heavy work, climbing, loading, etc.
Conceptual and thinking	Verbal knowledge	Knowledge and understanding of language	
	Word fluency	Rapid selection and production of words	
	Numerical ability	Facility in handling numbers	
	Concept fluency	Availability and recall of concepts	
	Discovery of principles	Ability to make verbal or figural analyses, complete number series, etc.	Design, development, etc.
	General reasoning	Comprehension of structure of problems	
	Seeing implications and consequences	Foresight	Planning
	Flexibility	Ability to reason, etc., 'laterally'	
	Symbol manipulation	Solution of problems requiring manipulation of symbols	
	Logical evaluation	Deductive reasoning	
	Practical judgement	The use of concepts in making sensible decisions	

Clearly the increasing performance of a worker during the initial learning period is in some way related to the increase in his skill in doing his job. Learning is associated with skill development, so much so that many writers, in discussing skills, deal solely with learning curves, etc. Our purpose in this section is to investigate a further cost source affecting task design. We are really only concerned with the wage cost of skill and therefore with the *basic skill* (sometimes called *ability*) requirements of tasks. Basic skills in this context are considered to be the stored potentials or *abilities* of people that influence both their attainable performance on tasks and their ease of learning such tasks. The manner and extent to which skills are developed during the learning period has been discussed in the previous section. Thus we are here concerned with the identification of the basic skills required of workers for the efficient performance of tasks, and with the means by which it might be established whether or not individuals possess such basic skills. Here, even more so than in the previous section, we are dealing with subjects about which little is known. Consequently our discussion will be brief.

For the purposes of illustration, the method of classification provided by Fleishman and Gagne (1959) will be adopted. Their classification of some basic abilities is summarized in Table 9.4, from which it can be appreciated that motor skills are generally of greatest importance in manual-flow-line work. Adequate motor skills are a prerequisite for the efficient performance of virtually all manual work, their relative importance depending, of course, on the nature of the work task.

Kinaesthetic skill (knowledge of the position of the limbs and objects in space) is present in most motor skills, and is clearly an important prerequisite for many production tasks in so much as it relates to the use and deployment of items in the working area, the manipulation of components, the positioning of items, etc.

Fine manipulative abilities are likely to be essential in virtually all types of bench machine and assembly work, where coordination and precision are also of importance. *Gross motor skills* are of comparatively more importance in heavier work, for example on many moving-belt-type lines. Inspectors working on manual flow lines will normally be required to demonstrate proficiency in *visual discrimination* and *perceptual speed* as well as certain types of *conceptual* and *memory skills*, the latter also being important in certain types of flow-line work such as long-cycle serial-type tasks. Clearly *memory, discrimination, identification* and, to a lesser extent, *perceptual* skills are more important on mixed-model and multimodel lines, while motor skills such as fine-control precision, *response concentration* and *reaction* time are of more importance in the operation of machines, the use of instruments, and in making adjustments and rectifications.

Appropriate, reliable and validated *psychometric tests* have two principle applications in the design and operation of manual-flow-line systems. First, such tests, used in conjunction with job or skills analyses, might be used for the selection of workers for flow-line work, and, secondly, the results of such tests might be used to predict the performance of workers and thus the performance of the flow-line system. Such tests, to be of any value, should cover all aspects known to affect operator learning and performance. Consequently the test batteries employed would be considerably larger than a mere skills battery. Some of the personal characteristics known or thought to affect operator performance will be discussed in the next section, but here it may be worth noting that some research has been conducted in an attempt to use skills tests to predict worker performance. One study dealt with the prediction of elemental motion times, elements being defined using the methods-time measurement (m.t.m.) system (Poock, 1968). Four m.t.m. motions were considered: reach, move, grasp and position. Eight skills or abilities were used to attempt to predict worker performance: visual acuity, kinaesthetic sense, forearm motorability, eye–hand coordination, decision-making ability, recoding ability, finger dexterity and tactile sense. Multiple regression was used to identify the extent to which the skills operated as predictors of elemental performance. The following summary is taken from the report of the study:

'The present research has shown that it is possible to obtain a methodology that shows promise for predicting human performance based on sensory, motor and psychomotor abilities. These ability parameters, as represented by reliable apparatus measurements in the context of this research, can be combined into regression equations which predict performance on elemental motions of the m.t.m. system. Prediction of elemental performance gives the flexibility to predict performance on any bench type operation to which an m.t.m. standard can be applied.

The methodology could be used to determine which employees already in the organization who could fill job openings. The methodology could also be used to determine what other jobs unacceptable performers could perform successfully before a decision was made to dismiss them. It could be very possible that they simply do not have the abilities required for successful performance of their *present* job.'

In discussing task design and the problems of learning, we suggested that, although certain aspects of task design had been found to bear some relation to certain aspects of learning, such relationships were not close enough to be of any practical predictive value. Much the same situation applies with respect to basic skills. It might be demonstrated that certain skills bear a relationship with task performance, but it is unlikely that such relationships alone will ever permit accurate and reliable prediction of work performance, since the latter is clearly affected by all manner of other factors, some of which are listed on p. 189, and are now discussed. This point is underlined by Poock's concluding remarks. He accepts that, to improve the efficiency of elemental motion prediction, some account must be taken of workers *motivation*.

INDIRECT COST SOURCES

It is often argued that the continued rationalization of work is likely to have the effect of increasing unit production costs. The justification for this point of view lies in the importance of indirect cost sources. There is little doubt that, from a direct-cost point of view, the policy of work rationalization that has been applied throughout the industrialized world during the last century has given rise to improvements in productivity. It is now argued, however, that a continued increase in productivity from this policy is largely illusory, since the resultant increase in indirect costs is likely to more than offset any direct-cost savings.

Such indirect costs include the cost of operator absence, lateness, turn-over, disputes, etc., the incidence of which are said to derive from workers' attitudes to their rationalized work tasks. It is argued that rationalized manual work is no longer able to provide satisfaction for workers, who therefore withdraw from their work situation either temporarily or perma-nently, and/or seek other means of involvement. This argument commands a certain amount of attention, and certainly appears to be supported by the trends evident over the past century. During this period educational levels have increased, and the economic situation has become one of reasonably full and secure employment. As a result, it is conceivable that financial and security needs are now of comparatively less importance to workers, who pay increasing attention to the need for personal involvement, fulfilment, and, perhaps to a greater extent than ever before, seek employ-ment situations which utilize their intellectual capacities. During this same period, however, there has been a continuing trend towards the rationalization of all work—a trend that is in conflict with the develop-ments that have been outlined.

The job attitudes of workers and their resultant behaviour have been the subjects of fairly extensive research over the pasty thirty or forty years.

A great deal of information is available, but the size and importance of the subject is such that these efforts have done little to settle the disputes and controversy which continue to rage in this subject area. In the following section we will attempt to précis some of the relevant information, concentrating, of course, on the problems of work design as they apply to manual flow lines. We shall attempt to concentrate on the nature of the *work* done, rather than the *job* as a whole, since the latter contains considerably more than mere work, encompassing features such as payment systems, supervision, social relations, etc. Work cannot be dealt with in isolation, however, and we shall have to return to the position of *work design* in the larger context of *job design* at a later stage.

In this section we shall examine the relationship of work characteristics with operator attitudes, and the relationship of these attitudes with operator behaviour.

One might argue that the provision of favourable attitudes (i.e. satisfaction) is not a sufficient objective in the design or redesign of work, and that the adoption of alternative principles of work design is only justified if operator behaviour which is beneficial to productivity can be shown to result. In view of this argument, we shall deal, in reverse order, with behaviour and attitudes, looking first at the attitudinal bases of certain aspects of operator behaviour.

Operator behaviour

Quite considerable evidence is available to support the hypothesis that voluntary *labour turnover* is related to overall or general job satisfaction (Vroom, 1964). The results of one recent study conducted among female manual operatives engaged on repetitive flow-line work, are shown in Table 9.5 (Wild and Hill, 1970). Fifty-two per cent of the leavers were found to have quit their jobs voluntarily, and voluntary leaving was

Table 9.5 Turnover against job satisfaction [reproduced from R. Wild and A. B. Hill (1970). *Women in the Factory*, Inst. Pers. Mgrs., London]

	Generally satisfied with job	Generally dissatisfied with job	Total
Voluntary leavers	55	67	122
Involuntary leavers	97	17	114
Total	152	84	

Table 9.6 Absenteeism against job factors [based on C. R. Walker
and R. H. Guest (1952). *The Man on the Assembly Line*, Harvard
University Press, Boston, Mass.]

	Below median job-factor score (%)	Above median job-factor score (%)	Total (%)
Lower than median absentee record (0–6 points)	39·3	60·7	100
Higher than median absentee record ($\geq$ 7 points)	62·8	27·2	100

found to be strongly related to overall job dissatisfaction. Similarly, a
certain amount of information is available that suggests that absenteeism
is also influenced by overall job dissatisfaction, although the evidence
here is slightly less convincing.

If we look at the relationship of operator behaviour to various job

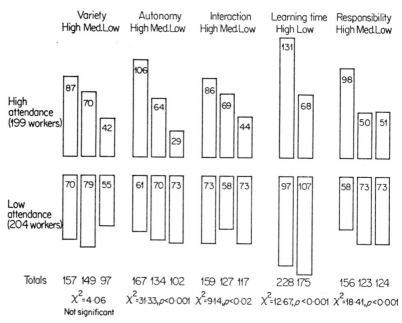

Figure 9.3 Major task attributes in relation to attendance (403 workers)
[reproduced from A. N. Turner and P. R. Lawrence (1965). *Industrial Jobs
and the Worker*, Division of Research, Harvard Business School, Boston]

factors, i.e. omitting the intermediate step in the model job–attitudes–behaviour, we can find more direct evidence to support the suggestion that indirect cost factors are important in work design. For example, Table 9.6 (Walker and Guest, 1952) derives from an early classic study conducted among 175 male automobile-flow-line workers. The figures here show the percentage of those workers with high and low absence records engaged on jobs with high and low job-factor scores (a measure of the degree of repetitiveness and pacing of the work, the skill required, frequency of breaks and social interaction in the job and the size of the work group). Clearly a larger proportion of the operatives engaged on jobs with low scores had a poor absence record. Figure 9.3 (Turner and Lawrence, 1965) provides similar data, this time deriving from a study conducted among more than 400 male operatives working in ten different industries. Here we see a consistent tendency for workers with good attendance records to be engaged on jobs with high task-attribute scores. The association between attendance and task attributes is particularly strong in respect of the autonomy and responsibility required of the worker, and the work learning time.

Operator attitudes

It is by no means true that all operatives engaged on repetitive rationalized work dislike such work; indeed, it is not even proven that a majority of such operatives express a dislike for their work. For example, the figures shown in Table 9.7 relate to female flow-line workers. These figures, which show the percentage of the total sample expressing satisfaction with certain aspects of their work, demonstrate that, in most respects, a

Table 9.7 Attitudes of female operatives to repetitive work (2159 workers) [based on R. Wild and A. B. Hill (1970). *Women in the Factory*, Inst. Pers. Mgrs., London]

Aspect of work done	Workers experiencing satisfaction with aspect of work (%)
Interest	60·5
Satisfaction	75·5
Extent of feelings of depression	64·5
Sense of achievement	60·0
Use of abilities	66·8
Variety in work	44·0
Tiring	43·6
Use of brains	63·3

clear majority are satisfied with their tasks. Such information, however, is of limited practical value, since the attitude of operatives to their work is a comparative thing, and hence, unless a person has experienced different types of work, he may have no real basis on which to judge his present task.

For this reason it will be useful to compare job attitudes. The study among male automobile-flow-line workers mentioned previously provided the results given in Table 9.8 in which operators' attitudes or interest in the work are related to work complexity as approximated by the number of operations performed. Here it can be seen that an increase in 'complexity' is associated with an increase in interest. On a slightly different level, several investigators have studied the relationship of *work* design to *job* attitudes, particularly overall or general job satisfaction,

Table 9.8 Interest against work complexity [based on C. R. Walker and R. H. Guest (1952). *The Man on the Assembly Line*, Harvard University Press, Boston, Mass.]

Number of operations performed in task ('complexity')	Attitude	
	Very or fairly interesting (%)	Not very or not at all interesting (%)
1	33·5	66·6
2–5	43·7	56·3
>5	69·4	30·6

and the relationship of 'satisfaction with work' with job satisfaction. The results of such studies might be considered to be of more practical value, in so much as a general attitude (overall job satisfaction) is more likely to influence operator behaviour than a specific attitude in respect of one aspect of the job. Table 9.9 (Wild and Hill, 1970) derives from the same data used in the construction of Table 9.7 and shows the relationship of attitudes to work and overall job satisfaction.

Here it can be seen that satisfaction with work, particularly the psychological effects of work characteristics, is substantially more prevalent among overall satisfied workers than among those who are generally dissatisfied with their jobs. Indeed, it was found in this study that attitudes to the work done provided the greatest discrimination between overall satisfied and dissatisfied workers. Several similar results have been reported, substantiating the hypothesis that operators' attitudes to their work are a substantial factor in determining overall or general job satisfaction.

Table 9.9 Work attitudes against job satisfaction for female operatives (total number of overall satisfied workers is 454; total number
of overall dissatisfied workers is 1705) [based on R. Wild and A. B.
Hill (1970). *Women in the Factory*, Inst. Pers. Mgrs., London]

| Aspect of work done | Workers expressing satisfaction with aspect of work (%) | |
	Overall dissatisfied workers (%)	Overall satisfied workers (%)
Interest	16	71
Satisfaction	34	86
Extent of feelings of depression	21	76
Sense of achievement	25	69
Use of abilities	42	73
Variety in work	22	50
Tiring	31	47
Use of brains	52	66

We have presented evidence which supports the following propositions:

(1) Overall job satisfaction is related to operator behaviour such as absence and turnover.
(2) The nature of the job done is related to job satisfaction.
(3) The nature of the work content and method influences both job satisfaction and operator behaviour.

Despite evidence of this type, these relationships remain generally unproven. Not all absence and turnover derives from job dissatisfaction (see Table 9.5), nor are all generally dissatisfied workers liable to such types of behaviour. Nor has it been demonstrated that all operatives engaged on repetitive work express a dislike for their tasks (Table 9.7). Taking a simpler approach to the problem, it is by no means generally proven that operatives engaged on repetitive tasks *are* more liable to absence and turnover than those engaged on apparently more demanding tasks [see, for example, Kilbridge (1961)].

Our survey of the literature in this field has presented us with a rather confusing situation, characterized by a lack of generally proven and reliable relationships. While such a situation is unfortunate, particularly from the behavioural scientist's point of view, it is not necessarily unduly inconvenient from our point of view, especially if we are prepared to make one assumption. We must concede that one valid and viable object in work design is the provision of satisfaction for the operatives concerned. The only justifications for this objective are first that job satisfaction is desirable in its own right, and secondly that there is very strong evidence that for at least a significant proportion of workers such an attitude may militate against turnover and absence, thus helping to minimize production costs. If we accept this objective, we can concentrate on identifying those factors which affect and determine job dissatisfaction.

Susceptibility to dissatisfaction

Flow-line workers who experience dissatisfaction with their tasks often describe them as being monotonous, boring, uninteresting, depressing, providing no sense of achievement, etc. It is impossible to be precise about the meaning of such terms, since they are interrelated and overlapping. One might argue that some are the consequence of others, for example that depression is a possible consequence of monotony and boredom. Semantic difficulties abound in this field, and for our purposes it is sufficient to accept such terms as applying to subjective phenomena experienced by workers. Semantic difficulties also occur when we consider the task characteristics which give rise to such phenomena. From an industrial-engineering point of view, it would be helpful to have some objective measure of characteristics such as variety, repetitiveness, pacing, etc., but, from a behavioural point of view, such features are subjective phenomena. Thus two workers may consider the same task to offer different degrees of variety, their subjective perceptions being influenced by their individual characteristics, experiences, circumstances, etc.

In this section we shall attempt to avoid the finer points of definition, and will look in general terms at some of the factors which are considered to influence susceptibility to dissatisfaction with rationalized flow-line-type work. We shall look at two classes of factors, first those inherent to the worker, and, secondly, those external to the work situation.

Biographical factors have been found to be closely related to dissatisfaction with rationalized manual work, dissatisfied operatives typically being younger and single. Length of service has often been found to be related to dissatisfaction for both males and females, dissatisfaction being typically less prevalent among new recruits and among long-service employees. The nature of work done as a determinant of overall job satisfaction is generally of paramount importance for all biographical groups, although its importance has been found to reduce with increasing length of service and also to be related to age, but in a somewhat more complex manner (Wild and Dawson, 1972). Despite extensive investigation, no practical and general relationship has been found between *intelligence* and susceptibility to dissatisfaction with rationalized work.

The importance of *personality* factors is less clear cut, although the concensus here inclines towards suggesting that dissatisfaction when engaged on rationalized work is more likely in operatives who are more emotional and extroverted. Susceptibility has also been found to be higher among workers exhibiting greater restlessness in their daily habits and greater dissatisfaction with their home and personal lives (Smith, 1955).

Declared *job needs* are themselves related to several of the factors mentioned above, as well as having been found to be related to the occurrence of dissatisfaction with rationalized work. Most workers place importance on financial and social needs (Table 9.1), while dissatisfied workers place comparatively more importance on the need for self fulfilment and achievement.

Certain *size factors* external to the work situation have been found to be related to the prevalence of dissatisfaction. The proportion of workers expressing dissatisfaction with rationalized manual tasks has been found to be positively related to work-group, department and plant size. Furthermore, *factors external* to the plant have also been found to be related to the extent of job dissatisfaction. Other things being equal, it has been found that workers in rural non-industrialized communities are less tolerant of such work than those in urban areas (Wild, 1972).

In summary, therefore, it would seem that the workers who are particularly prone to dissatisfaction when exposed to rationalized flow-line-type work are likely to be achievement orientated, comparatively emotional labile and extroverted, restless and perhaps given to dissatisfaction with their home and personal life. Furthermore, the evidence which is available suggests that dissatisfaction is aggravated or accentuated in larger departments and plants and in non-industrialized communities.

Work restructure and worker selection

The criticism of the present policy in work design—that of continued rationalization—has given rise to quite widespread restructuring of existing work, i.e. the enlargement of work tasks so as to provide more challenge, variety, greater use of worker skills, etc. Such restructuring is often referred to as job enlargement or enrichment, although, as we have indicated previously, work is but one part of any job. Thus the enlargement of an existing job might be accomplished without changing the work content or method. For example, more challenge, variety, interest and greater use of abilities might be provided by requiring an operative to be responsible for his own inspection, machine setting and adjusting, etc. Indeed, in theory at least, it is possible for work rationalization and job enlargement to exist concurrently.

In practice, however, job enlargement normally relies heavily on work restructuring. Numerous job/work enlargement exercises have been undertaken in many industries. The following example, described by Conant and Kilbridge (1965), is typical. The product being manufactured was a washing-machine pump consisting of 27 parts. The assembly was originally done by six men working on a flow line, each operator having a work cycle of 0·30 min, involving six work elements. The job was changed to a one-man operation, with each operator being responsible for 35 work elements. There was no work pacing, and each operator was responsible for the quality of his output. The result of this change was a reduction in the percentage defective output from 2·9 to 1·4, and an increase in the productive labour time.

In this exercise the results were beneficial to productivity, although not startingly so. Many exercises, in which the results have been far more impressive, have been reported from time to time, but, equally, several exercises have been undertaken from which no beneficial results have emerged. In some cases results have been counterproductive.

Studies of the evidence in this field (e.g. Hulin and Blood, 1968) reveal one important point—that the restructuring of existing rationalized manual tasks is likely to be beneficial for some, but not all, workers, and in some, but not all, situations. This perhaps rather obvious, but often ignored, point, supports the observations made in the previous section, namely that not all workers express dissatisfaction when exposed to flow-line-type work. Furthermore, it tends also to support the belief (p. 205) that the attitudes expressed by workers are relevant in developing principles of work design, even though such workers may have had few opportunities to compare their work with the available alternatives.

In view of the widespread controversy in this area, it is perhaps worth reiterating this point. We would argue that, from an economic point of view, work restructuring is justified only when dissatisfaction is evident. Others argue that existing attitudes are of little value in assessing the merit of restructure and enlargement. There is some evidence to support this latter view, in respect of non-manual workers, but little evidence in relation to manual workers.

Clearly, if possible, one must avoid exposing certain types of worker (identified previously) to highly rationalized, repetitive, short-cycle work, but at the same time it is probably impractical and unnecessary to think in terms of either enlarging all existing rationalized work, or of completely avoiding the creation of new work of this type. Ultimately, therefore, the problem is one of selection, i.e. how to select and place a worker so that he is not only capable of performing his work efficiently, but that in doing so he does not experience monotony, boredom and dissatisfaction. We will look briefly at this problem shortly, but before doing so we should recognize that, since all practical selection procedures are liable to error, we are unlikely to avoid the situation in which job dissatisfaction occurs. Consequently the need to restructure existing work or redeploy existing workers is likely to remain. Adoption of either of these policies is dependent on an ability to identify the need, i.e. the occurrence of dissatisfaction, a responsibility which rests with management, either personnel management, who might choose to use surveys, interviews, etc., or factory supervision, who should be in close contact with production workers. If a sufficient variety of task is available, it becomes possible to transfer dissatisfied workers to tasks which are more consistent with their needs. Otherwise it may be necessary to adopt a policy of selective work restructure and job enlargement.

The manner in which either work is structured or existing work restructured is likely to be influenced, and perhaps determined by, the circumstances which prevail. However, whatever these circumstances, the principal concern is the content and 'meaning' of the work. Increase in content and meaning is not obtained by mere manipulation of the work cycle, i.e. giving more of the same type of work to an operative, but requires consideration of factors such as:

(1) The *variety* offered by the task. This might be measured by the number of different work elements or operations to be performed, or the number of tools used.
(2) The *challenge* afforded by the task, e.g. the number of different skills or abilities used and the extent of their use.
(3) The amount of *discretion* afforded to the worker, e.g. the extent to which a worker must make decisions in the performance of his tasks, the extent of his responsibility for quality, scheduling.
(4) The extent of *freedom from control*, e.g. the extent of work pacing, or the extent of enforcement of work methods and output.

For these reasons multimodel and mixed-model lines are, in general, likely to be more acceptable to workers prone to dissatisfaction than single-model lines. Further, on occasions it may be possible to utilize such problems as absenteeism to effect an increase in the content of jobs by providing responsibility for the reallocation of work to the work group. Additionally, the occurrence of absenteeism provides an opportunity for the voluntary *job rotation* of workers on the line, thus providing more variety and discretion.

Few companies operate in a labour market in which there is a substantial surplus. Consequently most firms, in recruiting labour—especially unskilled and semiskilled labour, are unable to adopt selection policies which lead to the rejection of a substantial proportion of applicants. Thus the problem of ensuring that the 'right person is given the right job' is one of *selection and placement*. This in turn means that a company which has a variety of types of task, types of flow line, etc., is at an advantage, since for them there is greater scope in placing selected operatives. There are situations in which the available technology severely restricts design freedom, but for most companies some choice of systems and work design will be available. The desirability of ensuring that a variety of work situations are available does not detract from the use of manual-flow-line systems of production. Few companies will find it necessary to minimize their use of flow lines to provide the variety of situations necessary to accommodate the available labour force, but most companies will probably need to consider the nature of the flow lines they use. We have seen in earlier chapters how several design variables serve to structure the nature of the work situation (e.g. method of operation, cycle time, buffer distribution and capacities, model mix, batch sizes, launching disciplines and sequences, manning methods at stations, etc.). Clearly the manipulation of such variables is likely to influence both direct and indirect cost aspects of line productivity.

The problem of selecting and placing operatives extends considerably beyond the use of skills or aptitude tests, which, although necessary, must be supplemented by psychological tests aimed at establishing the individual's suitability for different types of work. As we have seen, such tests are likely to concentrate on the emotional and extraversion aspects of personality and on the structure of work used, in particular the relative importance of achievement motivation.

At the present time few companies adopt such comprehensive testing programmes—perhaps a reflection of the neglect of the importance of indirect cost factors. Various psychometric tests are available, many of which, although probably appropriate for use in selection and placement, are perhaps too broad and certainly too time consuming to administer. It is unlikely that the use of a single 'one-factor' instrument such as an introversion/extroversion test will prove to be a sufficiently accurate and reliable instrument for placement, but equally it is likely that, for most firms, the time and cost involved in the administration of a complex personality inventory will be unacceptable. Furthermore, since the local situation, both within and beyond the plant, plays a significant part in determining the nature and extent of absenteeism, turnover, etc., it is likely that effective test batteries will be 'situation specific' and developed locally, perhaps using features of proprietary tests.

References

Sayles, L. R., and Strauss, G. (1966). *Human Behaviour in Organizations*, Prentice Hall, New York.

Wild, R., and Hill, A. B. (1970). *Women in the Factory*, Inst. Pers. Mgrs., London.

Learning

Bayha, F. H., and Karger, D. W. (1969). *Engineered Work Measurement*, 2nd ed., Industrial Press, New York, Chap. 20.

Chaffin, D. B., and Hancock, W. M. (1966). *Factors in Manual Skill Training*, MTM Research Studies, Report 114, MTM Association, Mich., U.S.A.

Cochran, E. B. (1969). 'Learning: new dimensions in labour standards', *Ind. Eng.*, 1, No. 1, 38–47.

Deese, J. (1958). *The Psychology of Learning*, McGraw Hill, New York.

Hancock, W. M., Clifford, R. R., Foulke, J. A., and Krystynak, L. F. (1965). *Learning Curve Research on Manual Operations*, MTM Research Studies, Report 113, MTM Association, Mich., U.S.A.

Hancock, W. M. (1967). 'The prediction of learning rates for manual operations', *J. Ind. Eng.*, XVIII, No. 1, 42–47.

Hancock, W. M., and Foulke, J. A. (1963). *Learning Curve Research on Short Cycle Operations*, MTM Research Studies, Report 112, MTM Association, N.J., U.S.A.

Holding, D. H. (1965). *Principles of Training*, Pergamon, New York.

Kilbridge, M. D. (1962). 'A model for industrial learning costs', *Mgt. Sci.*, 8, No. 4, 516–527.

Kilbridge, M., and Wester, L. (1966). 'An economic model for the division of labour', *Mgt. Sci.*, 12, No. 6, B255–B269.

Nadler, G., and Smith, W. D. (1963). 'Manufacturing progressing functions for types of processes', *Int. J. Prod. Res.*, 2, No. 2, 115–134.

Thomopoulos, N. T. (1969). 'The mixed model learning curve', *A.I.I.E. Trans.*, 1, No. 2, 127–132.

Skills and abilities

Anastasi, A. (1961). *Psychological Testing*, Macmillan, New York.

Gagne, R. M., and Fleishman, E. A. (1959). *Psychology and Human Performance*, Holt, Rinehart and Winston, New York.

Poock, G. K. (1968). *Prediction of Elemental Motion Performance using Personnel Selection Tests*, MTM Research Studies, Report 115, MTM Association, Mich., U.S.A.

Roff, H. E., and Watson, T. E. (1961). *Job Analysis*, Inst. Pers. Mgrs., London.

Seymour, W. D. (1966). *Industrial Skills*, Pitman, New York.

Indirect costs

Conant, E. H., and Kilbridge, M. D. (1965). 'An interdisciplinary analysis of job enlargements technology, costs and behavioural implications', *Ind. & Lab. Rel. Rev.*, **18**, No. 3, 377–395.

Dunnette, M. D. (1966). *Personnel Selection and Placement*, Tavistock, London.

Hulin, C. L., and Blood, M. R. (1968). 'Job enlargement, individual differences and worker responses, *Psy. Bull.*, **69**, No. 1, 41–45.

Kilbridge, M. D. (1961). 'Turnover, absenteeism and transfer rates as indicators of employee dissatisfaction with repetitive work', *Ind. & Lab. Rel. Rev.*, **15**, No. 1, 21–32.

Smith, P. C. (1955). 'The prediction of individual differences in susceptibility to industrial monotony', *J. App. Psy.*, **39**, 332–339.

Turner, A. N., and Lawrence, P. R. (1965). *Industrial Jobs and the Worker*, Division of Research, Harvard Business School, Boston, Mass.

Vroom, V. (1964). *Work and Motivation*, Wiley, New York.

Walker, C. R., and Guest, R. H. (1952). *The Man on the Assembly Line*, Harvard University Press, Boston, Mass.

Wild, R. (1970). 'The design of jobs', *Chartered Mech. Engr.*, **17**, No. 6, 225–228.

Wild, R. (1972). 'Influence of community and plant characteristics on job attitudes of manual workers', *J. App. Psy.*, **56**, No. 2, 106–113.

Wild, R., and Dawson, J. A. (1972). 'The relationship of specific job attitudes with overall job satisfaction and the influence of biographical variables', *J. Mgt. Studies* (forthcoming).

Part 5
Bibliography

The references presented have been categorized approximately according to their principal contents. Details of the coding used are:

A Automation of processes, computer control of lines, etc.

B Line balancing—simple lines, i.e. single-model lines and excluding the influence of work-time and service-time variability —review articles.

B' Line balancing—complex lines, i.e. considering influence of service-time variability—mixed-model and multimodel lines— comparison of efficiencies of balancing methods.

C Conveyor systems—transfer lines.

D Division of labour and economic analysis.

G Group technology and cell manufacture, i.e. production of families of components using flow-line principles.

H Human aspects of flow-line design, e.g. learning, morale, job enlargement, etc.

L Layout of facilities.

M Mixed-model and multimodel lines.

P Pacing, work-time distributions and operator performance.

X Buffer stocks and line efficiency.

Z Generalities, history and principles of flow-line production, etc.

The literature relevant to categories A, D, G, H and Z is too diverse to be represented exhaustively and only selected references have been provided. References to group technology are confined largely to books—all original works in this field. References relevant to human aspects of line design relate to the division of labour, task learning, attitudes and morale and the policies of job enlargement. Papers which discuss task learning with respect to the design and operation of flow lines are listed, while the other papers listed (taken from industrial engineering publications) relate to the nature of skills acquisition in manual tasks. No attempt has been made to deal comprehensively with flow-line worker attitudes or job enlargement, since relevant reviews and bibliographies can be found elsewhere [e.g. Vroom, V. (1964). *Work and Motivation*, Wiley; Hulin, C. L., and Blood, M. R. (1968)., *Psy. Bull.*, **69**, No. 1, 41–55].

With the above exceptions, it is hoped that this bibliography provides a comprehensive coverage of material in the English language generally available at the time of writing.

Aberdeen, A. (1961). 'Physio-psychological differences between paced and unpaced work', Department of Engineering Production, University of Birmingham.   P

Anderson, D. R. (1968). 'Transient and steady-state minimum cost in-process inventory capacities for production lines', *Ph. D. Dissertation*, School of Industrial Engineering, Purdue University, Lafayette.   X

Anderson, D. R., and Moodie, C. L. (1969). 'Optimal buffer storage capacity in production line systems', *Int. J. Prod. Res.*, **7**, No. 3, 233–240.   X

Arcus, A. L. (1963). 'An analysis of a computer method of sequencing assembly line operations', *Ph.D. Thesis*, University of California, Berkeley.   B′

Arcus, A. L. (1966). 'COMSOAL—a computer method of sequencing operations for assembly lines', *Int. J. Prod. Res.*, **4**, No. 4, 259–277   B′

Avi-Itzhak, B. (1965). 'A sequence of service stations with arbitrary and regular service times', *Mgt. Sci.*, **11**, 565–571.   X

Avi-Itzhak, B., and Yadin, M. (1965). 'A sequence of two servers with no intermediate queue', *Mgt. Sci.*, **11**, 553–564.   X

Barten, K. A. (1962). 'A queueing simulator for determining optimum inventory levels in a sequential process', *J. Ind. Eng.*, **XIII**, No. 4, 245–252.   X

Bartlett, T. E. (1967). 'Determining optimal machine configurations for multi-stage machine processes', *Prod. Inventory Mgt.*, **8**, No. 1, 76–88.   D

Van Beek, H. G. (1961). 'Working on assembly lines', Philips Company Report, Eindhoven.   HX

Van Beek, H. G. (1964). 'The influence of assembly line organisation on output, quality and morale', *Occ. Psy.*, **38**, 161–172.   HX

Beightler, C. S., and Crisp, R. M. (1968). 'A discrete-time queueing analysis of conveyor-serviced production stations', *Operat. Res.*, **16**, No. 5, 986–1001.   C

Bellman, R. (1957). 'Formulation of recurrence equations for shuttle process and assembly line', *Nav. Res. Log. Quart.*, **4**, 321.   X

Bevis, F. W., Finniear, C., and Towill, D. R. (1970). 'Prediction of operator performance during learning of repetitive tasks', *Int. J. Prod. Res.*, **8**, No. 4, 293–305.   H

Bolenbacher, R. L. (1971). 'Line balancing made easier', *Ind. Eng.*, **3**, No. 11, 36–39.   B

Boling, R. W. (1965). 'Models for designing continuous sequential crew systems', *Unpublished Ph.D. Dissertation*, University of California, Stanford.   X

Boling, R. W. (1970). 'How to analyse sequential crew systems', *Ind. Eng.*, **2**, No. 2, 12–18.   B'

Bowman, E. H. (1960). 'Assembly line balancing by linear programming', *Operat. Res.*, **8**, No. 3, 385–389.   B

Brady, W., and Drury, C. G. (1969). 'The dependence of the coefficient of variation of the work time distribution on the number of elements in the work task', *Int. J. Prod. Res.*, **7**, No. 4, 311–315.   P

Brennecke, D. (1968). 'Two parameter assembly line balancing model'. In M. P. Hottenstein (Ed.), *Models and Analysis for Production Management*, International Textbook Co., Scranton, Penn.   B'

Bryton, B. (1954). 'Balancing of a continuous production line', *M.S. Thesis*, Northwestern University, Evanston, Ill.   B

Buffa, E. S. (1961). 'Pacing effects in production lines', *J. Ind. Eng.*, **XII**, No. 6, 383–386.   P

Burbidge, J. L. (Ed.) (1969). *Group Technology*, Proceedings of conference held at International Centre for Advanced Technology and Vocational Training, Turin.   G

Burbidge, J. L. (1971). *Production Planning*, Heinemann, London.   G

Burgeson, J. W., and Daum, T. E. (1958). 'Production line balancing', 650 Program Library, File 10.3.002, IBM, Akron, Ohio.   B

Burgess, A. R. (1968). 'A study of economic factors governing the selection of serial versus parallel production layouts', *Ph.D. Thesis*, University of Texas, Austin.   BXHD

Burke, P. J. (1956). 'The output of a queueing system', *Operat. Res.*, **4**, No. 6, 699–704.   X

Buxey, G., Slack, N. D., and Wild, R. (forthcoming). 'Production flow line design—a review'.   BB'DH
                                                                                                                                                 MPX

Buzacott, J. A. (1966). 'Automatic transfer lines with buffer stocks', *Int. J. Prod. Res.*, **5**, No. 3, 183–220.   CX

Buzacott, J. A. (1968). 'Prediction of the efficiency of production systems without internal storage', *Int. J. Prod. Res.*, **6**, No. 3, 173–188.   CX

Buzacott, J. A. (1969). 'Methods of reliability analysis of production systems subject to breakdowns', NATO Conference on Reliability, Turin, 1969.   C

Buzacott, J. A. (1971). 'The role of inventory banks in flow line systems', *Int. J. Prod. Res.*, **9**, No. 4, 425–436.   X

Cauley, J. M. (1968). 'A review of assembly line balancing algorithms', *Proceedings of the 19th conference of A.I.I.E.*, *New York*, 1968.   B

Chaffin, D. B., and Hancock, W. M. (1966). *Factors in Manual Skills Training*, MTM Research Studies, Report 114, MTM Association, Mich., U.S.A.   H

H§

Church, J. (1967). 'Model for determining low cost configurations of job shop assembly lines', *Ph.D. Thesis*, Illinois Institute of Technology.   MHD

Cochran, E. B. (1960). 'New concepts of the learning curve', *J. Ind. Eng.*, **XI**, No. 4, 317–327.   H

Cochran, E. B. (1969). 'Learning: new dimensions in labour standards', *Ind. Eng.*, **1**, No. 1, 38–47.   H

Coetsier, P. (1966). 'An approach to the study of the attitudes of workers on conveyor belt assembly lines', *Int. J. Prod. Res.*, **5**, No. 2, 113–135.   H

Colley, J. R. (1969). 'A daily system for balancing and sequencing a mixed-model assembly line', *Proceedings of the 5th Conference on Operations Research*.   B′

Conrad, R. (1954). 'Comparison of paced and unpaced performance at a packing task', Report 219/54, Medical Research Council (A.P.U.), Cambridge.   P

Conrad, R. (1954). 'The rate of paced man–machine systems', *J. Inst. Prod. Eng.*, **33**, No. 10, 562.   P

Conrad, R. (1955). 'Setting the pace', Report 232/55, Medical Research Council (A.P.U.), Cambridge.   P

Conrad, R. (1955). 'Setting the pace', *The Manager*, **23**, September, 664–667.   P

Conrad, R., and Hille, B. A. (1955). 'Comparison of paced and unpaced performance at a packing task', *Occ. Psy.*, **29**, No. 1, 15–28.   P

Conrad, R. B. (1970). 'The effect of interruption on standard time', *A.I.I.E. Trans.*, **2**, No. 2, June, 150–156.   P

Crisp, R. M. (1967). 'An analysis of conveyor-serviced production stations', *Ph.D. Dissertation*, University of Texas, Austin.   C

Crisp, R. M., Skeith, R. W., and Barnes, J. W. (1969). 'A simulated study of conveyor serviced production stations', *Int. J. Prod. Res.*, **7**, No. 4, 301–309.   C

Davis, L. E. (1966). 'Pacing effects on manned assembly lines', *Int. J. Prod. Res.*, **4**, No. 3, 171–184.   PB

Deming, D. D. (1959). 'When to shift to straight-line production', *Harvard Bus. Rev.*, **37**, No. 6, November/December, 62–68.   Z

Demyanyuk, F. S. (1963). *Technological Principles of Flow-line and Automated Production*, Vols. 1 and 2, Pergamon, Oxford.   G

Deutsch, D. F. (1967). 'The theory of blocking', *Ind. Eng. Res. at Arizona State University*, Bull. No. 3, January, 16–29.   X

Dudley, N. A. (1955). 'Output patterns in repetitive tasks', *Ph.D. Thesis*, University of Birmingham.   P

Dudley, N. A. (1958). 'Output pattern in repetitive tasks. Parts I, II, III and IV', *Prod. Eng.*, **37**, Nos. 3, 4 and 5, 187–206, 257–264, 303–313, 382–384.   P

Dudley, N. A. (1961). 'Simulation of paced work performance', Ford Faculty Seminar Working Paper No. 2, Carnegie Institute of Technology, Pittsburgh. P

Dudley, N. A. (1962). 'The effect of pacing on worker performance', *Int. J. Prod. Res.*, **1**, No. 2, 60–72. P

Dudley, N. A. (1963). 'Work time distributions', *Int. J. Prod. Res.*, **2**, No. 2, 137–144. P

Dudley, N. A. (1968). *Work Measurement: Some Research Studies*, Macmillan, London. PH

Durie, F. R. E. (1970). 'A survey of group technology and its potential for user applications in the U.K.', *Prod. Eng.*, **49**, No. 2, 51–61. G

Edwards, G. A. B. (1971). 'Group technology', *Mgt. Accountancy*, February, 57–60. G

Edwards, G. A. B. (1971). *Readings in Group Technology*, Machinery Publishing Co., Brighton. G

Evans, R. V. (1967). 'Inventory control of a multi-product system with a limited production resource', *Nav. Res. Log. Quart.*, **14**, No. 2, 173–184. AP

Ford, H., with Crowther, S. (1924). *My Life and Work*, Rev. Ed., Heinemann, London. Z

Ford, H. (1931). *Moving Forward*, Heinemann, London. X

Franks, I. T., Gillies, G. J., and Sury, R. J. (1969). 'Buffer stocks in conveyor based work', *Work Study Mgt. Serv.*, February, 78–82. XP

Franks, I. T., and Sury, R. J. (1966). 'The performance of operators in conveyor based work', *Int. J. Prod. Res.*, **5**, No. 2, 97–112. P

Franks, I. T., and Sury, R. J. (1966). 'Operator response in conveyor based work', *Int. J. Prod. Res.*, **5**, No. 2, 97–112. P

Freeman, D. R. (1968). 'A general line balancing model', *Proceedings of the 19th conference of A.I.I.E.*, 230–235. BX

Freeman, D. R., and Jucker, J. V. (1967). 'The line balancing problem', *J. Ind. Eng.*, **XVIII**, No. 6, 361–364. B

Freeman, M. C. (1964). 'The effects of breakdown and interstage storage on production line capacity', *J. Ind. Eng.*, **XV**, No. 4, 194–200. CX

Glover, J. H. (1965). 'Manufacturing progress functions—1', *Int. J. Prod. Res.*, **4**, No. 4, 279–300. H

Glover, P. C., and Norman, J. T. (1965). 'Assembly line balancing', *Assy. Engineering*, October, 28–32. B

Goode, H., and Saltzmann, S. (1962). 'Estimating inventory limits in a station-grouped production line', *J. Ind. Eng.*, **XIII**, No. 6, 485–490. X

Gosnay, M. V. (1959). 'The effect of pacing on the quality of worker performance', Department of Engineering Production, University of Birmingham.   PQ

Gould, A. F. (1965). 'Choosing a method of assembly line balancing', *Proceedings of the 16th Conference of A.I.I.E.*, 1965   B

Gutjahr, A. L., and Nemhauser, G. L. (1964). 'An algorithm for the line balancing problem', *Mgt. Sci.*, VII, No. 2, 308–315.   B

Haggan, A. M. (1962). 'Comparative study of paced and unpaced work', *Ph.D. Thesis*, University of Birmingham.   P

Hancock, W. M., Clifford, R. R., Foulke, J. A., and Krystynak, L. F. (1965). 'Learning curve research on manual operation', MTM Research Studies, Report 113, MTM Association, Mich., U.S.A.   H

Hancock, W. M. (1967). 'The prediction of learning rates for manual operations', *J. Ind. Eng.*, XVIII, No. 1, 42–47.   H

Hancock, W. M., and Foulke, J. A. (1963). 'Learning curve research on short cycle operations', MTM Research Studies, Report 112, MTM Association, N.J., U.S.A.   H

Harry, G. T. (1965). 'Conveyor based working with buffer stocks', *M.Sc. Dissertation*, Department of Engineering Production, University of Birmingham.   X

Hart, L. W. (1963). 'Activity sequencing—a bibliography', *J. Ind. Eng.*, XIV, No. 4, 221–222.   B′

Hatcher, J. M. (1969). 'The effect of internal storage on the production rate of a series of stages having exponential service times', *A.I.I.E. Trans.*, 1, June, 150–156.   X

Held, M., and Karp, R. M. (1962). 'A dynamic programming approach to sequencing problems', *J. Soc. Ind. Applied Maths.*, 10, No. 1, 196.   B

Held, M., Karp, R. M., and Shareshian, R.: 'Assembly line balancing —dynamic programming with precedence constraints', *Operat. Res.*, 11, No. 3, 442–459.   B

Helgeson, W. B. (1960). 'Planning for the use of overhead mono-rail non reversing loop type conveyor systems for storage and delivery', *J. Ind. Eng.*, XI, No. 6, 488–492.   C

Helgeson, W. B. (1964). Letter to the Editor, *J. Ind. Eng.*, XV, No. 6, 322.   B

Helgeson, W. B., and Birnie, D. P. (1961). 'Assembly line balancing using the ranked positional weight technique', *J. Ind. Eng.*, XII, No. 6, 394–398.   B

Helgeson, W. B., and Kwo, T. T. (1956). Letter to the Editor, *Mgt. Sci.*, 3, No. 1, 115.   B

Heskia Heskiaoff (1968). 'A heuristic method for balancing assembly lines', *Western Electric Engineer*, October, 9–17.   B

Heuertz, N. E. (1962). 'Computer speeds balancing of assembly line workload', *Machine and Tool Blue Book*, **57**, No. 11, 101–114.   B

Hillier, F. S., and Boling, R. W. (1966). 'The effect of some design factors on the efficiency of production lines with variable operation times', *J. Ind. Eng.*, **XVII**, No. 12, 651–658.   X

Hillier, F. S., and Boling, R. W. (1967). 'Finite queues in series with exponential or Erlang service times—a numerical approach', *Operat. Res.*, **15**, No. 2, 286–303.   X

Hoffman, T. R. (1963). 'Assembly line balancing with a precedence matrix', *Mgt. Sci.*, **9**, No. 4, 551–563.   B

Hollier, R. H. (1963). 'The layout of multi-product lines', *Int. J. Prod. Res.*, **2**, No. 1, 47–57.   GL

Hunt, G. C. (1956). 'Sequential arrays of waiting lines', *Operat. Res.*, **4**, No. 6, 674–683.   X

Hu, T. C. (1961). 'Parallel sequencing and assembly line problems', *Operat. Res.*, **9**, No. 6, 841–848.   X

Ignall, E. J. (1965). 'A review of assembly line balancing', *J. Ind. Eng.*, **XVI**, No. 4, 244–254.   B

Ivanov, E. K. (1968). *Group Production Organisation and Technology*, Business Publications, London.   G

Jackson, J. R. (1956). 'A computing procedure for a line balancing problem', *Mgt. Sci.*, **2**, No. 3, 261–271.   B

Johnston, J. (1956). 'A statistical analysis of one use of conveyors in industry', *Work Study Ind. Eng.*, December.   C

Kay, E. (1972). 'Buffer stocks in automatic transfer lines', *Int. J. Prod. Res.*, **10**, No. 2, 155–165.   C

Keay, D. R. (1959). 'The effect of pacing on output patterns', Department of Engineering Production, University of Birmingham.   P

Kilbridge, M. D. (1961). 'Non-productive work as a factor in the economic division of labour', *J. Ind. Eng.*, **XII**, No. 3, 155–159.   D

Kilbridge, M. D. (1962). 'A model for industrial learning costs', *Mgt. Sci.*, **8**, No. 4, 516–527.   H

Kilbridge, M. D., and Wester, L. (1961). 'A heuristic method of assembly line balancing', *J. Ind. Eng.*, **XII**, No. 4, 292–298.   B

Kilbridge, M. D., and Wester, L. (1962). 'The balance delay problem', *Mgt. Sci.*, **8**, No. 1, 69–84.   BD

Kilbridge, M. D., and Wester, L. (1962). 'A review of analytical systems of line balancing', *Operat. Res.*, **10**, No. 5, 626–638.   B

Kilbridge, M., and Wester, L. (1966). 'An economic model for the division of labour', *Mgt. Sci.*, **12**, No. 6, B255–B269.   DH

Klein, M. (1963). 'On assembly line balancing', *Operat. Res.*, **11**, No. 2, 274–281.   B

Knott, A. D. (1967). 'The efficiency of series production lines', *Ph.D. Thesis*, University of New South Wales.   X

Knott, A. D. (1970). 'The inefficiency of a series of work stations— a simple formula', *Int. J. Prod. Res.*, **8**, No. 2, 109–119.   X

Koenigsberg, E. (1959). 'Production lines and internal storage— a review', *Mgt. Sci.*, **5**, No. 4, 410–433.   CX

Kraemer, S. A., and Love, R. F. (1970). 'A model for optimizing the buffer inventory storage size in a sequential production system', *A.I.I.E. Trans.*, **II**, No. 1, 64–69.   X

Kwo, T. T. (1959). 'A theory of conveyors', *Mgt. Sci.*, **5**, No. 1, 51–71.   C

Lehman, M. (1969). 'What's going on in product assembly', *Ind. Eng.*, April, 41–45.   Z

Lehman, M. (1969). 'On criteria for assigning models to assembly lines', *Int. J. Prod. Res.*, **7**, No. 4, 269–285.   M

Lind, W. E. (1953). 'A statistical analysis of work-time distributions', *M.S.I.E. Thesis*, Georgia Institute of Technology.   P

Lindsay, G. F., and Bishop, A. B. (1964). 'Allocation of screening inspection—a dynamic programming approach', *Mgt. Sci.*, **10**, No. 1, 342–352.   Q

Mansoor, E. M. (1964). 'Assembly line balancing—an improvement on the ranked positional weight technique', *J. Ind. Eng.*, **XV**, No. 2, 73–77.   B

Mansoor, E. M. (1964). 'Assembly line balancing extensions and discussions', *J. Ind. Eng.*, **XV**, No. 6, 322–323.   B′

Mansoor, E. M. (1968). 'Assembly line balancing—a heuristic algorithm for variable operator performance levels', *J. Ind. Eng.*, **XIX**, No. 12, 618–629.   B′

Mansoor, E. M., and Ben-Tuvia, S. (1966). 'Optimizing balanced assembly lines', *J. Ind. Eng.*, **XVII**, No. 3, 126–132.   BP

Mariotti, J. (1970). 'Four approaches to manual assembly line balancing', *Ind. Eng.*, June, 35–40.   B′

Mastor, A. A. (1966). 'An experimental investigation and comparative evaluation of production line balancing techniques', *Ph.D. Dissertation*, University of California, Los Angeles.   B′

Mastor, A. A. (1970). 'An experimental investigation and comparative evaluation of production line balancing techniques', *Mgt. Sci.* (*Theory*), **16**, No. 11, 728–746.   B′

Maxwell, W. L. (1964). 'The scheduling of economic lot sizes', *Nav. Res. Log. Quart.*, **11**, 89–124.   M

Mayer, H. E. (1960). 'An introduction to conveyor theory', *Western Electric Engineer*, **4**, No. 1, 42–47.   C

Mertens, P. (1967). 'Assembly line balancing by partial enumeration', *Ablauf-und Planungforschung*, **8**, 429–433.   B

Mills, M. (1961). 'A study of optimum assembly runs', *Operat. Res.*, **9**, No. 1, 30–38.   DM

Mitchell, J. (1957). 'A computational procedure for balancing zoned assembly lines', Research Report No. 6–94801–1–R3, Westinghouse Research Laboratories, Pittsburgh, Penn.   B'

Mitrofanov, S. P. (1955). *Scientific Principles of Group Technology*, National Lending Library for Science and Technology, Boston Spa.   G

Moodie, C. L., and Young, H. H. (1965). 'A heuristic method of assembly line balancing for assumptions of constant or variable work element times', *J. Ind. Eng.*, **XVI**, No. 1, 23–29.   B'

Moreno, C. W. (1965). 'A technique for simulating transient sequential queues in production lines', *Ph.D. Dissertation*, School of Industrial Engineering, Purdue University, Lafayette.   X

Mukherjee, S. K., and Basie, S. K. (1963). 'Application of assembly line balancing in an Indian industry', *Proc. Inst. Mech. Eng.*, **178**, 11.   B

Murrell, K. F. H. (1962). 'Operator variability and its industrial consequences', *Int. J. Prod. Res.*, **1**, No. 2, 39–55.   P

Murrell, K. F. H. (1963). 'Laboratory studies of repetitive work—I: paced work and its relationship to unpaced work', *Int. J. Prod. Res.*, **2**, No. 3, 169–185.   P

Murrell, K. F. H., and Forsaith, B. (1963). 'Laboratory studies of repetitive work—II: progress work on results from two subjects', *Int. J. Prod. Res.*, **2**, No. 4, 247–264.   P

Murrell, K. F. H. (1965). 'A classification of pacing', *Int. J. Prod. Res.*, **4**, No. 1, 69–74.   P

Nadler, G., and Smith, W. D. (1963). 'Manufacturing progress functions for types of processes', *Int. J. Prod. Res.*, **2**, No. 2, 115–135.   H

Newell, G. F. (1955). 'Statistical analysis of sequences of operations', Brown University, Providence, Rhode Island.   X

Nissen, R., Kallem, L., and Christianson, P. (1968). 'Loading techniques for the multi-product assembly line', *J. Ind. Eng.*, **XIX**, No. 5, 243–246.   M

Patterson, R. L. (1964). 'Markov processes occurring in the theory of traffic flow through an N-stage statistic service system', *J. Ind. Eng.*, **XV**, No. 4, 188–193.   X

Payne, S., Slack, N., and Wild, R. (1972). 'A note on the operating characteristics of "balanced" and "unbalanced" production flow lines', *Int. J. Prod. Res.*, **10**, No. 1, 93–98.   XB

Petrov, V. A. (1968). *Flow Line Group Production Planning*, Business Publications, London.   G

Prenting, T. O. (1964). 'Better selection of workers for repetitive work', *Personnel*, **41**, No. 5, 26–31. H

Prenting, T. O. (1966). 'Automatic assembly: the economic considerations', *Mech. Eng.*, August, 29–31. AD

Prenting, T. O. (1966). 'Efficient manual assembly operations', *Automation*, September, 97–100. A

Prenting, T. O. (1967). 'Research and development of analytical systems to reduce product assembly costs', *J. Ind. Eng.*, XVIII, No. 1, 101–105. Z

Prenting, T. O. (1970). "Why automatic assembly needs I.E.'s", *Ind. Eng.*, December, 25–31. A

Prenting, T. O., and Battaglin, R. (1964). 'The precedence diagram: a tool for analysis in assembly line balancing', *J. Ind. Eng.*, XV, No. 4, 208–213. B

Prenting, T. O., and Kilbridge, M. D. (1965). 'Assembly: the last frontier of automation', *Mgt. Rev.*, February, 4–19. A

Pritsker, A. A. B. (1966). 'Application of multichannel queueing results to the analysis of conveyor systems', *J. Ind. Eng.*, XVII, No. 1, 14–21. C

Prizan, P. M., and Jackson, J. T. R. (1967). 'A dynamic programming application in production line inspection', *Technometrics*, **9**, No. 1, 73–81. Q

Ramsing, K., and Downing, R. (1970). 'Assembly line balancing with variable element times', *Ind. Eng.*, January, 41–43. B′

Reich, E. (1957). 'Waiting time when queues are in tandem', *Ann. Math. Stat.*, **28**, 768–772. X

Reis, I. L., Brennan, J. J., and Crisp, R. M. (1967). 'A Markovian analysis of delay at conveyor-serviced production stations', *Int. J. Prod. Res.*, **5**, No. 3, 201–211. C

Reis, I. L., Dunlap, L. L., and Schneider, M. H. (1963). 'Conveyor theory: the individual station', *J. Ind. Eng.*, XIV, No. 4, 212–217. C

Reis, I. L., and Hatcher, J. M. (1963). 'Probabilistic conveyor analysis', *Int. J. Prod. Res.*, **2**, No. 3, 186–194. C

Reiter, R. (1969). 'On assembly line balancing problems', *Operat. Res.*, **17**, No. 4, 685–700. B′

Richman, E., and Elmaghraby, S. (1957). 'The design of in-process storage facilities', *J. Ind. Eng.*, VIII, No. 1, 7–9. X

Salveson, M. E. (1955). 'The assembly line balancing problem', *Trans. A.S.M.E.*, **77**, No. 6, 939–948. B

Salveson, M. E. (1955). 'The assembly line balancing problem', *J. Ind. Eng.*, **6**, No. 3, 18–25. B

Sarafin, E. E. (1964). 'Multiple computer system controls manufacturing line', *Control Eng.*, December, 83–92. A

Sawyer, J. H. F. (1970). *Line Balancing*, Machinery Publishing Co., Brighton.   BP

Seymour, W. D. (1956). 'The pattern of improvement with practice in a simple assembly task', Final report on M.R.C. and D.S.I.R. project on the nature and acquisition of industrial skills, Appendix A, D.S.I.R., London.   H

Singleton, W. T. (1962). 'Optimum sequencing of operations for batch production', *Work Study Ind. Eng.*, **6**, No. 3, 100–110.   GL

Sury, R. J. (1964). 'Operator performance in conveyor based work systems', *Ph.D. Thesis*, University of Birmingham.   P

Sury, R. J. (1964). 'An industrial study of paced and unpaced operator performance in a single stage work task', *Int. J. Prod. Res.*, **3**, No. 2, 91–102.   P

Sury, R. J. (1965). 'The simulation of a paced single stage work task', *Int. J. Prod. Res.*, **4**, No. 2, 125–140.   P

Sury, R. J. (1965). 'L'execution du travail à allure cadences par un convoyeur', *L'Etude du Travail*, October, No. 166.   P

Sury, R. J. (1967). 'Operator performance in conveyor based working', *Work Study Mgt. Serv.*, January, 12–15.   P

Sury, R. J. (1971). 'Aspects of assembly line balancing', *Int. J. Prod. Res.*, **9**, No. 4, 501–512.   B′

Svestka, J. A., and Nair, K. P. K. (1972). 'Parallel operation of sequential service lines with interline transfer', *Trans. A.I.I.E.*, **4**, No. 1, 29–35.   B′

Taylor, J., and Jackson, R. R. P. (1954). 'An application of the birth and death process to the provision of spare machines', *Operat. Res. Quart.*, **5**, 95–108.   C

Teugels, J. (1970). 'Simultaneous success-run chains', *Operat. Res.*, **18**, No. 1, 132–144.   B′

Thangavelu, S. R. (1970). 'Assembly line balancing by 0–1 integral programming', *Master's Thesis*, Georgia Institute of Technology.   B

Thangavelu, S. R., and Shetty, C. M. (1971). 'Assembly line balancing by zero-one integral programming', *A.I.I.E. Trans.*, **III**, No. 1, 61–68.   B

Thomopoulos, N. T. (1967). 'Line balancing—sequencing for mixed model assembly', *Mgt. Sci.*, **14**, No. 2, October, B59–B75.   MB′

Thomopoulos, N. T. (1968). 'Some analytical approaches to assembly line problems', *Prod. Eng.*, July, 345–351.   MB′

Thomopoulos, N. T. (1970). 'Mixed model line balancing with smoothed station assignments', *Mgt. Sci. (Theory)*, **16**, No. 9, 593–603.   MB′

Thomopoulos, N. T. (forthcoming). 'The mixed model similarity index'.   M

Thomopoulos, N. T., and Lehman, M. (1969). 'The mixed model learning curve', *A.I.I.E. Trans.*, **1**, No. 2, 127–132.   MH

Tonge, F. M. (1960). 'Summary of a heuristic line balancing procedure', *Mgt. Sci.*, **7**, No. 1, 21–42.   B

Tonge, F. M. (1961). *A Heuristic Program for Assembly Line Balancing*, Prentice Hall, New York.   B

Tonge, F. M. (1965). 'Assembly line balancing using probabilistic combinations of heuristics', *Mgt. Sci.*, **11**, No. 7, 727–735.   B

Tuggle, G. (1969). 'Job enlargement: an assault on assembly line inefficiency', *Ind. Eng.*, **1**, No. 2, 26–31.   H

Walker, C. R., and Guest, R. H. (1952). *The Man on the Assembly Line*, Harvard University Press, Boston, Mass.   H

Walker, J. R. (1959). 'A study of element independence in work cycles', *M.S. Thesis*, Georgia Institute of Technology.   P

Wester, L., and Kilbridge, M. D. (1960). 'The assembly line problem', 2nd International Conference on Operations Research, Aix-en-Provence, France, September 1960, pp. 213–225.   D

Wester, L., and Kilbridge, M. D. (1961). 'Analytical systems of line balancing', First National Joint Meeting of TIMS/ORSA, San Francisco, November, Operations Research Society of America, Baltimore, Md.   B

Wester, L., and Kilbridge, M. D. (1962). 'Heuristic line balancing: a case', *J. Ind. Eng.*, **XIII**, No. 3, 139–149.   B

Wester, L., and Kilbridge, M. D. (1964). 'The assembly line model-mix sequencing problem'. In *Proceedings of 3rd International Conference on Operations Research*, 1963, *Paris*, Dunod, pp. 247–260.   M

White, L. S. (1966). 'An analysis of a sample class of multistage inspection plans', *Mgt. Sci.*, **12**, No. 5, 685–693.   Q

White, L. S. (1969). 'Shortest route models for the allocation of inspection effort on a production line', *Mgt. Sci.*, **15**, No. 5, 249–259.   Q

White, W. W. (1961). 'Comments on a paper by Bowman' [*Operat. Res.*, **8**, No. 3 (1960)], *Operat. Res.*, **9**, No. 2, 274–276.   B

Wiberg, M. (1947). *Work-Time Distribution*, McClure, Haddon and Ortman, Chicago.   P

Wild, R., and Slack, N. D. (1972). 'The Operating Characteristics of "single" and "double" non-mechanical flow lines', *Int. J. Prod. Res.* (forthcoming).   B′X

Williams, P. F. (1961). 'The application of manufacturing improvement curves in multi-product industries', *J. Ind. Eng.*, **12**, No. 2, 108–112.   H

Woollard, F. G. (1925). 'Some notes on British methods of continuous production', *Proc. Inst. Automobile Eng.*, **19**, February, 419–442.   Z

Woollard, F. G. (1954). *Principles of Mass and Flow Production*, Iliffe, London.   Z

Woollard, F. G. (1956). 'Flow production and automation', Industrial Administration Group, Birmingham.   Z

Wyatt, S., and Fraser, J. A. (1929). 'The effect of monotony at work', I.F.R.B. Report No. 56, H.M.S.O., London.   H

Wyatt, S., and Langdon, J. N. (1938). 'The machine and the worker— a study of machine-feeding processes', I.H.R.B. Report No. 83, H.M.S.O., London.   H

Young, H. H. (1964). 'Time, inventory and balance in the production line'. In *Proceedings of the 15th Conference of A.I.I.E.*   B′X

Young, H. H. (1966). 'Digital computer control of an automated multiproduct line'. In *Proceedings of the 17th Annual Inst. Conf. and Convention of A.I.I.E.*, San Francisco, May 1966.   XM

Young, H. H. (1966). 'Digital computer control of an automated multiproduct production line', *Ph.D. Dissertation*, Department of Industrial Engineering, Arizona State University.   XM

Young, H. H. (1967). 'Optimisation models for production lines', *J. Ind. Eng.*, **XVIII**, No. 1, 70–78.   XM

Name Index

Subject Index

Those subjects marked * recur throughout the text—only key entries are listed here.

Human problems, *see* Behavioural
problems

Idle time, *see* Balancing delay,
Balancing loss, Blocking, Starv-
ing
Incentive payments, *see* Payment
systems
Industrial Revolution 6
Inspection 83–5, *see also* Quality
control
Interchangeable parts 7, 13, 24–33
in arms manufacture 24–7

Job attitudes 188–202, 205–8
Job design 203

Labour placement, *see* Selection and
placement
Labour selection, *see* Selection and
placement
Labour turnover 92, 193, 202–3
Launching 50, 136, 156–63
Layout, *see* Machine layout
Learning 189–97
Learning curves 189–92
Linear programming 61, 144
Line balancing* 14, 46–8, 53–4
aids to 77–82
comparison of methods 74–5
Comsoal method 72–4
factors affecting 54–9
heuristic methods of 62–74
largest-candidate rule 72, 103
methods of 61–75
of mixed-model lines 151–5
of multimodel lines 139–40
of simple lines 53–83
practice 82–3
ranked positional-weight method
of 67–71
with variable element times 102–7
Line of balance 155

Machine grouping 175–7
Machine layout 175–7
Manufacture 3
Mass production*, concepts of 3–18

developments in Britain 29–33
developments of 19–43
early use of 19–24
nature of 3–18
prerequisites of 14–6
systems 8
technologies, developments of 12
Method study 87–8
'Model T' Ford 35–8
Morris Company 40
Morris Engines Ltd. 40
Motion study, *see* Method study
Motivation 190, 202, *see also* Behavioural problems

Oldsmobile 33
Operator behaviour 203–5, *see also*
Behavioural problems
Operator response 126–8, *see also*
Pacing
Operator variability 48–9, 88–93
in paced work 90–1
in unpaced tasks 89–90

Pacing 48–9, 89–91, 93, 95–101, 109,
125–8, 184
Payment systems 184–6
'Penny press' 28
Placement, *see* Selection and place-
ment
Precedence constraints 47–8
Precedence diagram 62, 67–8, 80,
152, *see also* Precedence con-
straints
Predetermined-motion-time systems
89, 106
Production 3
types of 4–5
Production-flow analysis 173–4
Production line, *see* Flow line
Production management* 3–4
problems 4, 9

Quality control 83–5
Quantity production 4–12, 23
Queueing theory 109